THE COMPLETE BOOK OF FASHION ILLUSTRATION

SHARON LEE TATE

MONA SHAFER EDWARDS

UNIVERSITY OF CALIFORNIA, LOS ANGELES, UNIVERSITY EXTENSION

PERENNIAL LIBRARY

Harper & Row, Publishers
New York, Cambridge, Philadelphia, San Francisco
London, Mexico City, São Paulo, Singapore, Sydney

TO
ALLISON, KEVIN,
MARISA,
AND MARC

A hardcover edition of this book is
published by Harper & Row, Publishers, Inc.

THE COMPLETE BOOK OF FASHION
ILLUSTRATION. Copyright © 1982 by Harper
& Row, Publishers, Inc. All rights reserved.
Printed in the United States of America. No
part of this book may be used or reproduced
in any manner whatsoever without written
permission except in the case of brief
quotations embodied in critical articles and
reviews. For information address Harper
& Row, Publishers, Inc., 10 East 53rd Street,
New York, N.Y. 10022. Published
simultaneously in Canada by Fitzhenry
& Whiteside Limited, Toronto.

First BARNES & NOBLE BOOKS edition
published 1984.

**Library of Congress Cataloging in
Publication Data**

Tate, Sharon Lee.
    The complete book of fashion
    illustration.
    Includes index.
    1. Fashion drawing.   I. Edwards, Mona
Shafer, 1951-   II. Title.
TT509.T37   741.67'2   81-7103
ISBN 0-06-464085-X   AACR2

89 90   10 9 8 7

CONTENTS

CHAPTER
SIX
RENDERING FABRICS   **122**

CHAPTER
SEVEN
**RENDERING TECHNIQUES
AND MATERIALS**   **170**

CHAPTER
EIGHT
**DESIGNING THE
ILLUSTRATION 194**

CHAPTER
NINE
SOURCES OF INSPIRATION 225

CHAPTER
TEN
DRAWING MEN 266

Planning a career in fashion? Knowing how to draw a fashion figure may be one of the skills you need. Drawing a fashion sketch is a necessary skill for designers and patternmakers. Buyers who can sketch have a tool for recording the merchandise they see at market. The professional fashion illustrator, of course, has the most developed graphic skills and uses them to earn a livelihood by illustrating apparel for a wide range of clients. Whatever your career goals and drawing abilities, you can use *The Complete Book of Fashion Illustration* to learn to draw the fashion figure. Relatively undeveloped sketchers will learn the basics. Intermediate-ability sketchers will learn to improve and refine their skills.

The Complete Book of Fashion Illustration may be used as a self-teaching manual, because the demonstration pages break sketching skills down into simple steps. Each step builds your confidence and ability and moves you towards a more advanced drawing ability. This book is a *do* book. You must work through each exercise to master a specific skill. All the lessons build your ability so you can produce a competent fashion sketch.

Chapters One through Four stress basic figure drawing skills. Combining these lessons on proportion and body structure with drawing from life will begin to develop your awareness of how to draw and move the female fashion figure.

Chapters Five and Six demonstrate how to draw clothing and render fabrics. After completing these chapters, you will easily be able to communicate a design or illustration concept graphically.

Chapters Eight and Nine introduce intermediate graphic skills. These chapters show you how to present the fashion figure in a dynamic, appealing way to capitalize on the drawing ability you have developed in the primary stages. Chapter Nine, "Sources of Inspiration," guides you to contemporary and period art that will inspire you to continue to refine and develop your fashion drawing skills.

Chapters Ten through Twelve deal with specialized illustration categories. Men's and children's fashions are covered in detail, as is the art of drawing and rendering accessories.

The last two sections (Chapters Eight through Twelve) enhance your graphic skills. Once you have mastered the basic skills you go on to more advanced art problems, with the goal of producing a finished illustration.

Fashion Illustration can be used by the first time drawer or an advanced illustrator who wants to specialize in fashion. The only prerequisite, and the constant demand of this text, is that you desire to develop good drawing skills. Apply yourself consistently and thoroughly to the exercises and demonstrations presented here, and you should end up being able to communicate fashion concepts graphically.

ACKNOWLEDGMENTS

This book could not have been written without the contributions of many outstanding artists, and others in the fashion industry. Special thanks go to the following people:

☐ Mia Carpenter, Gregory Weir-Quiton, Steve Bieck, David Horii, Paul Lowe, Marie D. Shafer, Robert Passantino, Steve Stipelman, Cynthia Willoughby, Linda Trapp, Richard Rosenfeld, Catherine Clayton Purnell, Antonio, John C. Jay, and the artists whose period illustrations were gleaned from the pages of twentieth-century fashion publications.

☐ Charles Bush, photographer extraordinaire, for his fashion photographs.

☐ *Vogue* and *Harper's Bazaar*, who kindly allowed me to research their back issues for outstanding artists.

☐ Edwin Mader and Florence Currant of the Los Angeles County Museum of Art, Textile and Costume Department, for their counsel.

☐ UCLA, which allowed me access to the fine graphics in the Grunwald Graphic Art Collection and to their fine students, who inspired both Mona and me to do this book.

☐ Francine Horn and Pat Stimack of *Here and There,* a fashion reporting service, for their work and talents.

☐ And, last but not least, Mona Edwards, who persevered as the major illustrator of this text. We were better friends when we completed the manuscript than we had been when we began.

Sharon Lee Tate

CHAPTER
ONE

BEGINNING
TO
DRAW

WHO CAN DRAW?

Look at the objects that surround you. Every piece of furniture, every building, every household tool, every garment—in fact, every manufactured object—began as a designer's sketch. This sketch captured an idea's first physical reality. It was the plan from which the object was constructed. It was the symbol of the designer's thought. The skill behind that sketch —the ability to draw—can be learned. Once learned, drawing skills can develop to the point where designers can use them to present unique interpretations of the world. The talent and persistence to develop drawing from a basic skill to such a highly specialized art form is not within every person's grasp. But most people do have the potential to sharpen their graphic ability to the point where they are able to use drawing as a tool to communicate their ideas.

Children have an innate ability to draw. They relish capturing an image. They find it thrilling to draw with a bright pencil, to splash paint on a clean piece of paper. Children enjoy creating a drawing more than evaluating the final product. To them the creative act is enough fun in itself. Unfortunately, many adults impose their product-oriented goals on the spontaneous creativity of their children. "Johnny, leaves aren't blue." "Sally, the people in your picture shouldn't be larger than the houses." These value judgments often discourage children from continuing their graphic experiments.

Skills in writing are stressed in children's early years in school. Verbalizing and writing are the important building blocks of a classic education.

Imagine how different your drawing ability would be if you had spent years of early education practicing figure drawing or pencil-shading techniques, instead of the ABCs.

Many people have to begin with very simple approaches to drawing to regain the spontaneity of their childhood creativity. Before they can enjoy and develop their native drawing ability, they have to overcome their negative feelings of being unable to draw. Begin to draw, develop simple graphic skills, and do not worry about producing a professional image. The product will improve as you relax and begin to enjoy sketching.

The first human figure a beginner draws usually reflects his or her own physical and mental image. A man tends to draw figures with large shoulders and slim hips. A large woman will often draw large women. A beginner with low personal esteem will tend to draw a figure with a small, pointed head—or a tiny, cramped, thin figure. One of the first steps in drawing a fashion figure is to neutralize your self-image and study a typical fashion figure. As beginners' sketching skill develops, they may start to incorporate desirable personal traits into their drawings.

WHAT IS FASHION DRAWING?

Fashion drawing differs from regular descriptive drawing. Exaggeration and idealism are standard methods of enhancing the fashion image. Realism, sometimes a goal of other drawing disciplines, is greatly modified in fash-

Children draw with a natural, bold line and an eager enthusiasm that provide the basis for developing drawing into a skill.

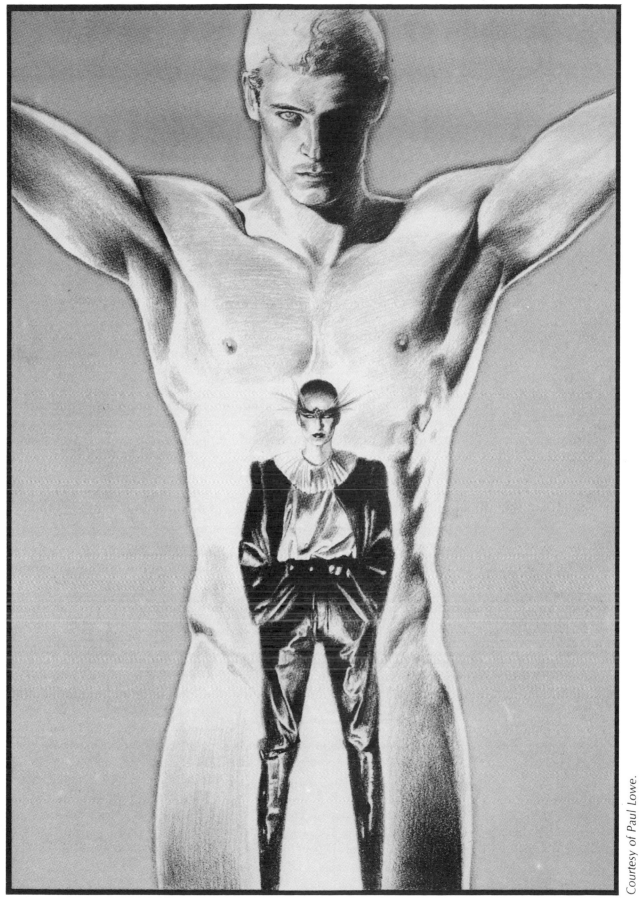

3

ion drawing. Current ideals of beauty are emphasized in a fashion drawing, to create a stylized version of reality. Good fashion drawing is very dependent on knowing what the current ideal of beauty is and how clothing is used to enhance the human body.

Developing drawing skills is the important first step for drawing the fashion figure. As skills evolve, developing a sense of what is currently fashionable is critical to upgrading the development of good fashion drawing. Also important is developing a taste level—your own personal point of view about the way an object or design should look. Today this means being aware of lifestyle trends, as well as apparel fashion. Many facets of life affect the ways people live. Reading newspapers, books, and magazines that reflect lifestyle trends in home furnishings, sports, literature, graphics, and fine arts—as well as apparel— will broaden your taste level. Creativity is the ability to combine several things into something new—to synthesize and organize elements in a unique way. Be sensitive to the way other art forms relate to apparel fashion design and illustration.

FASHION CAREERS THAT REQUIRE SKETCHING

Many careers in fashion use drawing skills. Designers sketch their ideas so they can be interpreted by a patternmaker. This working sketch, or *croquis* (cro-key), must accurately show the silhouette and style details. The size of the collar, cuffs, and trims must be drawn to scale, so the actual garment can be constructed in fabric.

Often, notes will indicate technical details to the patternmaker and samplemaker. This sketch does not have to be exciting. It should have a minimum of exaggeration. The designer's working sketch should relate directly to the product to be created. The croquis transfers the designer's mental image to a graphic reality from which it may be constructed and evaluated by other people.

Illustrators have a different purpose in drawing a garment. They want to emphasize the style details so they are an enhancement of the original design concept. Fashion illustrators are creating the image of a fashionable product—not the garment itself—so they will often omit details and exaggerate the silhouette to make a fashion point. Illustrations stimulate customers into projecting themselves into the garment. Photographs are more realistic, but probably less effective in helping customers transpose themselves into the image of a live model.

The kind of garment and how the illustration will be used influences how the drawing is done. A product advertisement drawn to sell the garment will often be more realistically rendered than a sketch that is being used to emphasize the fashion image of the garment, designer, or store advertising it.

Buyers who can sketch will often make picture notes of garments they are purchasing. Most handbag buyers must have a rough sketching ability, because of the difficulty in describing similar products. Visual merchandisers draw layout sketches of proposed window and interior displays. Commerical artists who specialize in figure work often train with fashion illustrators to become more aware of current trends in figure illustration.

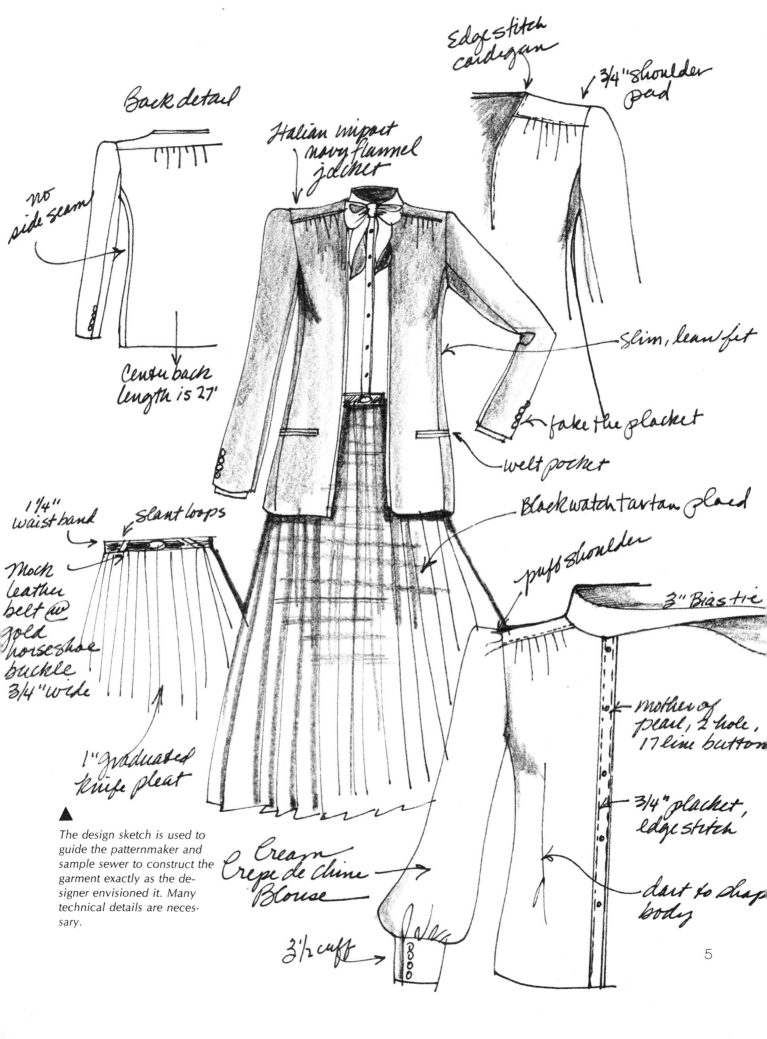

Back detail

no side seam

Center back length is 27'

Italian import navy flannel jacket

Edge stitch cardigan

3/4" shoulder pad

slim, lean fit

fake the placket

welt pocket

Black watch tartan plaid

puffs shoulder

3" Bias tie

mother of pearl, 2 hole, 17 line button

3/4" placket, edge stitch

dart to shape body

1 1/4" waist band

slant loops

Mock leather belt w/ gold horseshoe buckle 3/4" wide

1" graduated knife pleat

Cream Crepe de Chine Blouse

3 1/2 cuff

▲ The design sketch is used to guide the patternmaker and sample sewer to construct the garment exactly as the designer envisioned it. Many technical details are necessary.

5

The store advertisement presents the garment so a consumer can identify with the illustration and be motivated to buy the outfit. The style is enhanced, but not overly exaggerated.

◄

The editorial illustration is primarily illustrated to present an exciting fashion concept where details are less important than impact.

▼

Drawing skills begin with knowledge of the body, interpreted as a fashion figure. Today, the ideal man or woman has a tall, slim, athletic figure. Drawing clothes is the next technical skill to master. Techniques of drawing apparel and rendering fabrics can be learned by observation and practice.

As drawing skills develop, more complicated media (paint, felt pens, pencils, and so forth) should be used to achieve different effects. Learn the techniques of other illustrators by imitating their work, then adapt them to your own style. After experimenting with many different media and techniques, a backlog of results enables the artist to more quickly and accurately sketch and render a concept. As the image becomes easier to draw, the student should begin to design the whole page. A figure floating on a blank page has a very amateurish look, when compared to an illustration that is designed to relate to the whole page. Finally, the student can expand to drawing related fashion figures. Children and men are specialities that are relatively easily mastered after a firm basis in female body proportion has been developed. The differences are ones of emphasis and do not require that the student relearn total structure.

Drawing is a skill that can be mastered by constant practice. The early products are less important than doing the sketch. Don't be critical of your early work. Appreciate the successful parts of your drawing. Work on repeating these good elements and improving the weaker aspects on your next sketch. When you have mastered one style or technique, try another. Do not be afraid of copying a drawing you like. Trace or draw it, trying

to analyze how and why the artist created the image. Then use these techniques to illustrate a different garment in another pose. Use what you see to enhance your own drawing ability and style. Never limit yourself to one style. An artist who is to have a longevity of more than one season should always be open to change and expansion.

BEGINNING DRAWING SUPPLIES

The most important way to learn to draw is to do it. Carry a small sketch book and doodle. Draw on the mar-

gins of paper. Whenever you have to wait, look around for an interesting face or object and sketch it. Next time you visualize something you want to make or purchase, try and sketch it. Substitute a drawn image for a word description of an object. But, of course, before you can begin, you must have the proper materials. You will find a detailed discussion of equipment in Chapter 7. For now, though, the following list of materials should be adequate.

PAPERS

1. Overlay or vellum tablets are durable transparent paper to use for tracing and reworking sketches. A pad 14-by-17 inches is a handy size.

2. Bond paper is an inexpensive, semitranslucent paper that is an all-purpose paper for pencils and marking pens. Buy a 14-by-16-inch or larger pad.

3. A 6-by-8-inch sketch book with plain pages is easy to carry, yet large enough for quick sketches.

MARKERS AND PENCILS

1. Buy a dozen package of #2 soft lead pencils and sharpen all 12. Change pencils as the points become blunt.

2. Fine-line red markers are used for correcting and redrawing your sketch exercises.

3. Fine-line black markers ("razor point") or a Rapidograph with changeable points are used for detailed line drawings. Buy ink if you are using a Rapidograph.

4. Prisma pencils are available in a wide variety of colors. The beginner should buy two or three blacks, a white, and several shades of grey for basic work.

5. Markers should be purchased in several shades of cool grey with a blunt or chisel point. The tones of grey are numbered. The lower the number, the lighter the tone. A #2, #4, #6, and #8 will make a good basic selection. Buy a pointed black marker for a heavier line than the fine-point markers.

6. A portable pencil sharpener is handy and saves time.

OTHER EQUIPMENT

1. Drawing board—buy a light-weight, masonite board with clips and a hand hold for portability. This board should be at least 18-by-26 inches.

2. Ruler—a 12-inch ruler is needed to do the basic exercises.

3. Masking tape—$\frac{3}{4}$-inch wide tube is a basic tool.

4. Kneaded erasers—these are necessary for corrections.

5. Matt knives—basic tools for cutting paper, illustration board, and tape.

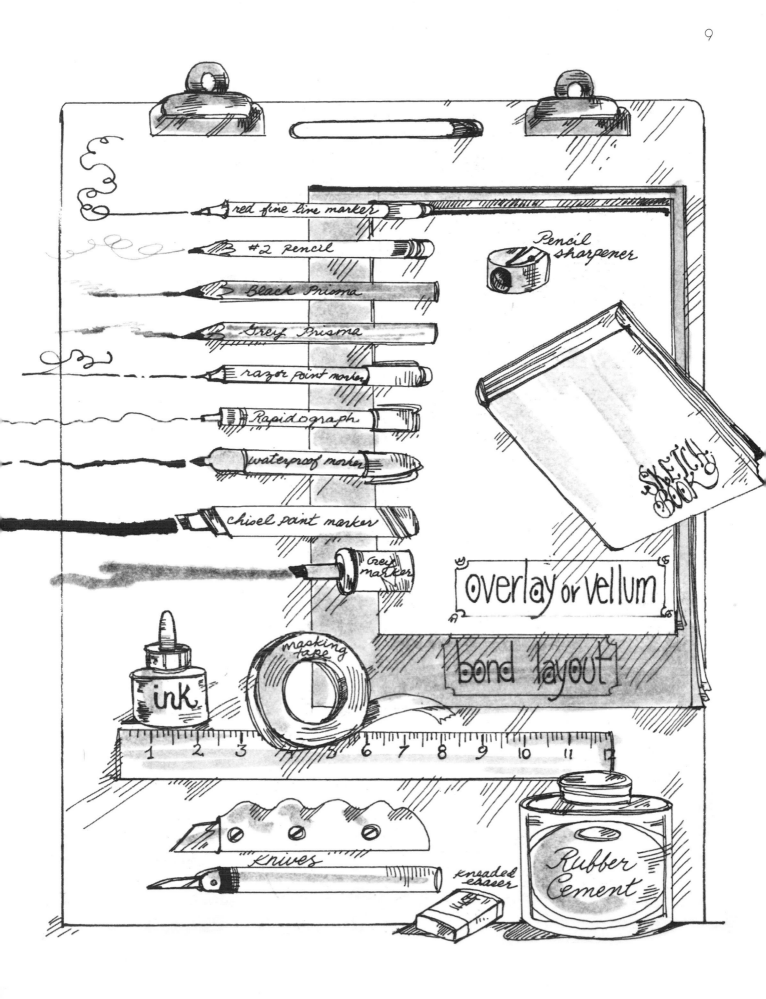

red fine line marker

#2 pencil

Black Prisma

Grey Prisma

razor point marker

Rapidograph

waterproof marker

chisel paint marker

Grey marker

Pencil sharpener

SKETCH BOOK

overlay or vellum

bond layout

ink

masking tape

1 2 3 4 5 6 7 8 9 10 11 12

Knives

kneaded eraser

Rubber Cement

CHAPTER TWO

FASHION FIGURE PROPORTION

THE CURRENT FASHION FIGURE

Fashion illustration of every period emphasizes the ideal of beauty for the age. Today's ideal figure for showing apparel is a tall (5'7" to 5'11"), slender, athletic, young woman. She has a small bosom and broad shoulders, so clothes hang easily over her lithe silhouette. She wears a size six to ten. Her face, hair, and body have a natural look when she is showing casual or active sportswear. The mood of her hairstyle and makeup is more stylized when wearing suits, evening wear, and more expensive apparel.

The fashion ideal is far from the proportions and appearance of most bodies. Today's American woman is taller than yesterday's, but average height is still only about 5'4". Nor is the typical woman as slender as the fashion model.

DRAWING THE EIGHT-HEAD FIGURE

Fashion drawing changes the average figure to the modern ideal by lengthening the body to eight head lengths as a minimum height. This means the total body length is eight times the length of the head. The figure is lengthened at the neck and legs and the proportion of the torso remains fairly realistic. Fashion illustrators often attenuate the figure even more, making it eight and one-half to ten heads high. These illustrations of tall women have a very sophisticated look. Optical illusions to heighten the figure are also used by designers. For example, they dress their mannequins in high-heel or platform shoes, often covered by long pant legs or skirts.

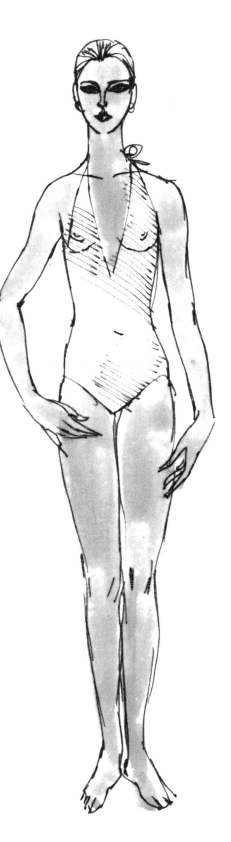

Eight-head figure most realistic— comes off looking too stocky for high fashion

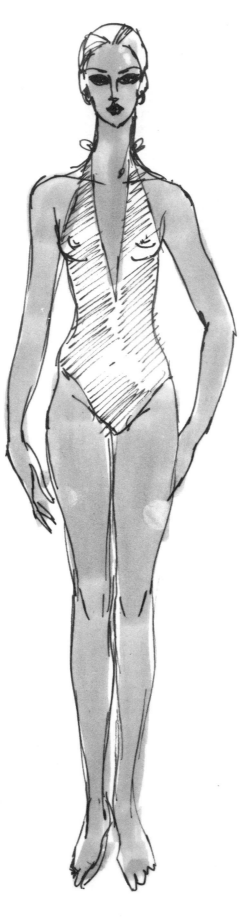

*Nine-head figure
less realistic —
still too heavy
and short for
editorial or
high fashion*

1. Study the geometric components of the eight-head figure on pages 14 and 15. Draw a straight line on a piece of overlay or tracing paper 8 inches long and mark the inches. Follow the diagrams as you draw the figure.

2. Draw an oval between the top line and the first inch mark. Divide the oval with the median line. Draw a slender cylindrical shape from the sides of the head to $\frac{1}{2}$ inch down from the first inch mark (this represents the neck). Draw the shoulder line from the bottom of this cylinder outward $\frac{3}{4}$ of an inch on either side of the median line. Connect the ends of the shoulder line to the neck, forming a shallow triangle.

3. Draw two small, narrow ovals at the end of the shoulder triangle representing the ball joints of the arm. Draw a tapered line from inside each arm's eye circle to within $\frac{1}{4}$ inch of the line 3 mark.

4. Draw a flexible line from the center of the rib cage block to $\frac{1}{4}$ inch below line 3. Draw the pelvic block at the base of this line. The top is the same one-head length as the bottom of the rib cage and flares out slightly as it ends at line 4. Draw two flat ovals at the bottom of each side of the pelvic wedge representing the hip joints.

5.   Finish drawing the arm by placing the wrist circle slightly below line 4 and connecting it to the elbow circle with two straight lines. Draw a square and lines to represent the hand and fingertips which end at line 5. Draw two circles representing the knees on line 6. Connect to the hip joint with straight lines on each side.

6.   Draw two smaller circles $\frac{1}{4}$ inch above the bottom line to represent the ankles. Connect these to the knee circles with straight lines. Draw wedge shapes to represent the feet and notice how they extend slightly below the bottom line to visually support the figure.

Ten-head figure
ideal proportions
for editorial
and high fashion
sketches.

Chin — 1.

½ Shoulder — ½

Bust — 2.

Waist — 3.

Crotch — 4.

Fingertips — 5.

Knees — 6.

Calf — 7.

Heels — 8.

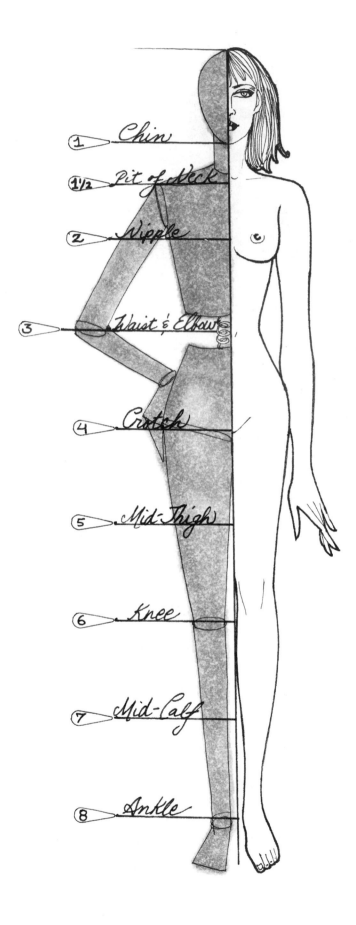

① Chin

①½ Pit of Neck

② Nipple

③ Waist & Elbow

④ Crotch

⑤ Mid-Thigh

⑥ Knee

⑦ Mid-Calf

⑧ Ankle

Put your sketch over the 8-inch figure on the preceding page to see how closely your drawing compares to the standard. With a colored felt pen, re-draw the areas that do not match the standard. Trace the figure several times, fleshing out the geometric components so your drawing looks like a figure. Make a conscious effort to draw the ideal and not to impose your body image into the sketch.

Hold your pencil with a relaxed, comfortable grip. A #2 soft pencil, kept very sharp, is the best tool for these basic exercises. Sharpen eight or ten pencils and pick up a new one as they become blunt. This will save you time and keep your drawing from getting smudged and dirty. Attach your practice piece of overlay paper to the book with a small piece of masking tape. (No damage will be done to the book.) Draw this figure many times, gradually eliminating the guidelines until you can sketch it freehand. Measure your drawings from the head to the crotch and make sure the legs are equal to or longer than this distance. The crotch line (line 4) is always at least the halfway point of any fashion sketch. The legs may be longer than four heads, but never shorter.

TORSO BONE STRUCTURE

Bone structure of a fashion model is important because she is very slender and the bones are visible at the joints, rib cage, and pelvic area. Compare the skeletons to the block figure. It is important to study skeletal structure to understand which parts of the body can bend. The arm can move at the shoulder, elbow, and wrist, but not in between, because of the straight solid humerus (upper arm), and radius and ulna (lower arm) bones. The leg moves from the hip, knee, and ankle joints only. Feel the joints of your own body to understand how they move. Look at yourself in the mirror, and test where your arms and legs can bend.

Trace over the front and profile skeleton drawings several times on overlay paper. Say the names of the major bones that are listed as you draw. On one sketch, draw all the straight bones with pencil and draw the moveable joints in fine-line red felt pens. Remember to include the spine and neck as flexible joints. The red areas will alert you to where you can move the body.

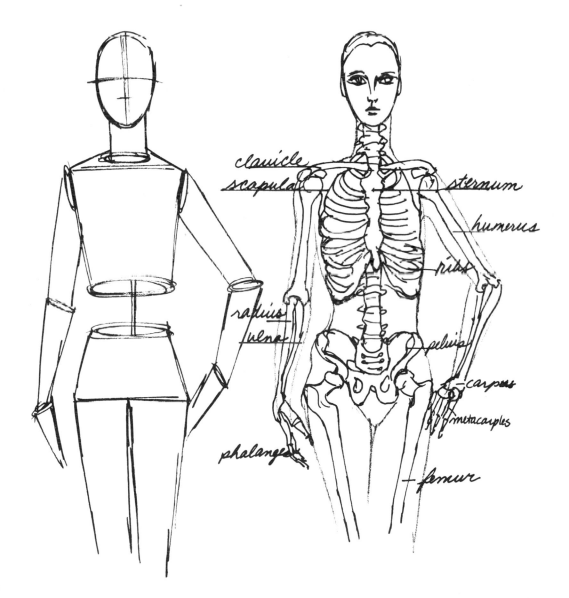

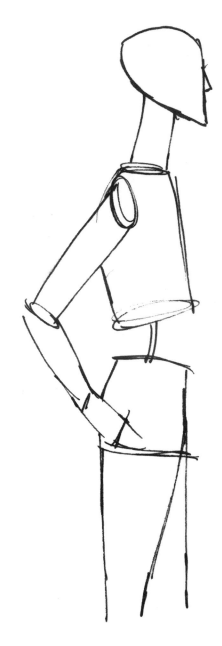

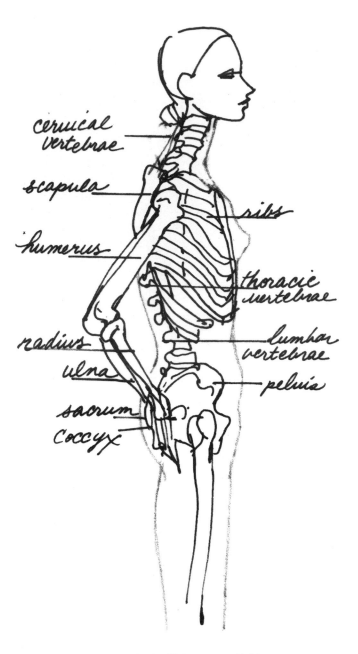

cervical vertebrae

scapula

humerus

radius

ulna

sacrum

coccyx

ribs

thoracic vertebrae

lumbar vertebrae

pelvis

TORSO MUSCLE STRUCTURE

The fasion model has long, lithe, healthy muscle structure, but it is not as defined as a man's. She has very little extra fat on her body. When an arm moves, the muscle will contract slightly, making a smooth curve.

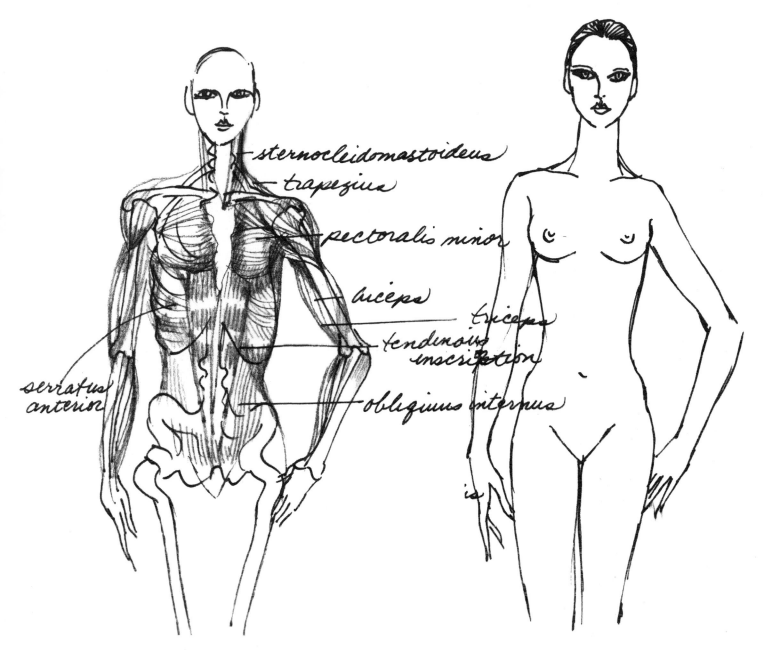

sternocleidomastoideus

trapezius

pectoralis minor

biceps

triceps

tendinous inscription

serratus anterior

obliquius internus

Place a drawing you have done of the bones over the drawing of the muscled body shown here. Notice how the skeleton supports and relates to the muscle structure of the body. Now move your tracing of the skeleton over the fleshed-out body, and compare the supporting bones with the body.

Practice drawing the finished figure

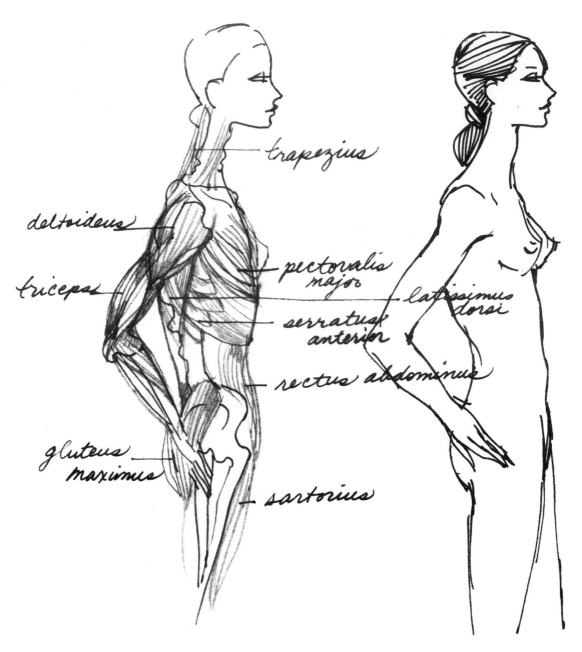

trapezius

deltoideus

triceps

pectoralis major

serratus anterior

latissimus dorsi

rectus abdominus

gluteus maximus

sartorius

and muscles shown here and on page 19. Follow these steps:

1. Trace the muscled figure several times. Say the names of the major muscles as you draw them.

2. Put a piece of overlay paper on one of your tracings of the muscles. Draw a fleshed-out figure over your drawing of the muscles. Take away the muscle drawing and compare your sketch to the figure in the book.

3. Draw over your sketch of the skeleton on a fresh sheet of overlay paper. Use the skeleton as a guide to proportion and draw a fleshed-out figure. Correct your drawing with a red marking pen, by comparing it to the finished figure in the book.

4. Do these exercises until it is easy to draw the shapes of the limbs in the correct proportion.

THE BACK TORSO

The back view of a fashion figure has the same proportion as the front. The bone and muscle structure differ. It is important to show back views to illustrate a garment with a back interest.

Practice drawing the back view following these steps:

1. Draw a line 5 inches long on a piece of overlay paper and mark the inches as you did in the first exercise on proportion. Sketch the geometric shapes of the figure freehand. Place your drawing over the block figure and correct your sketch with a red felt pen. Draw the block figure freehand until you do not have to make any corrections.

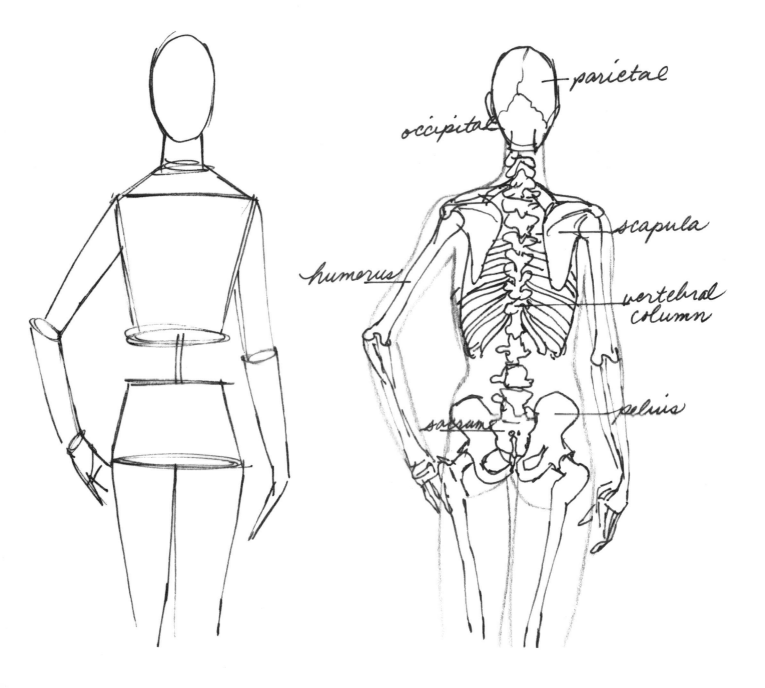

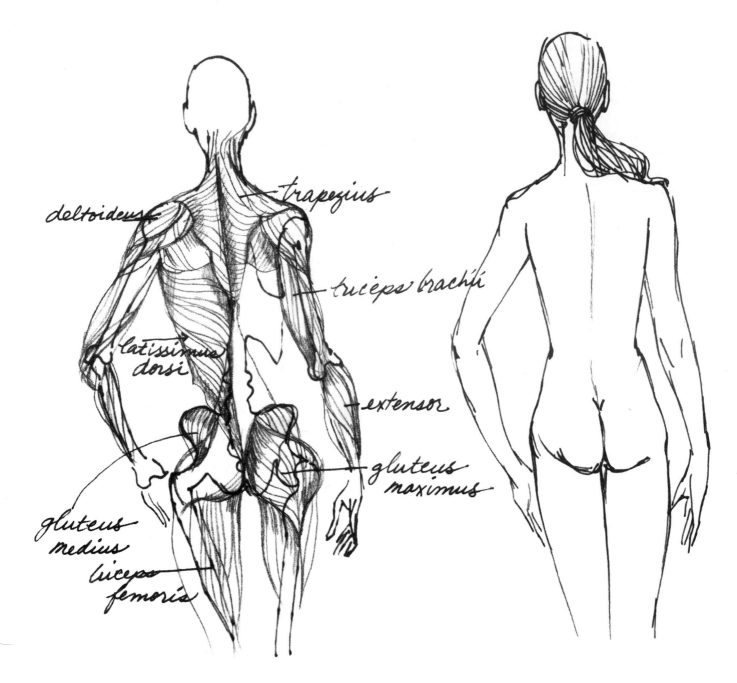

deltoideus

trapezius

triceps brachii

latissimus dorsi

extensor

gluteus maximus

gluteus medius

biceps femoris

2. Trace the back view of the skeleton on overlay paper. Say the names of the bones as you draw them.

3. Trace the back view of the muscles on overlay paper. Say the names of the muscles as you draw them. Line up your sketch of the muscles over the skeleton and compare them.

4. Put a fresh piece of overlay paper over the two sketches of the bones and muscles. Using these as a guide, draw a fleshed-out figure. Compare this sketch to the fleshed-out figure in the book, and make any corrections with red felt pen.

5. Repeat the last step until you are easily able to sketch a fleshed-out back-view figure.

STRUCTURE OF THE LEGS AND FEET

The structure of the legs and feet is important to a fashion sketch, because that structure supports the visual weight of the figure. Notice that the feet are sketched as if you were looking directly down on them. This gives the feet enough size to support the figure.

When the leg moves, the muscle controlling the movement contracts and makes the leg thicken slightly.

Use the following exercises to practice drawing legs:

1. Draw a line 5 inches long on a piece of overlay paper, and mark the inches as you did in the first exercise on proportion, starting with the top line as line 4. Using the first sketch as a guide, draw the geometric structure

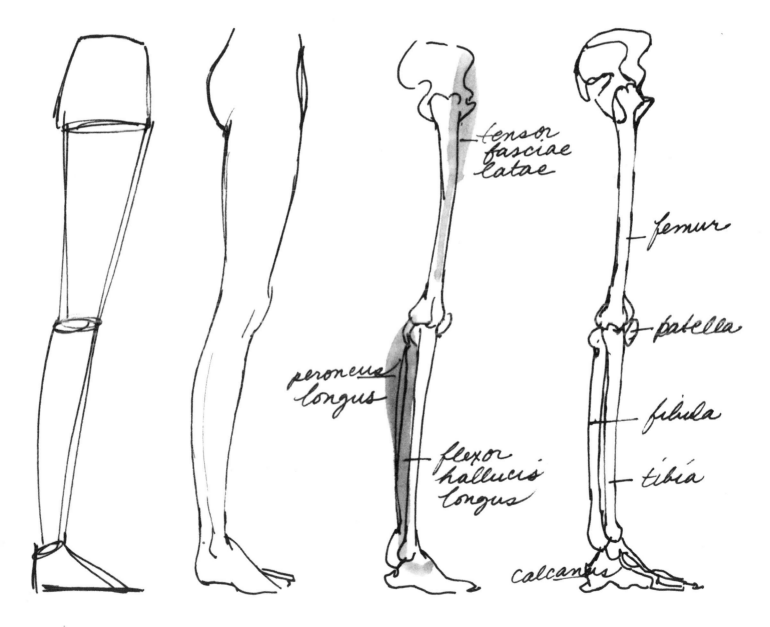

tensor fasciae latae

peroneus longus

flexor hallucis longus

femur

patella

fibula

tibia

calcaneus

of the legs from the pelvis block to the feet. Compare your sketch to the block figure, and make corrections in your sketch with a red felt pen.

2. Trace the diagram of the bone structure of the legs on overlay paper. Say the names of the major bones as you draw them.

3. Trace the muscle diagrams on overlay paper. Compare them to your skeleton diagram.

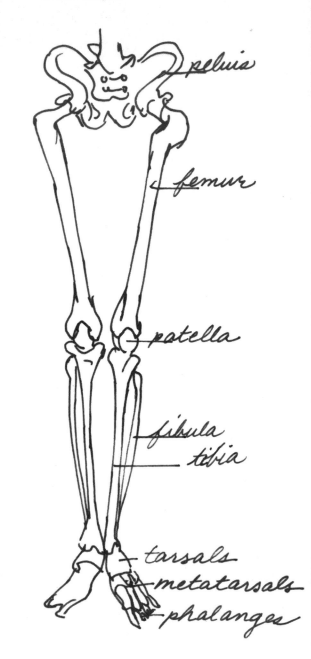

pelvis

femur

patella

fibula
tibia

tarsals
metatarsals
phalanges

4. Draw a finished fleshed-out sketch of the legs on a fresh sheet of overlay paper, using your drawing of the muscles as a guide.

5. Practice drawing legs and feet freehand. Try to imagine the bone and muscle structure of the fleshed-out legs as you draw them. Practice until you can draw a realistic leg and foot.

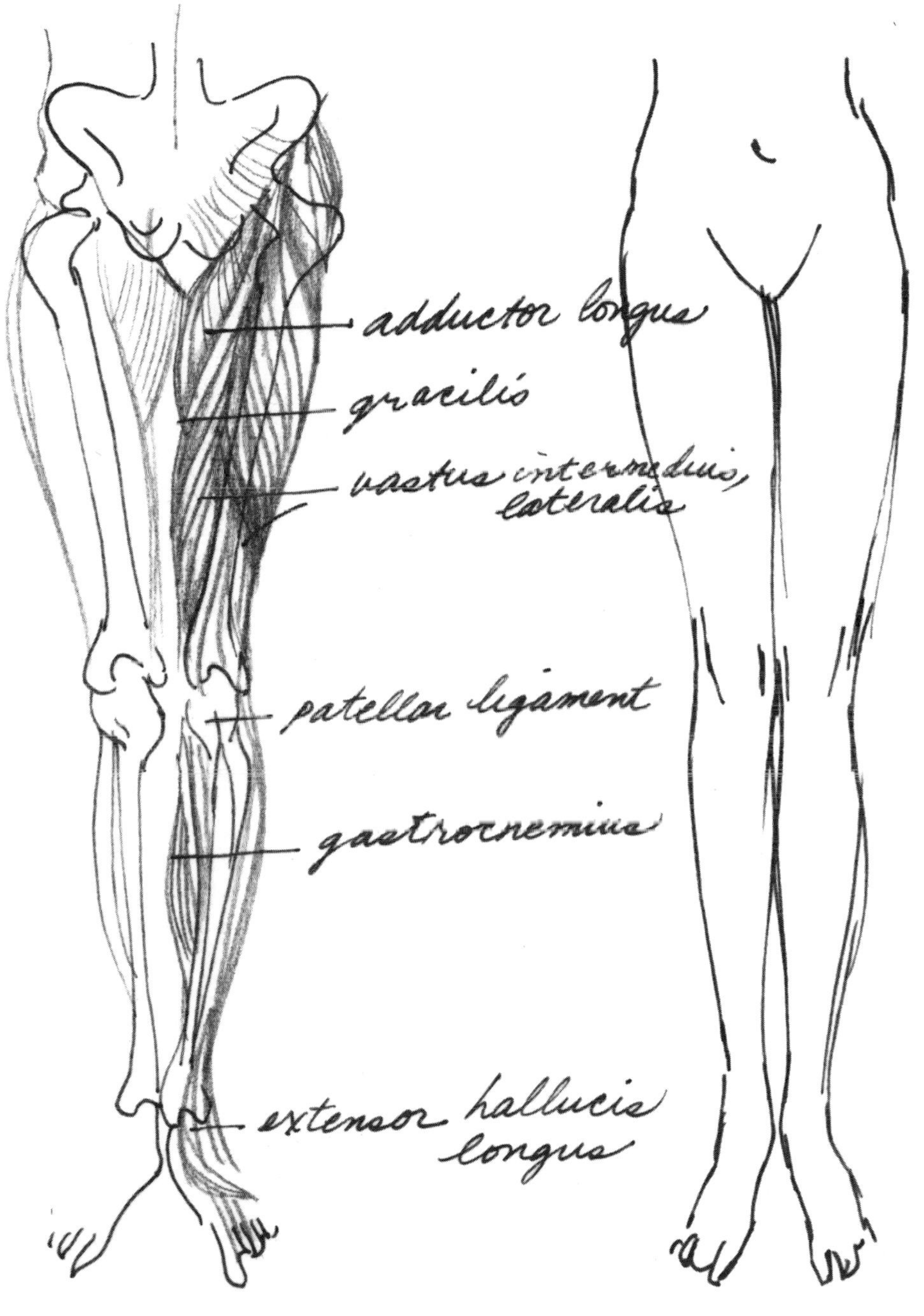

adductor longus

gracilis

vastus intermedius, lateralis

patella ligament

gastrocnemius

extensor hallucis longus

STRUCTURE OF THE HAND

The hand is a complicated area of the body to draw. You will find it easier to sketch the hand if you break it down into its three major components: the thumb, fingers, and hand proper (palm). Drawing the thumb position in the correct relationship to the hand and fingers is of primary importance to a realistic sketch. Trace the block hand and bone diagrams several times. Draw your own hand in a relaxed pose several times. The folds of skin over the knuckles are usually simplified in a fashion drawing. Draw the other hand studies shown here several times. The fashion hand should have a strong, poised look. The fingernails should be well groomed, but not exaggerated. The size of the hand is as large as the face from the chin to the eyebrows. Measure your own hand in relationship to your face. Observation and trial-and-error sketching are the best ways to improve drawing hands.

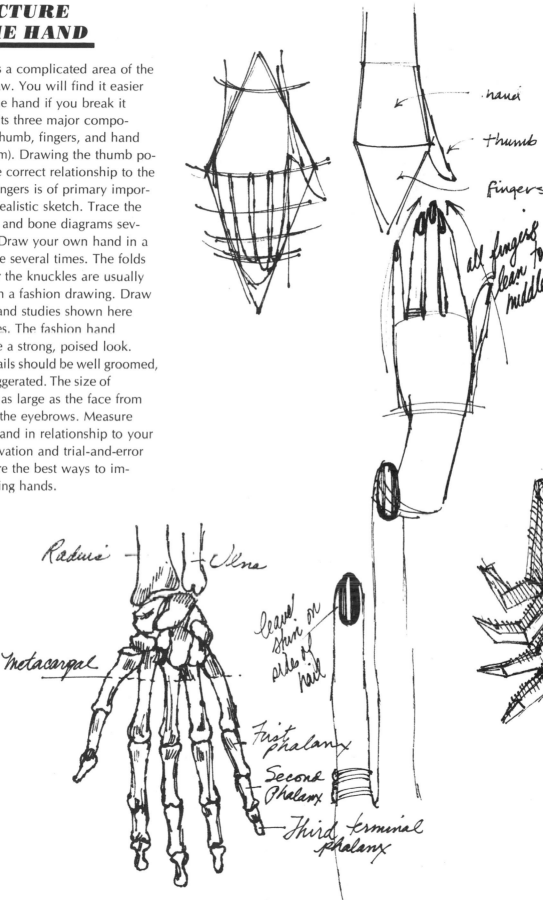

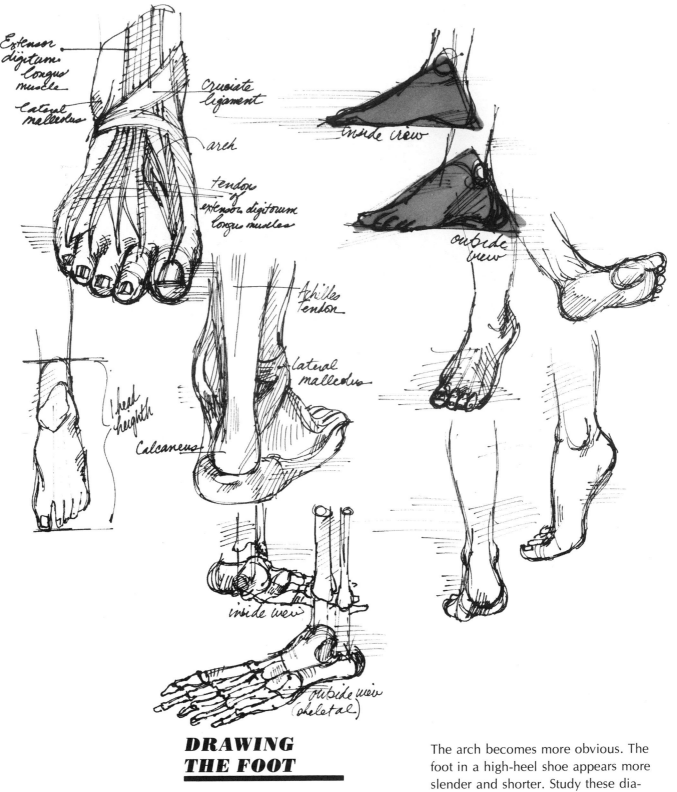

Extensor digitum longus muscle

Lateral malleolus

Cruciate ligament

arch

tendon of extensor digitorum longus muscles

inside view

outside view

Achilles tendon

Lateral malleolus

Calcaneus

heal heighth

inside view

outside view (skeletal)

DRAWING THE FOOT

The shape of the foot can be simplified to a wedge. A convincing fashion sketch should have a well-drawn foot, large enough to support the weight of the figure. The basic shape of the foot is altered when high heels are worn.

The arch becomes more obvious. The foot in a high-heel shoe appears more slender and shorter. Study these diagrams of the foot in a flat position and in shoes with heels. Trace the studies several times, then try to draw them freehand. Finally draw your own foot by looking straight down at it. Sketch shoes and an imaginary foot in them.

The shoe encases and wraps around foot

flat

arches

CHECK YOUR SKILLS

Collect the sketches you have made while working on the exercises in this chapter. Separate your freehand sketches from the exercises you have traced.

Line them up from your first effort to those completed at the end of the chapter. Analyze your progress. Compare your sketches to the following examples of student work. Identify any problems you may have from similar problems and review the solutions from the chapter.

As you progress with more complicated figure problems, continue to refer back to this chapter to help analyze proportion, muscle, and bone structure of the body.

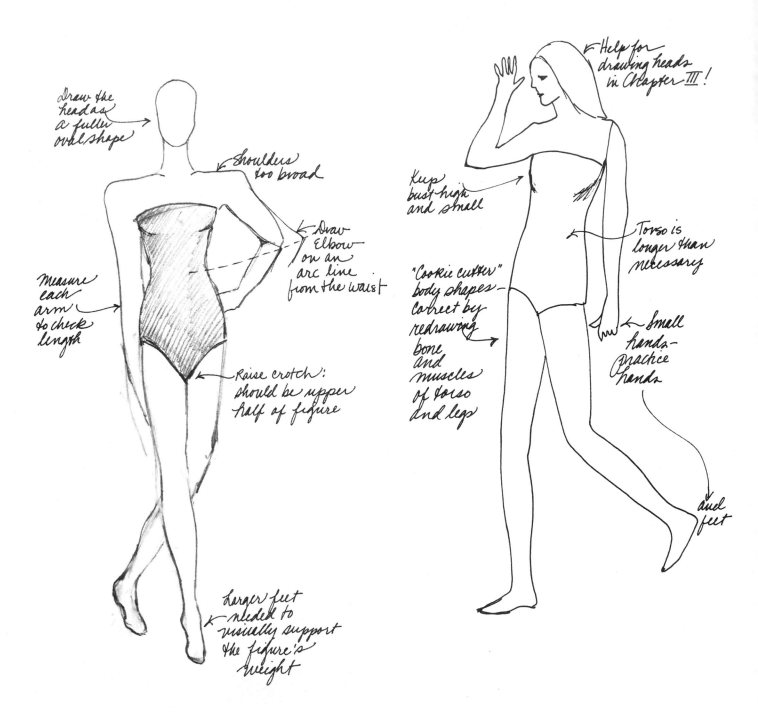

Draw the head as a fuller oval shape

Shoulders too broad

Draw Elbow on an arc line from the waist

Measure each arm to check length

Raise crotch: should be upper half of figure

Larger feet needed to visually support the figure's weight

Help for drawing heads in Chapter III!

Keep bust high and small

"Cookie cutter" body shapes—Correct by redrawing bone and muscles of torso and legs

Torso is longer than necessary

Small hands—practice hands

and feet

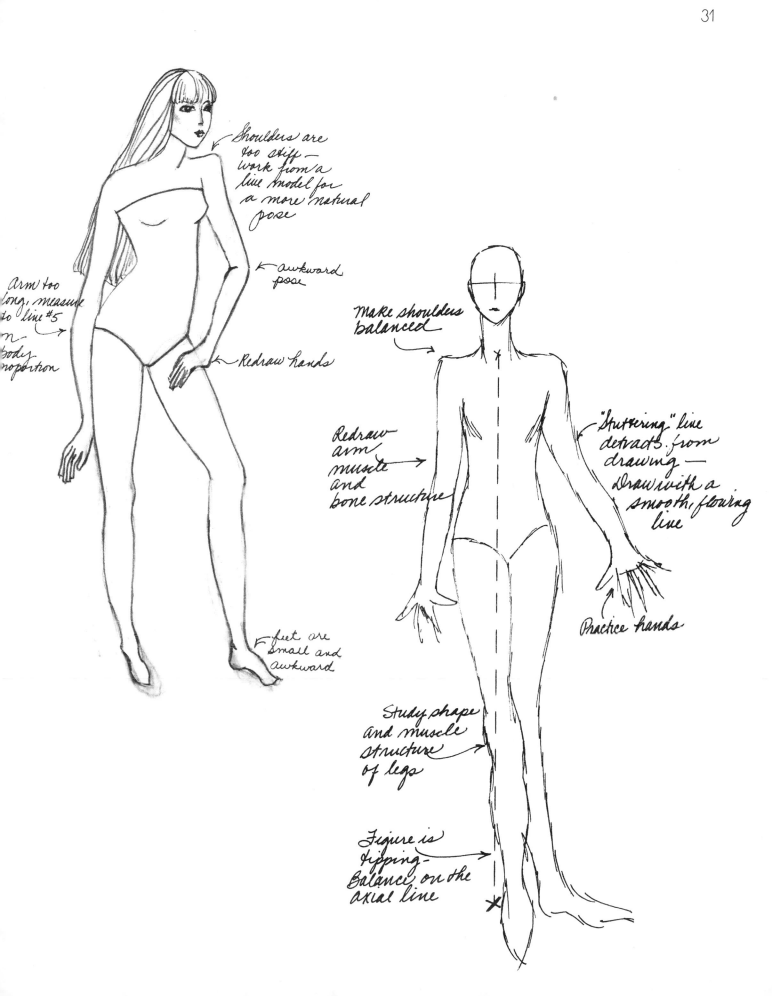

Shoulders are too stiff — work from a live model for a more natural pose

awkward pose

Redraw hands

Arm too long, measure to line #5 in body proportion

feet are small and awkward

Make shoulders balanced

Redraw arm muscle and bone structure

"Stuttering" line detracts from drawing — Draw with a smooth, flowing line

Practice hands

Study shape and muscle structure of legs

Figure is tipping — Balance on the axial line

CHAPTER THREE

DRAWING THE FASHION FACE

The fashion face gives an illustration definition and character. The face is a focal point in a picture and usually the first thing looked at. A child's first drawing is usually an attempt to draw a face, because a mother's face is the most important early human image. A poorly drawn face will detract from an otherwise good illustration, just as a well-drawn face will enhance a poor drawing.

The face establishes the age of a fashion figure. A youthful face has a natural look with a slightly rounded nose and full mouth, a natural hairstyle and little eye makeup. The sophisticated fashion illustration has sharper, more defined features, subtle but definite makeup, and a tailored hairstyle. Evening gowns are sketched on elegant models with very stylized makeup and hairstyles.

Usually a simple hairstyle and makeup is more effective, because the drawing of the face does not detract from the garment. Begin collecting scrap (photographs and sketches of faces and hairstyles) to inspire your drawing. Sketch from life and try to capture the personality of your model.

FACIAL PROPORTIONS

Study the face shown here.

The head is oval shaped, with the fuller end representing the forehead. The features are balanced symmetrically on either side of the vertical median (central) line.

The eyes are placed on the horizontal median of the head. They are almond shaped. There is almost the length of a whole eye between them. Eyebrows begin at the inside corner of the eye, arch over the midpoint of the almond shape, and extend slightly beyond the outer edge.

The nose falls at the lower one-third division of the face and lines up with the inner corner of the eyes. The mouth is centered below the nose. The chin should be slender and well defined.

The oval shape of the face is accented with prominent cheekbones defined by shadows. The top of the ears align with the eyes and end parallel to the mouth. The natural hairline curves around the skull above line 1. The neck lines up with the outer corner of the eyes, extending on the side lateral lines connecting to the head at the back of the neck.

Practice drawing smooth, even oval shapes with a #2 soft pencil between two vertical lines. Hold your pencil with a light, firm grip as you draw the ovals.

DRAWING THE FACE, STEP BY STEP

1. Draw a rectangle 6 inches long and 4 inches wide on a piece of overlay paper. Measure and mark the 6 inches on the sides of the rectangle. Fill the rectangle with an oval that touches the bottom and top and falls slightly inside the sides of the rectangle.

2. Divide the rectangle in quarters–2 inches on either side of the vertical median, 3 inches on either side of the horizontal median.

3. Measure 1½ inches on either side of the vertical median and lightly draw the two side lateral lines.

practice making smooth ovals

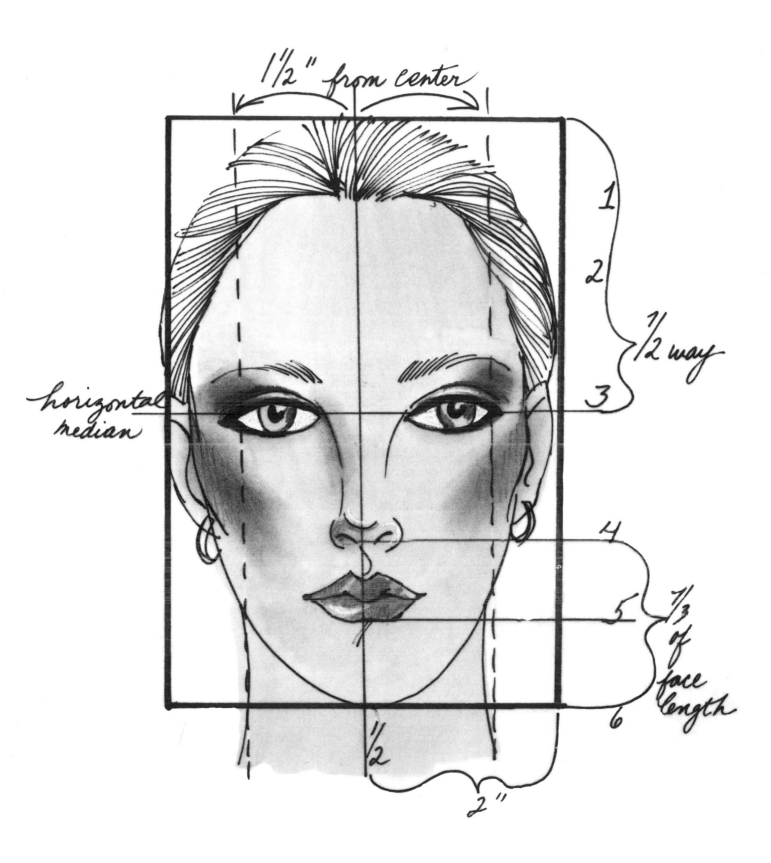

1½" from center

horizontal
median

1
2
3
} ½ way

4
5 } ⅓ of face length
6

½

2"

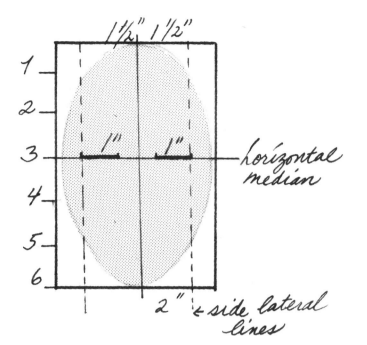

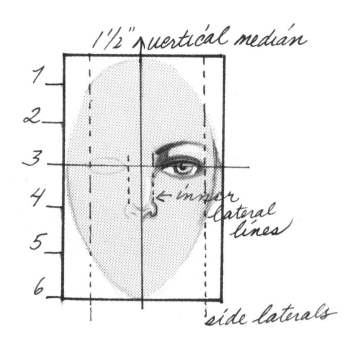

4. From the lateral lines inward along the horizontal median, draw two 1-inch-long almond-shaped eyes. Notice there is 1 inch in between the eyes.

5. Extend two light guidelines down from the inner corners of the eyes. Indicate the nostrils evenly balanced on either side of the vertical median (line 4).

6. Draw shallow ear shapes at the sides of the head between the eyes (line 3) and mouth (slightly beyond line 4).

7. Draw the mouth extending slightly beyond the inner lateral lines above line 5.

8. Curve the side lateral lines slightly inward and draw the neck.

9. Add cheekbone contours inside the ears and shade.

10. Draw eyebrows beginning at the inner corner of the eyes. Arch at the center and extend slightly beyond the outer edge of the eyes. Use light, short lines to imitate the way eyebrows really are. Hard pencil lines are passé.

11. Detail the eyes with lids and pupils.

12. Add the hairline above line 1, and extend to the sides of the ears.

13. Shade the eyes and the bridge of the nose.

Put your finished exercise over the face on page 35 and compare it. Make corrections in fine-line red felt pen. Practice the front face many times. Draw the eyes and mouth on the following pages. Draw faces from life, photographs, and other drawings. Develop personality and style for your illustrations.

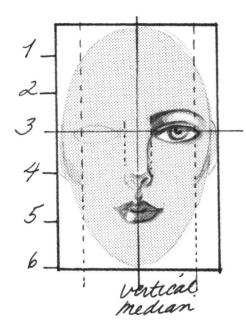

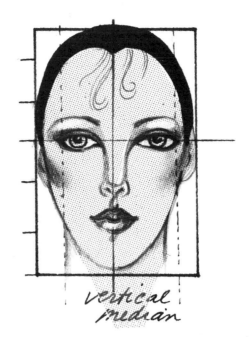

FEATURES

DRAWING THE EYE

1.   Draw an almond shape.

2.   Divide the top third of the almond with the curved lid line. Fill at least one-third of the eye with a round circle for the iris. Notice how the lid covers the top of the iris.

3.   Add the pupil to the center of the iris and shape the inner corner of the eye.

4.   Detail the eye with subtle lashes, highlights, and shadows.

DRAWING THE MOUTH

1.   Divide a small rectangle as shown. The top lip is usually smaller than the bottom lip.

2.   Draw two circles in the top part of the rectangle and a larger oval below these.

3.   Detail the shape of the mouth using the ovals as a guide and carrying the lines to the edge of the rectangle.

4.   Shade and shape the lips.

Notice the many ways the basic features can be drawn to create exciting and unique faces.

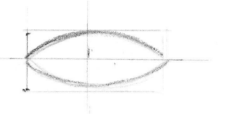

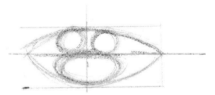

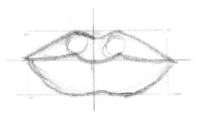

A Young Socialite look
— slightly bored and
blasé

Oriental face
Eyes have heavy
lids, flatter nose
hair looks best
a graphic shape

A smile shouldn't
be too toothy.
Never indicate
individual
teeth

Black
Face

High cheekbones
wider bridge of
nose and nostrils
Eyes are rounder
lips, fuller

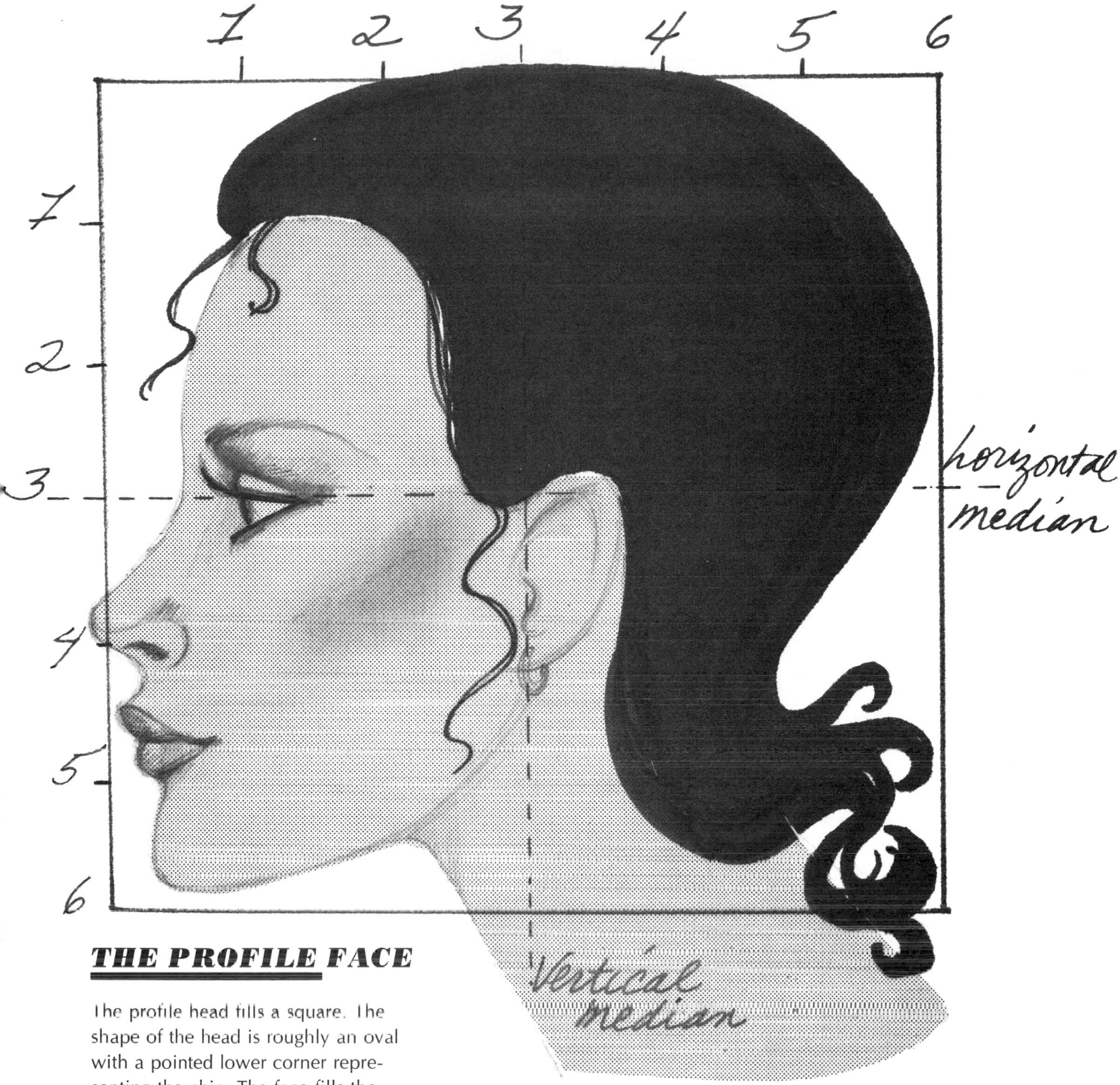

Numbered grid labels across top: 1 2 3 4 5 6

Numbered grid labels down left side: 1 2 3 4 5 6

horizontal median

Vertical median

THE PROFILE FACE

The profile head fills a square. The shape of the head is roughly an oval with a pointed lower corner representing the chin. The face fills the front diagonal half of the square. Notice how the feature placement relates to the front face. The eyes fall on the horizontal median. The nose falls at line 4. The lips are drawn in the same position, slightly above line 5, as on the front face. The placement of the ear is between the eyes and the mouth.

The hairline roughly conforms to the diagonal line through the square. Do not emphasize the jawbone, which connects to the neck behind the ear, as it will look too masculine.

Notice how the eye and mouth are drawn in profile (see pages 40 and 41). Practice drawing several of these features before you attempt the step-by-step profile drawing on the next pages.

39

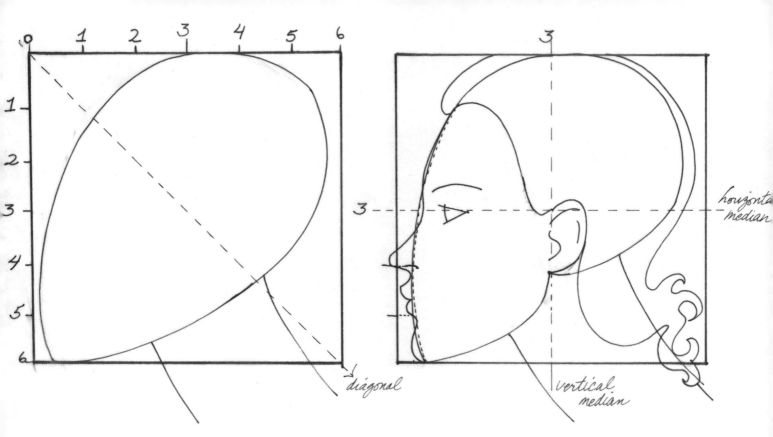

DRAWING THE PROFILE HEAD, STEP BY STEP

1. Draw a square 6 inches by 6 inches and mark a 1-inch grid in light pencil. Use overlay paper.

2. Draw an oval with the narrow end slanted towards the lower corner of the square.

3. Draw a diagonal guideline from corner to corner bisecting the square.

4. Divide the square into quarters with light lines.

5. Draw a wedge shape centered on the horizontal median, line 3. Indicate the profile eye shape here.

6. Shape the nose indenting it at line 3 and drawing the triangular shape ending at line 4.

7. Draw the ear between the eye and the mouth on the vertical median of the square.

8. Outline mouth and chin.

9. Draw the neck coming from behind the diagonal in a graceful curve.

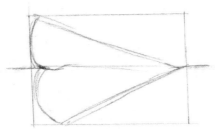

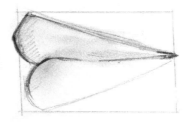

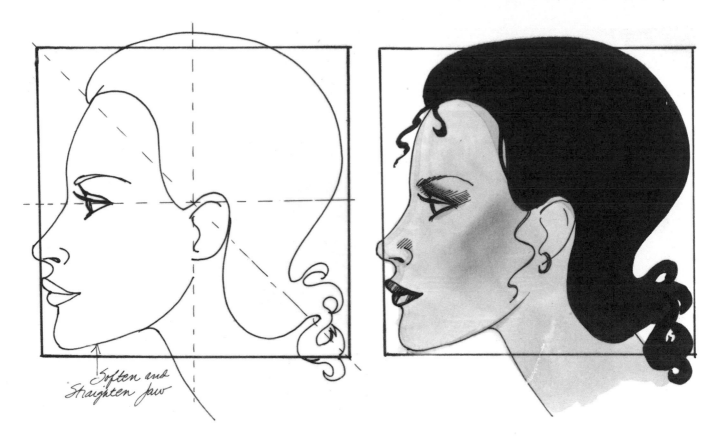

Soften and
Straighten Jaw

10. Draw the mouth above line 5.

11. Curve the chin: do not make it weak or too exaggerated.

12. The hairline corresponds roughly with the diagonal. Curve the hair around the ears and at the nape of the neck.

13. Detail the eye. Notice how the eyebrow arches over the front of the eye as it follows the skull's ridge over the eye socket.

14. Add the nostril and the outer curve of the nose. Refine the profile of the nose.

15. Detail and shadow the mouth. Shadow the cheekbones.

Place your sketch over the first profile drawing on page 39. Compare your drawing to the standard. Correct errors with a fine-line red felt pen.

Sketch profiles from life, photographs, and other drawings. Notice the infinite variety of shapes of faces and noses. Draw the profiles facing left and right, so that you will be able to draw them both ways. Beginners tend to face a profile in the direction of their weaker hand.

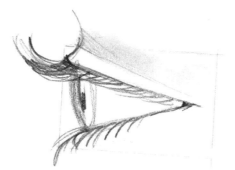

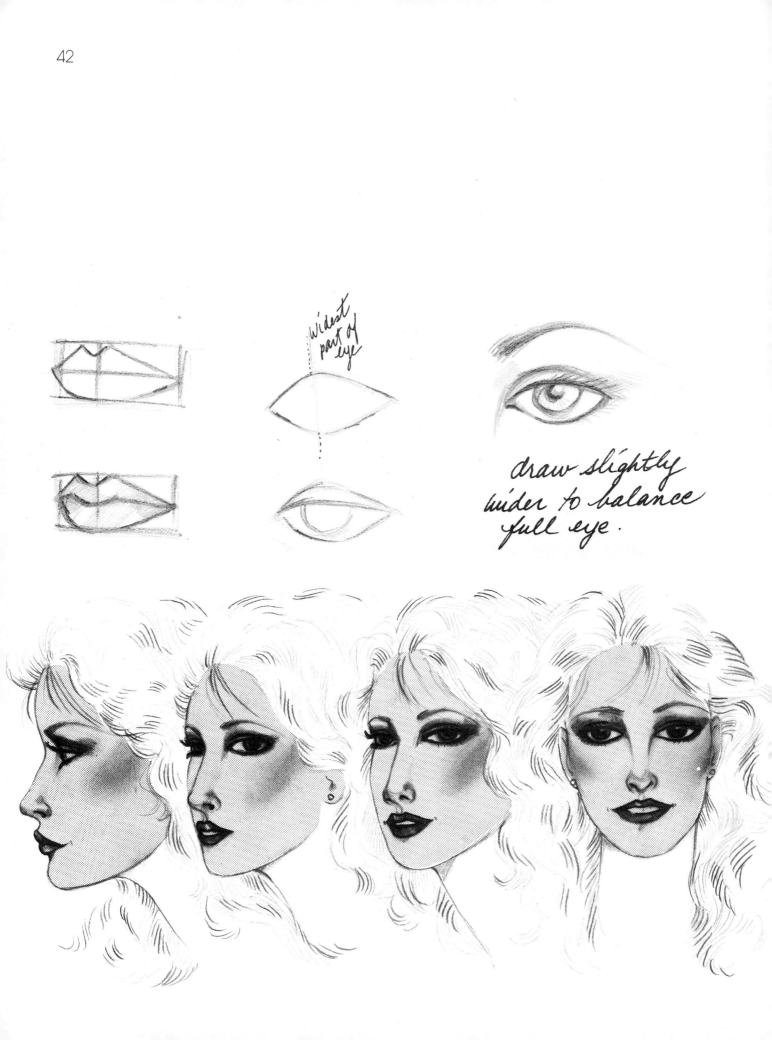

widest part of eye

draw slightly
wider to balance
full eye.

TURNING THE HEAD

The three-quarter head combines the elements of the full face and the profile head. Observing contours of the cheek and chin is an important part of drawing the face as it turns. The proportion and feature placement is consistent with the other faces—eyes on the horizontal median, nose at line 4, and mouth placement above line 5. Practice drawing eyes and mouth in their various positions.

1. Draw a 6-by-6-inch square.

2. Divide it in half horizontally.

3. Draw an oval in the square, with the smaller end tilted towards one corner.

4. Lightly draw a curved center line in the front quarter of the oval.

5. Place the almond-shaped eyes on the horizontal median. Notice how the inside corner of one eye is partially hidden by the curve of the nose. For balance, draw the eye on the far side of the nose slightly fuller than the closer eye.

6. Contour the cheekbone and chin.

7. Place the nose at line 4. It is a shallower triangle than that of the profile nose.

8. Draw a mouth wedge using the center line and the line 5 mark as a guide.

9. Detail the eyes. Notice how the far eyebrow follows into the curve of the bridge of the nose.

10. Detail the mouth, foreshortening the far side.

11. Draw the hairline above line 1 and frame the face at the ears and nape of the neck.

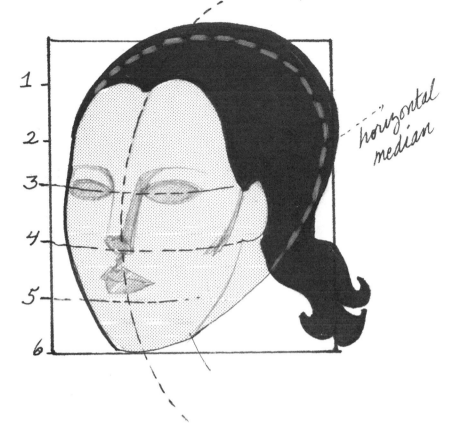

horizontal median

Line up Ear with base of Neck

More skull is visible

THE THREE-DIMEN-SIONAL HEAD

The head has volume that corresponds to a cube drawn in perspective. The features can be simplified to stylized indications, but a concrete idea of volume and structure is necessary to successfully draw more complicated and realistic faces.

Study the volume sketches, which show the nose and eyes in various positions. Notice how tilting the head up and down subtly alters the shape of the features.

You see more of the nose and lips when the head tilts upward

The direction of the curved lines determines head looking up or down

Sketch several heads using photographs as inspiration. Break down the structural elements of the head by outlining the shadowed areas. Always identify the part of the face closest to you because it has the truest proportion for the accurate placement of features. When you have a good rough drawing in a square, trace over it, leaving out the guidelines, and use light shadows done in a black prisma pencil to model the head. Draw the features with a fine-line black felt pen, a sharp prisma pencil, or a Rapidograph.

direct all lines to clasp

flow enhances long neck

DRAWING HAIR

Hairstyles change as rapidly as fashions. It is important to use a hairstyle that is appropriate for the age of the fashion figure and the garment she is wearing. A stylized, ornate hairstyle would be as out of place on a fashion model wearing a tennis dress as it would be on the tennis court.

To inspire your selection of hairstyles, observe and collect photographs (scrap) from fashion magazines. Look at people and study the way well-

shape!

follow shape of skull

subtle hairs at neckline

groomed hair looks. The hairstyle should not detract from the garment.

Hair grows out of the scalp. Your drawing lines should imitate hair's natural growth pattern. Draw the direction the hair grows with irregularly spaced lines that simplify and capture the volume of the style. Soft, fine hair

grows at the hairline, so render it with delicate light strokes.

Highlights give hair a sleek, healthy look. They are drawn by letting the white of the paper remain as the light accent, darkening in natural shadows, and then accenting the lines that show the direction the hair flows.

Block in face, features

DRAWING HAIR, STEP BY STEP

1. Draw a face with a light pencil line indicating the features and skull.

2. Block in the general silhouette of the hairstyle.

3. Erase the vague indication of the skull.

4. Draw directional lines starting at the hairline and flowing out to the edge of the silhouette. Make the lines irregularly spaced. Continue to detail the features as you work on the hairstyle.

Add tone, refine oval (face) define features more

5. Shadow and highlight the hair. Observe live hairstyles and photographs, noticing how the highlights occur in various styles and hair colors. A darker area around the face is an effective contrast devise.

6. Fully detail and shadow the features.

7. To render blond hair, use more highlight areas and fewer deep shadows. Do not eliminate all tone because the hairstyle will lack definition.

8. An upswept hairstyle accented with a dressy hair ornament is appropriate for a more sophisticated outfit.

*Add more tone,
Highlights
Add linework for
hair and accessories*

Drawing by Robert Passantino for Women's Wear Daily.

Sketch a series of ten hairstyles from magazine photographs. Experiment with the felt pens and prisma and lead pencils. Try using only line to illustrate some of the hairstyles. Illustrate a variety of ages. Try adding hair accessories like combs and ribbons to vary the effect.

Simple Hairdo

Light Eyebrows

Less defined cheekbones

Softer, Fuller Lips

Less Eye Make Up

Freckles

THE YOUTHFUL FACE
A young junior model should have a simple hairstyle and natural makeup. The cheeks are often shadowed on top of the cheekbone, so the face looks suntanned. A casual pose completes the natural look.

◀

Casual
Hairstyle
with movement

Little make-up

Sunglasses: an
effective prop

Casual,
easy linework
looking quite
effortless!

▲
THE ACTIVE FACE
*Active clothes look best on a
sport figure with a bright, active look. The hairstyle should
be very casual. Props appropriate to the sport and sunglasses help set the stage.*

THE DAYTIME HIGH-
FASHION FACE
*This model should have the
look of polished sophistication. A simple, but elegant,
hairstyle and makeup will not
detract from the clothes being
shown.*

Subtle
hairdo-
Close to the
head, simple
style

Shade less on brows

Eyes are
alert, less
eye make up

Soft shading
on cheekbones

Simple
earrings

Sophisticated
expression, yet
friendly

Lighter skin tones

52

THE SOPHISTICATED EVENING FACE

The drama of evening clothes is enhanced by a more stylized and defined makeup. Elaborate jewelry is appropriate. The hairstyle can be more flamboyant or stylized depending on the kind of evening dress illustrated.

simple hairstyle

heavier eye makeup

slightly pouting mouth

more heavily accentuated jewelry

54

Hair style is stiff and overworked

Soften eyes,

Detail the nose, show the curve of a nostril

Mouth is too low so chin looks weak

Practice aligning the features

Mouth should have a pleasant, relaxed look

Use a soft, feathered line for a natural eyebrow

Always finish the eye

Part of the outside eye is covered by bridge of nose

Contour the cheek bone

Study mouth shape

Hair is overworked

Chin is awkward

Keep a vision of the volume of the head as you draw hair

Study the contour of the 3/4 profile

Neck is a fluid, curved column

Collect the sketches you have made while doing the exercises on faces. Compare them to the student work shown here. Analyze the strengths and weaknesses of your work. Refer back to the pages that teach lessons that you need more work on.

Study line profiles and draw from life to emulate realism

Re-align features Eyes and nose are too high

Heavy, overworked rendering of hair

Keep whisps of hair soft and natural

Ear prominent for an upswept hair style

Chin and jaw too heavy

Slim, lythe neck is more graceful

Eye brows should be lightly feathered

One eye space between eyes

Detail the nostrils

Align the features Eyes too high

nose too high

mouth is awkward

Render the hair with smoother tones and lines to show direction of hair style

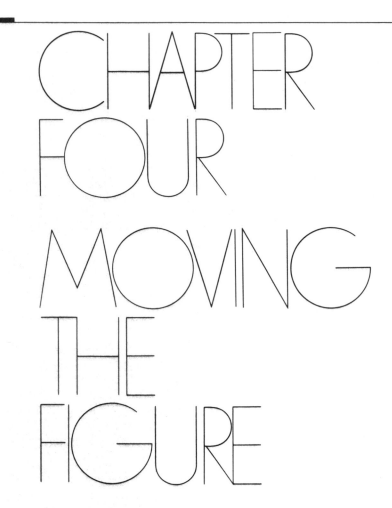

CHAPTER FOUR

MOVING THE FIGURE

TYPICAL POSES

Moving the fashion figure adds drama, excitement, and personality to a sketch. The construction of the body governs the way it moves. The base of the neck is the center of gravity that determines the vertical (or axial) balance line. When the figure is standing with the weight evenly distributed on both feet, the axial line falls midway between the feet. All the horizontal body lines, the shoulder, rib cage, pelvis, and knees, are parallel to the floor and form 90-degree angles with the axial line.

The one-leg stand is a typical fashion pose, because of the flowing body lines created. For this pose the figure relaxes one leg and puts most of the weight on the other leg. The axial line and horizontal body lines are re-aligned. It is important not to let the figure in this asymmetrical pose lean. To avoid this, draw a vertical axial line from the base of the neck perpendicular to the bottom of the page. This line must intersect the heel of the support leg or the figure will tilt. When a figure is leaning against a prop, the axial line falls between the support leg and the prop.

The slant of the shoulder and pelvis blocks are altered when the body's weight is supported mostly by one leg. The shoulder can align with the pelvic block. In this pose, the high shoulder is over the high hip.

THE AXIAL LINE
The axial line governs the balance of any figure. The axial line falls between both legs in a balanced stand when the weight is on both feet. The axial line starts at the base of the neck and lines up with the heel of the support leg in a one-leg stand.

▶

The classical one-leg stand has the rib cage tilted in opposition to the pelvic block. The high shoulder is over the low hip. A smooth S curve is created by opposing the direction of the body's two major masses. This pose is very flattering and shows clothes fluidly with very little distortion of detail and silhouette. Yet, there is a great deal of movement and action to the figure. Notice the axial line in both of the one-leg stands starts at the base of the neck and always falls at the heel of the leg supporting the majority of the body's weight.

Practice drawing these three figures several times. Concentrate on lining up the base of the neck with the supporting leg, and draw this axial line in a contrasting color felt pen.

DRAWING FROM
A LIVE MODEL

The beginner will often be confused when drawing from a live model. The subject looks complicated and difficult to draw after working from photographs.

Study the pose before you begin to draw. Analyze the slant of the shoulders and the hip bone. Notice how the head tilts and curves into the base of the neck. Determine which leg is supporting the major weight load. Draw an imaginary axial line from the base of the neck to the heel of the support leg, or hold up your pencil and squint to visualize the flow of the pose. Notice how the arms are posed and relate the elbows to an arc that passes smoothly through the waist.

Now you are ready to sketch the live model. Nothing substitutes for this analysis of the structural elements of the pose before you pick up your pencil. Follow the steps on the next page as you draw the sketch from the live model.

analyze the slant of shoulders and block out.

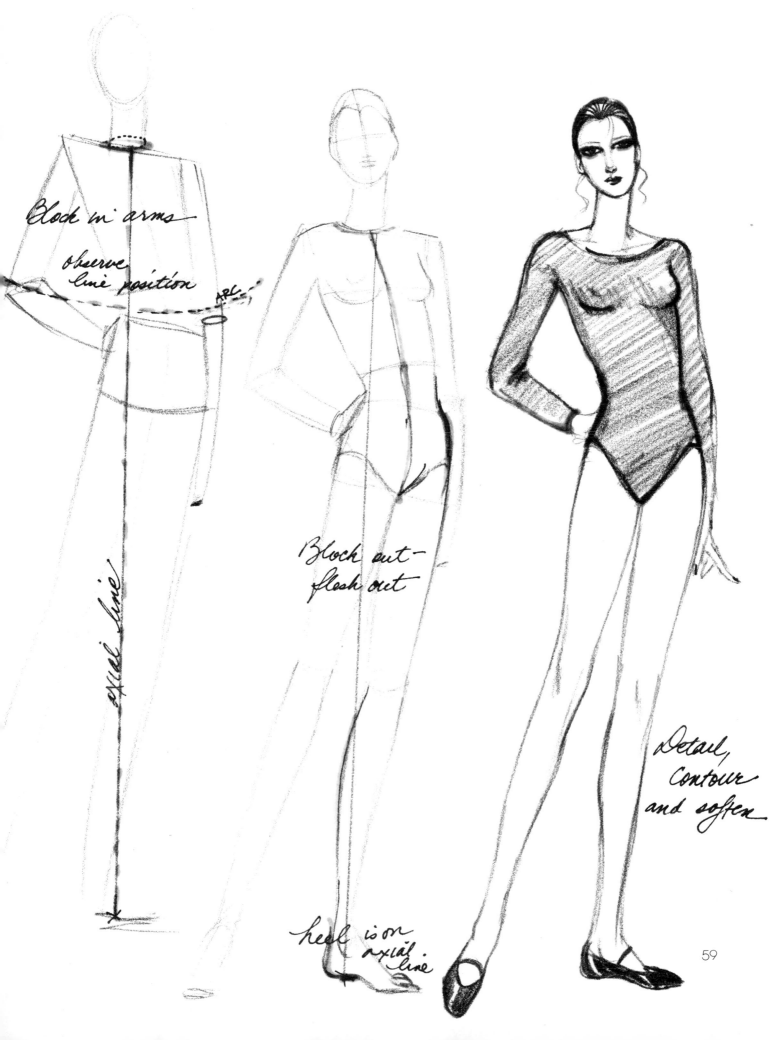

Block in arms

observe
line position

ARC

axial line

Block out –
flesh out

heel is on
axial line

Detail,
Contour
and soften

59

THE THREE-DIMENSIONAL BODY

As the figure turns, the body planes rotate and develop depth. Arms and legs are often partially or entirely hidden by the torso. When drawing from a live pose or photograph, evaluate the pose before beginning to draw. Trace the part of the body that is closest to you (the leading edge) with your eyes. Then begin to lightly sketch the head and the torso blocks, drawing the leading edges first. Notice how the torso may block the view of an arm or leg. Draw the arm nearest you first. Then draw the par-

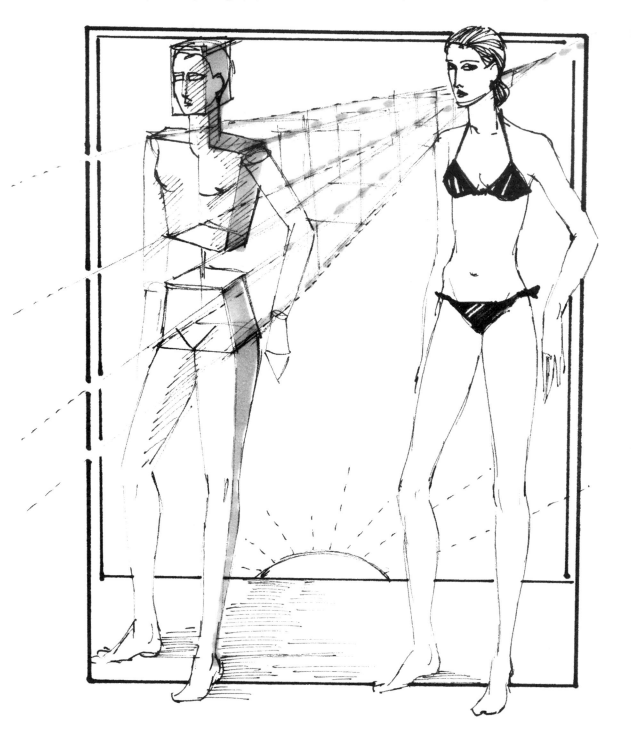

tially hidden arm. Draw the main support leg first. Make sure it falls on the axial line, so that your figure does not tip. Then draw the more relaxed balance leg.

Draw the median line (center) on the face and torso blocks. It will shift farther and farther to the side as the figure rotates. The median line is not used on a profile figure. On a back view, the median line corresponds to the spine.

Study these sketches and draw a series of three-dimensional figure studies from models in similar poses. Lightly draw the simple box figure blocks before fleshing out your sketch.

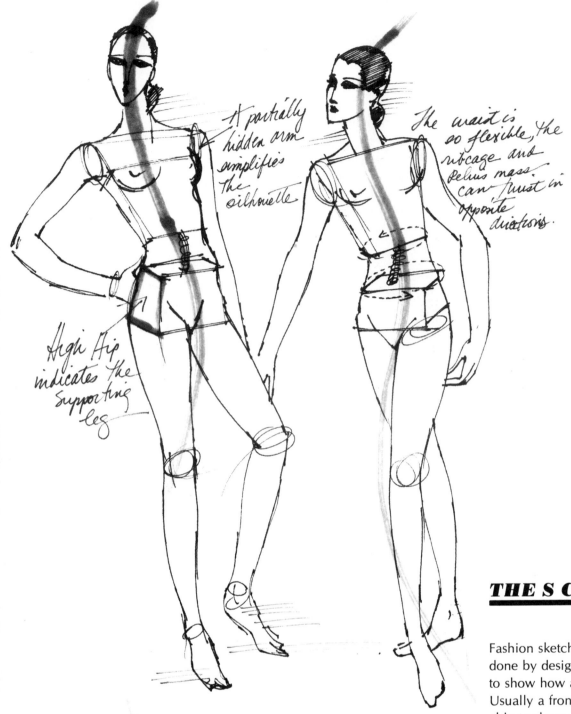

A partially hidden arm simplifies the silhouette

The waist is so flexible, the ribcage and pelvis mass can twist in opposite directions.

High hip indicates the supporting leg

THE S CURVE

Fashion sketching, especially when done by designers, is primarily used to show how a garment should look. Usually a frontal pose is the most suitable to show garment detail and silhouette. A rigid, straightforward pose can be repetitious and stiff. The figure can assume an exciting frontal pose when it follows a flowing S curve. The one-leg stand, with well posed arms that give the shoulders direction and thrust, will show a garment to its best advantage.

The rib cage and pelvis can twist in opposite directions, because the waist is very flexible. This twisting pose

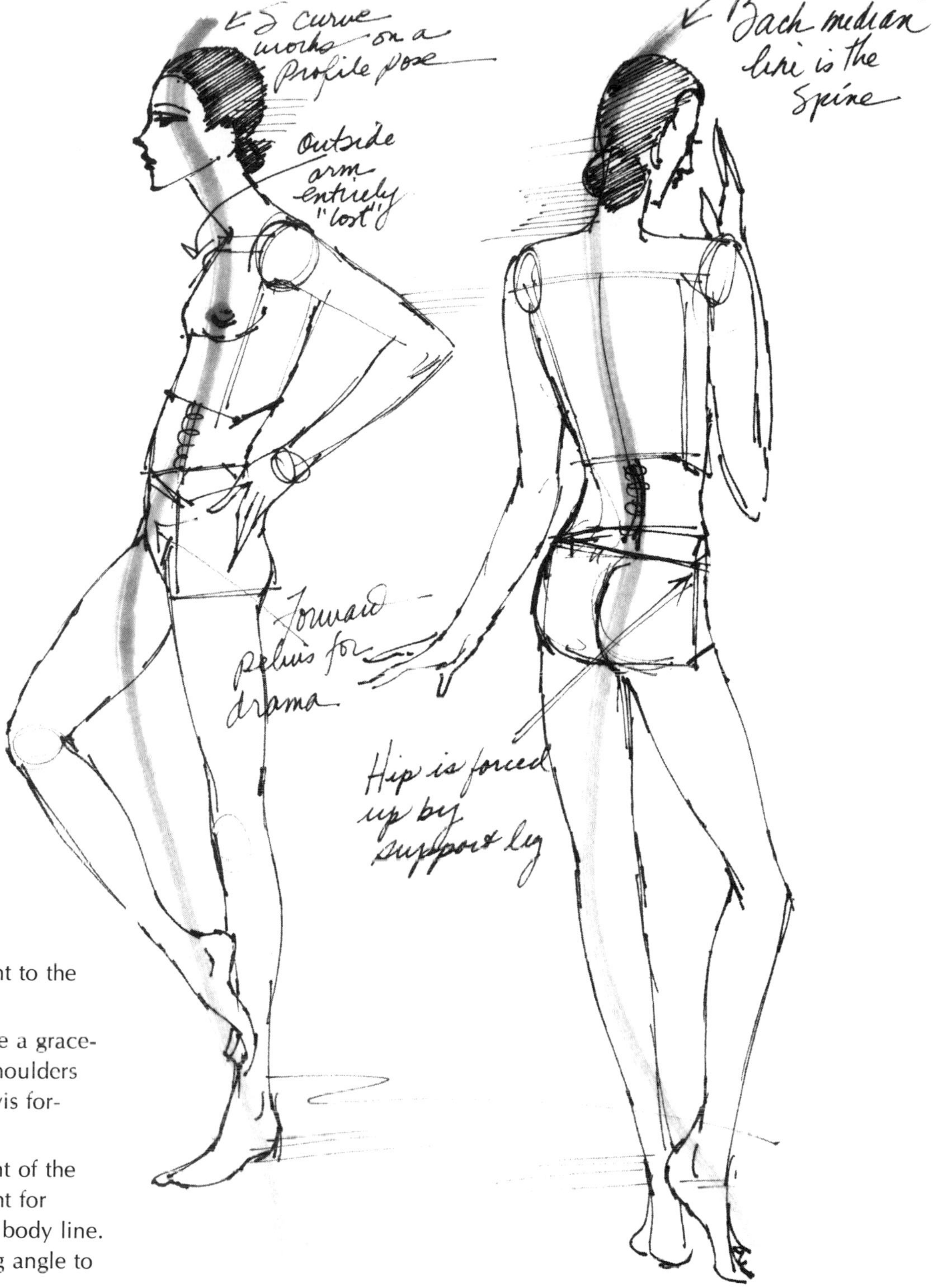

S curve works on a profile pose

Outside arm entirely "lost"

Forward pelvis for drama

Back median line is the spine

Hip is forced up by support leg

adds even greater movement to the one-leg stand pose.

A profile pose can also have a graceful S curve line when the shoulders are thrust back and the pelvis forward.

The direction and placement of the head and neck are important for creating a flowing, graceful body line. Draw the head at a pleasing angle to the rest of the body.

Practice drawing these figures many times: Start with a broad-nib light-grey felt pen and draw the S curve first. Then construct a body along this flowing line. Constantly check the axial line, and do not lose sight of the fact the axial line is a guide for realistic support of the flowing pose.

Courtesy of Charles Bush.

DRAWING FROM PHOTOGRAPHS

Fashion magazines, especially those from Europe, are an excellent source of figures for sketching. Foreign fashion magazines feature forward styling and innovative photography. Most illustrators and designers read and use the ideas presented in these specialized publications.

A pose is easily adapted from a swipe (magazine photograph) when it is used as a suggestion—not a tracing for a drawing. Analyze the photograph as you would a live pose. Determine the axial line of the figure before drawing a line. Notice the slant of the shoulders. Are the hips angled in opposition to the shoulders? Put a piece of overlay or tracing paper over the photograph and quickly rough in the body blocks. Do not trace directly from the photograph, because your figure will look stocky and awkward. Put another piece of tracing paper over the rough blocks you traced from the figure, and use them as a guide to sketch a finished figure. Refer back to the photograph to make sure the details are accurate.

Block out ten or more figures from magazine photographs. Select several of your favorite block figures to work into finished sketches. Experiment with drawing clothes by observing how the fabric drapes and flows over the body. Use the block figures as a

F·E·M·M·E cosmetics

guide and try to sketch the figure and garments without using further guidelines. Leave your work for several hours. Compare your sketch with the photograph. Turn the tracing or overlay paper over, so you can see the reverse image of your sketch or hold your drawing up to a mirror. Obvious mistakes will pop out at you. This is because your eye adjusts to a sketch that it sees develop over a period of time and tends to balance symmetrical elements. By reversing the image, the artist will have a new perspective on the sketch and can analyze its weaknesses.

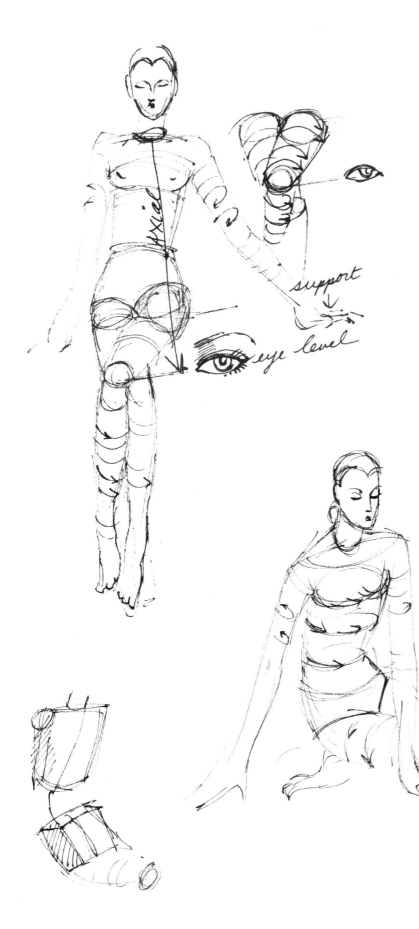

FORESHORTENING THE FIGURE

Visualizing complicated poses as a series of simple geometric forms will help the beginner to analyze and draw the sitting or reclining figure. The axial line for a seated pose relates the base of the neck to the seat. When the weight of the figure is partially supported by an arm, the axial line will fall at a point between the support arm and the seat.

Think of an arm or leg as a cylindrical shape when you want to foreshorten it. Draw the part closest to your eye first. Draw cylindrical, spiraling lines for the arm or leg curving back toward the body. Observation and practice are the surest teachers for mastering perspective. Quick sketches from life and photographs will sharpen your analytical eye and drawing ability.

Perspective plays an important part in drawing a three-dimensional pose. Establish the eye level of the figure you want to draw. At this line, your eye views a flat dimension. Above the eye-level line you will look up at the bottom of the geometric cubes representing the rib cage or pelvic block. Horizontal lines of the figure or garments will have a subtle upward arc. Below eye level the body blocks will be viewed from the top and horizontal lines will have a curve downward at the center.

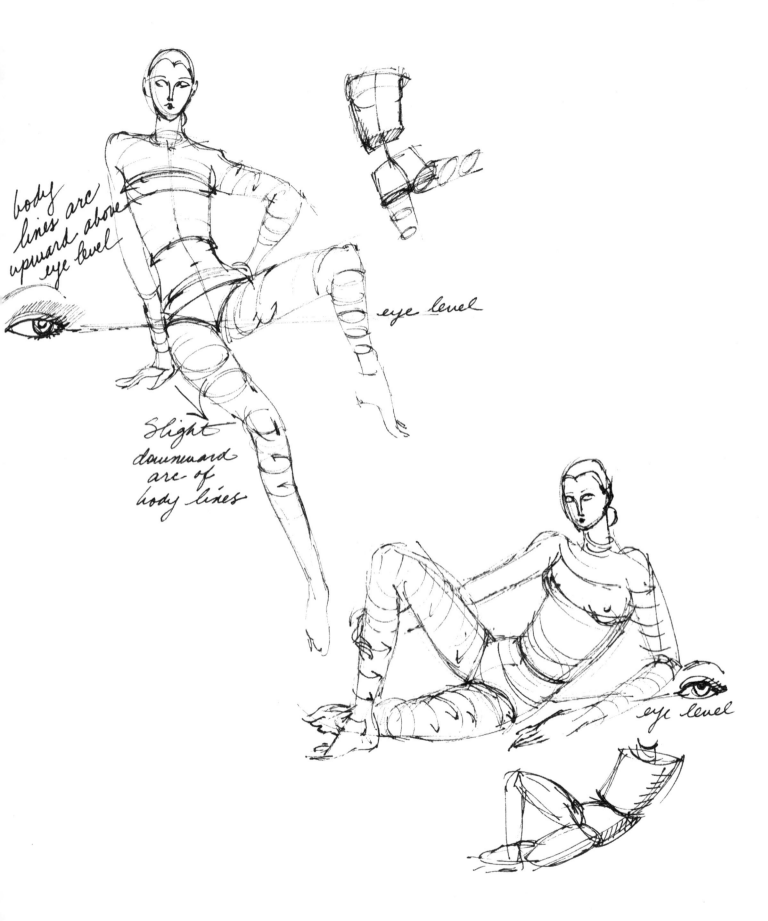

body lines arc upward above eye level

eye level

Slight downward arc of body lines

eye level

68

ADDING MOVEMENT TO THE FIGURE

The advanced illustrator is able to give figures realistic action that creates a dramatic drawing. "Loose" drawing has an immediate, spontaneous look that is not overly self-conscious about rendering details. To loosen up your drawing and give it a confident "loose" look, use the following techniques and sketch from life or photographs of an action figure.

Quickly sketch the body blocks and limbs with a broad-nib light-colored felt pen. Use as few strokes as possible to capture the action of the figure. Do not worry about details. Work quickly on poses lasting no longer than two minutes. If working from photographs, clip out ten or more and use a timer to tell you when to move on to the next sketch. Later, select the best action drawings and use them under a fresh sheet of overlay paper the way you used the tracings of the skeleton in the second chapter. Draw detailed figures with prisma pencils or fine-line markers, incorporating the movement of the block figure underneath.

Spiral drawing is another effective technique for loosening up your drawings. Start with the head and work through the body with quick spirals, never letting your pencil leave the paper. Practice several times, and rework the best examples as you did with the felt-pen action figures.

You may also loosen up your figures by drawing with a soft piece of charcoal. Wedge the end of the stick. Block in the masses with the broad part of the charcoal, and sketch the limbs with a single stroke.

Charcoal.

Soft pencil

broad tip Marker

Charcoal for S curve

Medium marker

Check the proportion of the figure to the crotch line, to make sure the legs are at least as long as the torso and head of your figure.

Still another technique is to start with an S curve line, drawn with a broad-nib light-color felt pen. Sketch the body around this curve with a soft pencil or fine-line marker. Emphasize the angles of the shoulders and pelvic block.

Whenever you feel stale or tight, review these techniques for putting action into your drawings. The most advanced illustrators will often feel stale or flat about their sketches and use these techniques to refresh their approach.

SCRAP

Start a clipping file of photographs and illustrations that you can use for inspiration. Search out many different ages and kinds of models and images that inspire you.

THE SKETCH BOOK

Use your sketch book every day. Carry it with you and doodle. Make quick sketches of all that interests you. Make drawing an enjoyable habit.

AN ACTION DRAWING BE-
COMES FINISHED ART
Block in a simple figure on a piece of vellum you have placed over an action drawing. Draw the clothes on the figure. Detail with pencil or felt pen. Try to capture the movement in your original sketch in the second drawing.

▼

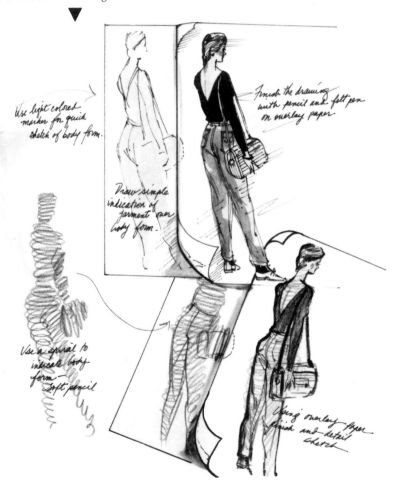

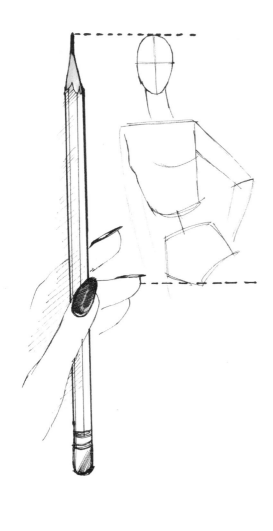

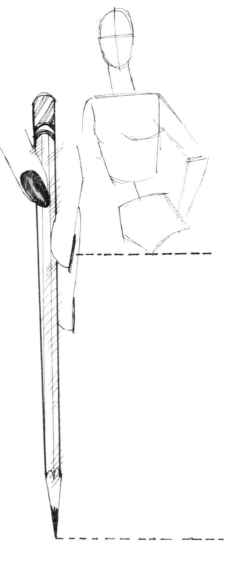

THE ARTIST'S MEASURE

As you work with more complicated figure problems, remember the basic proportion lessons from Chapter Two. Use a pencil to quickly measure the figure as you sketch. Measure the figure from head to crotch by lining up your pencil point with the top of the head and marking the crotch with your finger on the pencil. Drop the pencil down and indicate the length at the bottom of the figure as a guide

to where the feet must fall. This measuring technique can be used for arms and legs in complicated poses where the limbs do not automatically line up with the body. Use the body proportions to guide your pencil measure.

The pencil can also be used to measure and line up a live model's pose. Squint your eye and hold out the pencil to determine the axial line of a pose. Double-check the model's proportions and limb length, then bring the pencil down to your sketch and compare the visual image to your drawing.

Simpler hair style would be more flattering

Student has lost the body under the coat — The body form guides the fit of a garment

Arm is almost completly hidden

Balance the buttons and leading edge of the coat on either side of the median line of the body

Feet?

CHECK YOUR SKILLS

Collect the sketches you have made while doing the exercises. Compare them to the student work shown here. Analyze the strengths and weaknesses of your work. Refer back to the pages that teach lessons that you need more work on.

Bust too low

Angling the shoulders and hips would give more movement to this figure

oopps! Hiding hands? Review how to draw hands

axial line should fall under support leg

and feet

Hair style is too fussy for active Sports wear

Give neck a firm, yet supple Column

Arm too short

Flex Elbow on an arc Extending from waist

Median line will help to draw clothes

Hands should be large enough to relate to figure

Sketch with body structure more firmly drawn

Far leg would be partially hidden

Review bone structure

Even the width of the Shoulders

Sitting poses are difficult to show elaborate garments because the silhouette is distorted

axial line should fall between seat and supporting hand

Feet need to be larger to support the figure

Foreshortened legs look awkward

Measure length of leg in relation to head size — Should be about 2½ heads long

Practice feet !

CHAPTER FIVE

DRAWING CLOTHES

WHAT IS FASHION?

Fashion is a way of life that is accepted by a specific group at a given time period. Fashion is constantly changing. Fashionable clothes are a continuing evolution of garment styles and an infinite variety of ways to combine this apparel within a framework of the current "in fashion" looks for the audience accepting that way of dressing.

Fashion illustrators must constantly update their knowledge of current fashion apparel. They should know the trends of the sophisticated designer creations, as well as lesser priced categories of domestic RTW (ready to wear). Apparel designers must be aware of forward, innovative foreign and domestic apparel and lifestyle trends, so they can create appropriate apparel for their specific, specialized customers. Exposure to many sources of fashion media and events is essential to every person who illustrates or creates apparel. Train yourself to see what clothes people are wearing and how they are wearing them. Observe the total effect and the specific details that make up a unique outfit. Get in the habit of sketching a detail or garment that you admire. Make drawing a method of recording your impressions.

Clothes abound in infinite variety. They identify and adorn the people who surround us. Stores are stages where appealing apparel is displayed. Shop apparel stores and look carefully at the clothes. Try to remember what you see on the rack and sketch it when you leave the store. Draw directly from window displays. The attractive mannequins are good stationary models to show how the latest apparel should fit and be accessorized.

Go to fashion shows. Sketch the clothes and models as they parade the latest styles. Notice how the clothing fits the ideal body of a professional runway model. Sketch the pose and apparel with quick jesture drawings in your sketch book.

Sit at a restaurant in a chic part of town. Observe customers and sketch them. Try to capture the current trends and how real people wear the fashion presented to them by the apparel media and industry.

Observing and being stimulated by fashionable lifestyle trends is an essential ingredient of developing a creative eye for illustrating and designing apparel.

Look at and collect any visual fashion drawings or photographs that appeal to you. Read trade publications that show coming fashion developments and consumer publications that feature apparel especially to stimulate the consumer. The following publications are important for their visual fashion coverage.

Drawing by Robert Passantino for Women's Wear Daily.

TRADE PUBLICATIONS

☐ *Women's Wear Daily (WWD)*— Fairchild Publications, 7 East 12th Street, New York, NY 10003. *WWD* is known as the "bible of the fashion industry," because it is the most important trade publication for women's clothing. Many artists are represented in the daily coverage of the domestic and foreign fashion scene. This newspaper is an excellent source of sketches and current fashion news.

☐ *California Apparel News*— California Fashion Publications, 1016 South Broadway Place, Los Angeles, CA 90015. This West Coast newspaper has extensive coverage of the Los Angeles market and features sketches by a variety of artists. The paper also publishes editions to cover midwestern and southern regional markets.

☐ *Fashion Showcase*—1145 Empire Central Place #100, Dallas, TX 75247. This regional newspaper has strong apparel editorial coverage, featuring sketches and photographs of national apparel manufacturers.

Tapestry jacquards:
Michael Milea's beautiful
one-upmanship.

Because when it comes to
knitting wool, Mr. Milea layers
it on thick, fine, and
fantastically!

Come meet this chieftain of
color-webbed knits today in
New York from 6 to 7 p.m.,
and see his wonder works
informally modeled from 5 to
7...ah, talk about delicious.

Here, just a taste of his all
so very affordable, in
deepest, darkest plum,
smokey blue, sapphire-teal
and sweet violet.

Short-cut tunic with soft
cowl 36.00.
Crewneck sweater, 28.00.
Both, for S-M-L.

New Editions Juniors on 2,
New York. And all our
fashion stores.

The Shop for Michael Milea at

bloomingdale's

CONSUMER NEWSPAPERS

☐ *Local newspapers*—daily newspapers feature advertisements for current merchandise and fashion editorial sections that are invaluable for the illustrator and designer. Develop an awareness of each major retailer's advertising format and style of illustration. Consider how each format and style relate to customers.

☐ *New York Times*—the great collections of major retailers that advertise daily in this newspaper make it an excellent source of sketches for the designer and illustrator. The Sunday edition often features a fashion supplement.

☐ *W*—this publication features the fashion coverage of *Women's Wear Daily* reprinted, often in color, for the consumer. Published twice monthly, this paper focuses on lifestyle articles. It is very well illustrated with sketches and photographs and is an excellent source of inspiration. Like *Women's Wear Daily,* it is published by Fairchild Publications.

◀ ▶

These superb illustrations by Antonio for Bloomingdales are typical of the high quality artwork run in the New York Times. *Fashion professionals throughout the nation subscribe to this newspaper. (Courtesy of Bloomingdales, illustrated by Antonio, art direction by John C. Jay.)*

SWEATER DRESSING
Eighties 'n Easy

Knits are news!

The witty shapes.
Fresh textures.
Bold patterns.
Attitudinal colors.

There's a ground swell
of new sweaterdressing—
right here, right now—
contemporary and beyond.

Expressing a Junior view:
the sweater that slinks below
the waist and stops short of
the knee—it's back on top.
A powerful statement in
favor of one-piece, sure-shot
dressing. Hooray!

Three city kickers,
from left to right:
The Thermal, knit to match
the texture of your favorite
ski undies, in navy, berry, steel
or lilac acrylic, 38.00.
Juniors on 2.

The Argyle, a whimsical
plaiding of black, blueberry
and cerise acrylic, 24.00.
Metro Juniors, Metro Level

The Stripe, a lean V-neck
in lavender/aqua/pink/maize
or green/navy/ruby/
chocolate acrylic, 38.00.
Juniors on 2.

New York. And a selection in
all our fashion stores.

Sweater Dressings Live at

bloomingdale's

SCOOP ON PRET: MILAN
Preview of Designs By: Soprani

(Soprani for Helyett)

(Soprani for Pims)

DESIGN REPORTS

Private subscription fashion reports are expensive but excellent sources of future fashion trends. Many designers and retailers and some fashion schools subscribe to these services to have an early prediction of what Europeans are designing and wearing on the streets. Some of the better fashion reports are *IM, Nigel French,* and *Here and There.*

DOMESTIC CONSUMER MAGAZINES (GLOSSIES)

☐ Children's and young girls' apparel—*Ladies Home Journal* has occasional articles on children's apparel. *Seventeen* is the publication that most influences teenage apparel (also filters down to children's wear).

☐ Young women—*Glamour* and *Mademoiselle* appeal to college age and young career women. Both of these magazines feature articles that promote high audience involvement through store show and guest editorships.

☐ General and high fashion magazines—*Vogue* and *Harper's Bazaar* cover American and foreign fashion styles for a mature, sophisticated customer.

☐ Specialized magazines with some apparel articles abound. Glance through current publications for special articles on apparel. Look at patternmaking and home-sewing books and magazines for different ideas.

Fashion reporting for the trade is often exaggerated, but careful attention is given to construction details. (Courtesy of Here and There, Fashion Reporting Service.)

FOREIGN FASHION PUBLICATIONS

Foreign publications offer many new perspectives on fashion through innovative design and photographs. Illustrators and designers avidly read them for inspiration. The following list covers the most influential and most readily available graphic magazines. Subscriptions are available and individual copies are often sold in major city book stores.

☐ *Elle* — 90, rue de Flandre, 75943, Paris Cedex 19, France. This trendy European fashion magazine features youthful apparel and accessories. Handicrafts offer additional inspirational input.

☐ *Lei* — Condé Nast, S.P.A., Piazza Castello, 27–20121 Milano, Italy. This magazine is the Italian counterpart of *Glamour* and *Mademoiselle*. Features youth-oriented clothing and accessories.

☐ *Harper's Bazaar* — this magazine is published in several countries. England has *Harper* and *Queen*. In Italy it is called *Bazaar Italia*. This is a leading graphic fashion publication and can be ordered from Bazaar Italia, Corso di Porta Nuova, Linia Italia, 46 Milano, Italy.

☐ *L'Officiel de la Couture et du Monde de Paris* — officiel de la Couture SZ, 226 Rue du Faubourg St Honore, Paris, 8e France. This magazine is published by a group of couture and prêt-à-porter (French RTW houses). *L'Officiel* is also published in an American edition at a lower cost. Features high fashion for the mature woman.

SCOOP ON PRET: PARIS
Preview of Designs By: France Andrevie

☐ *Vogue*—published by Condé Nast in French, English, Italian, and Australian editions. The French and Italian publications are the most forward. Condé Nast also publishes special magazines covering home furnishings (*Casa Vogue*), men's wear (*L'Uomo* and *Homme*), children's clothing *(Vogue Bambini),* and boating apparel (*Uomo Mare*), which represent current interesting lifestyle trends abroad. Condé Nast, S.P.A., Piazza Castello, 27–20121 Milano, Italy.

☐ Japanese fashion magazines—several excellent Japanese fashion magazines report on the European scene with a unique point of view. *So An* and *An An* cover the youth market. *High Fashion* reports on more sophisticated, trendier styles.

HOW GARMENTS FIT

Fit is the way a garment conforms to the structure of a body. How a garment fits depends a great deal on the weight and texture of the fabric it is made of. The silhouette (the outline of a garment) follows changing fashion cycles, in each of which the styling focuses on one part of the human anatomy. During the 1960s, for example, the focus was on the leg.

Short, youthful garments were popular. The silhouette shrunk to a small wedge shape that looked like a young girl's dress.

Fashion illustrators and designers draw garments to emphasize current fashion trends. The beginner should master drawing the body first. After the proportion of the figure becomes second nature, the sketches can integrate clothing into drawing the figure. The stance and movement of a figure will change the way a garment hangs. Fashion clothing has a subtle relationship to a model's body. The slender, idealized figure of a fashion model does not look overly voluptuous, even if illustrated in a tightly fitted bathing suit or evening gown.

Observing silhouettes and garment details is the surest way to master drawing clothes. Fashion will change the volume and shape of the current silhouette. Fabrics can be woven heavy or light, crisp or soft, to serve the fashion demands of any period. Details can be flamboyantly large and dramatic, or subtle and scaled to miniature. These are the dictums of current fashion that every illustrator must be aware of.

A knowledge of proportion and a basic understanding of garment construction rules will enable an illustrator to draw clothing and modify the techniques to illustrate fashion of any period.

DARTS

A commercial dress form is divided into symmetrical and balanced divisions. Style lines often follow these guidelines. The dart is one method for fitting a flat piece of fabric to the contours of a body. A dart is a wedge-shaped piece of fabric that is stitched out of the garments. Darts are used in a rigid fabric when the garment is meant to fit the body closely.

Darts are conventionally placed on the princess line. Darts stop about 1

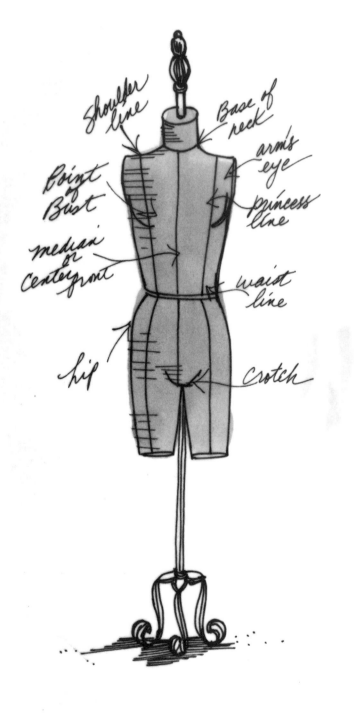

Shoulder line

Base of neck

arm's eye

Point of Bust

princess line

median or Centerfront

waist line

hip

crotch

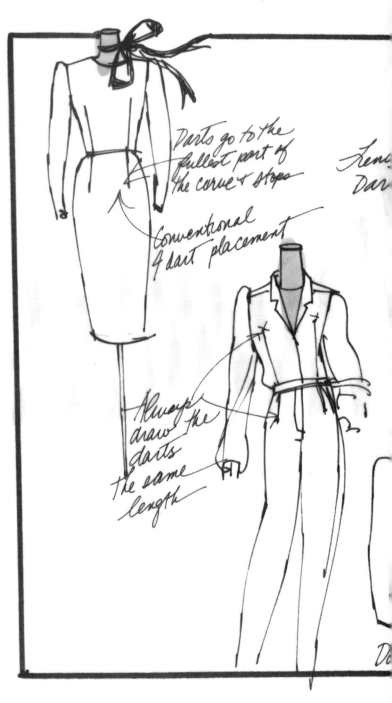

Darts go to the fullest part of the curve & stops

Conventional 4 dart placement

Always draw the darts the same length

inch away from the point of the bust (the highest part of the bust on a dress form), to avoid an exaggerated pointed shape. Many variations and combinations of novelty darts are also possible. Darts are used in pants and skirts to take care of the "drop" (the difference between the smaller waist and full hip).

Search out photographs of darted garments and sketch the garments as if they were on a body. See how many variations you can find. Look at your own clothes to see how darts are used.

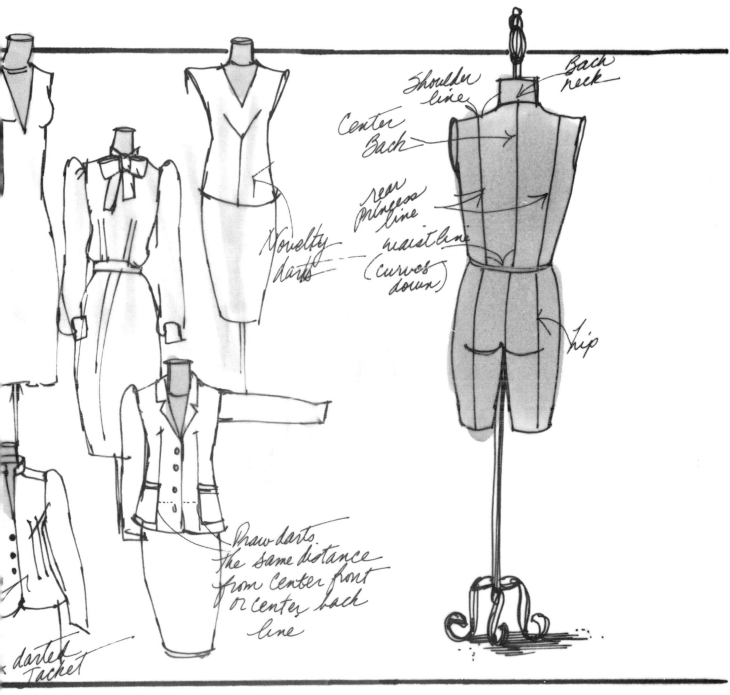

GORES

Gores are vertical divisions in a garment, often placed on the standard princess lines of the dress form. Gores are separate pieces of fabric, which are sewn together to shape the garment to the figure. Gores are also used to add fullness to a garment. Gores may be placed as novelty style lines wherever a designer may want to call attention to a part of the body.

Gores can be accented by stitching or piping for added emphasis. Gores can be combined with darts or ease for various effects. Pleats and slits can be added to the gores. When drawing a garment with gores, make sure the seam line is not broken and runs from one edge of the garment through to the other.

Practice sketching these examples of gores. Collect scrap of other gore treatments.

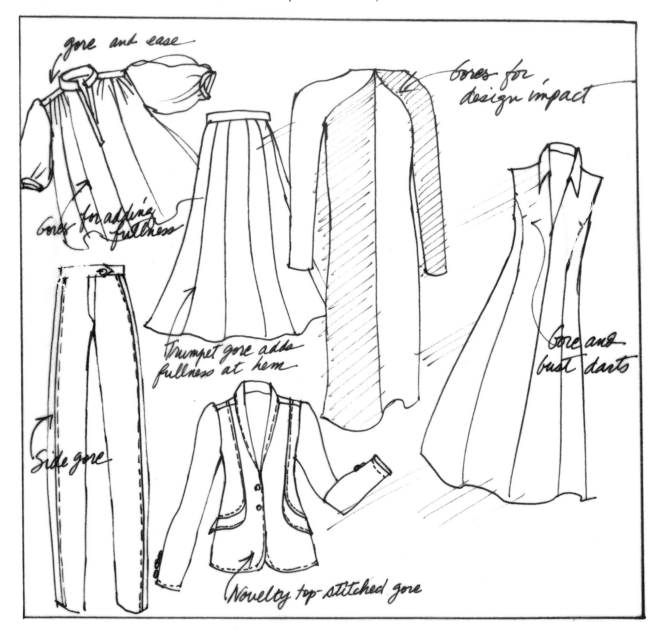

gore and ease

Gores for adding fullness

bores for design impact

Side gore

Trumpet gore adds fullness at hem

Novelty top-stitched gore

Gore and bust darts

Hip
yoke

Yokes + Ease
= flounces

Shoulder
yoke

Back
Yoke

Curved
Yoke

Western
Cowboy
shaped yoke

YOKES

Yokes are horizontal divisions in a garment; they are used for styling and fitting. Yokes are often found at the shoulder line. They are particularly effective when they are used to control ease (gathered or pleated fullness). Yokes can be shaped into curves or wedges. Cowboy shirts feature elaborately shaped front and back yokes.

The yoke line is often accented by top-stitching or contrast piping or color.

Hip yokes are used on pants, skirts, and dresses. Shirts styled as a series of tiers are based on yoke construction that is gathered together on horizontal style lines. These yoke details are important aspects of garment design and should be observed and sketched carefully.

EASE

Ease has two meanings in apparel construction. Simple or fit ease is the room that must be left between the body and a rigid fabric (one that does not stretch), so the body can move. Fabrics that naturally stretch can fit the body tightly. Most knits have a natural stretch because of the fabric construction, which allows it to expand and recover. When a stretch fiber like lycra spandex is added to any fabric, knit or woven, the garment will stretch to fit the body like a second skin, because the fit ease is built into the fabric. Leotards, bathing suits, and other active sportswear are often made from stretch fabric because great flexibility for vigorous activities is necessary.

Ease also means gathers, pleats, or extra fabric added to a garment for styling purposes. The ease must be controlled by a smooth area of fabric, a belt, a tie, or elastic insets. Yokes are often used in conjunction with ease to place the gathers where they are most effective. Fashion dictates the placement and quantity of ease. Fabrics tend to become lighter during periods when a full, easy silhouette is popular.

Baggy Pants

GARMENT DETAILS

OPENINGS

Buttons and zippers are the most frequently used fasteners for women's apparel. Usually the opening is at the center front or center back of a garment. To place the buttons on the median line of a garment, the buttonhole must extend slightly beyond the center front line. The button is pulled to the edge of the buttonhole, lining it up with the median line. The button placket extends beyond the median line. When bulky fabrics require large buttons, this extension should be wider to visually balance the size of the button. The front edge of the button placket is called the leading edge.

Functioning buttons are placed where the collar begins to roll and at the bust and waistline. Then additional buttons are added between these stress points so they are equally spaced.

Loop buttonholes are placed on the center front line. The side of the garment that carries the button has an extension. Loop buttonholes are placed at closer intervals, because in this way they serve decorative purposes and because they tend to gap.

Zippers are most often hidden, but may be used as decorative fastenings. They can be accented with top-stitching as in the slot zipper or classic trouser placket. Contrasting zippers are sometimes used in active sportswear.

Practice drawing the fastenings shown here. Search out more variations of buttonholing treatments. Sketch the details quickly for practice.

leading edge

median line

center front

Classic shirt placket vertical buttonholes

placket

asymmetrical opening with loop buttonhole

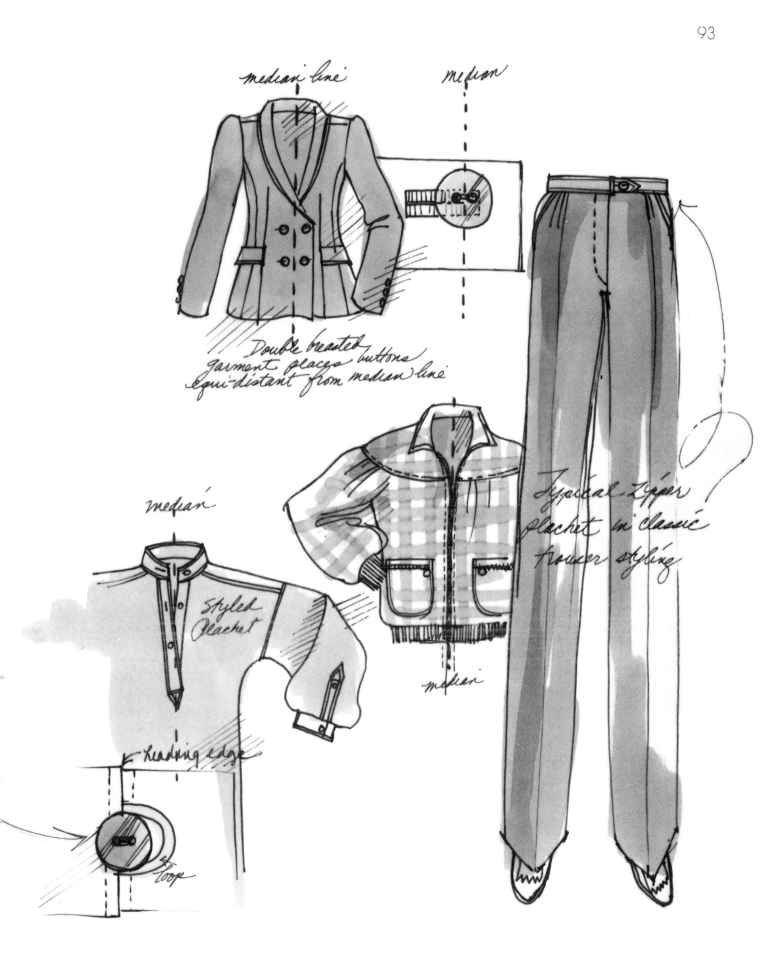

median line

median

Double breasted
garment places buttons
equi-distant from median line

median

Styled
Placket

Leading edge

Loop

Typical Zipper
placket in classic
trouser styling

median

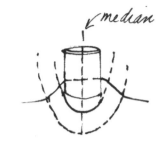

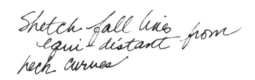

Sketch fall lines
equi-distant from
neck curves

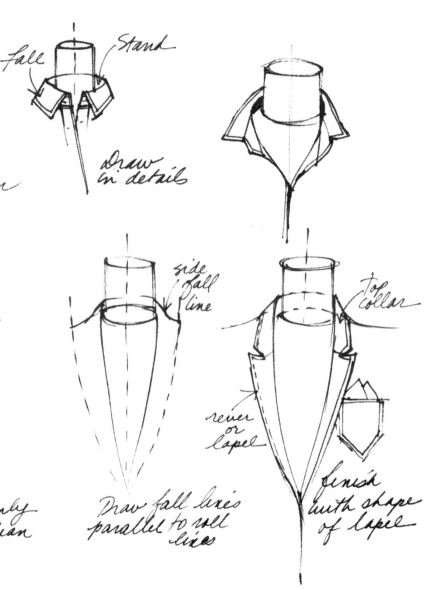

Draw
in details

Draw fall to shoulder · roll lines

Draw roll lines evenly
on both sides from median

Draw fall lines
parallel to roll
lines

Finish
with shape
of lapel

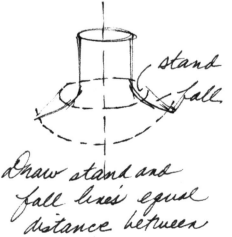

Draw stand and
fall lines equal
distance between
neckline curves

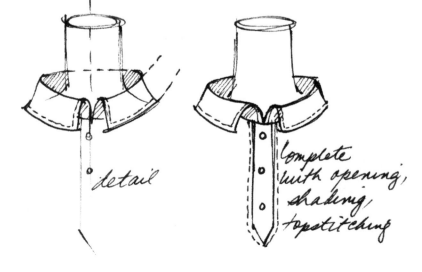

detail

Complete
with opening,
shading,
topstitching

COLLARS

A collar is an added piece of fabric that encircles the neck and frames the face. Fashion cycles determine the size and kinds of collars that are popular. The illustrator and designer should know the styling possibilities for collar shapes and sizes and interpret them as fashion of the period dictates. The collar is an important detail that must be carefully drawn to capture the garment exactly.

Most collars are equally balanced on either side of the median line. Start drawing the back of the collar following the neckline curve in an even arc. Next draw the roll or opening shape. Detail the collar evenly on both sides of the neck. Practice sketching these collars step by step. Sketch collars from magazines and then try some from your imagination.

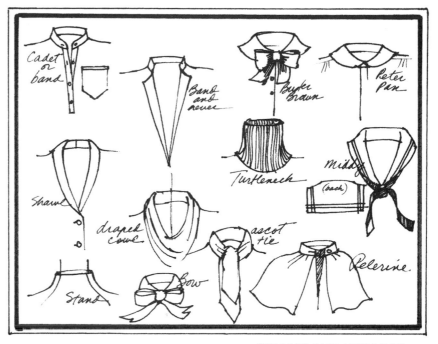

COLLARS AND NECKLINES

Study these collars and neck lines. Collars that have equal sides are called symmetrical. Asymmetrical collars and necklines are different on each side of the garment.

▼

SLEEVES

Sleeves are tubes of fabric that surround the arms. The most common type is set in at the shoulder line with a seam. Altering the position of the seam from the standard at the top of the shoulder can alter the silhouette of the garment. An artist should notice where and how the sleeve is set in and draw the silhouette and details carefully, because they effect the entire shape of the garment. The sleeve is also styled by changing its size (by adding ease at the shoulder and wrist), its shape, and its length.

A second type of sleeve—which includes raglan, doleman, and kimono sleeves—incorporates part of the bodice. To allow for freedom of movement, these sleeves are usually much looser than set-in sleeves.

Draw the sleeve length and shape relating to the arm. Carefully observe the sleeves shown here, and draw sleeves from photographs and life. Go through a good fashion magazine and draw each of the varieties of sleeves you see.

A drop shoulder line has a mature, casual look because the shoulders seem broader.

▼

A sleeve with a short shoulder seam looks more youthful that a regular set-in sleeve. The sleeve can be puffed without overexaggerating the shoulders.

▼

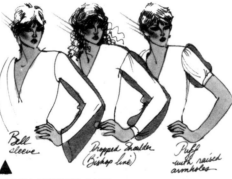

▲
SET-IN SLEEVES AND
SLEEVES INCORPORATING
THE BODICE
▼

SLEEVE VARIATIONS
▼

Puff

Raglan

Leg O' Mutton

Petal

roll sleeve + tof

Dropshoulder + Epaulette

Cape

Dolman

Kimono

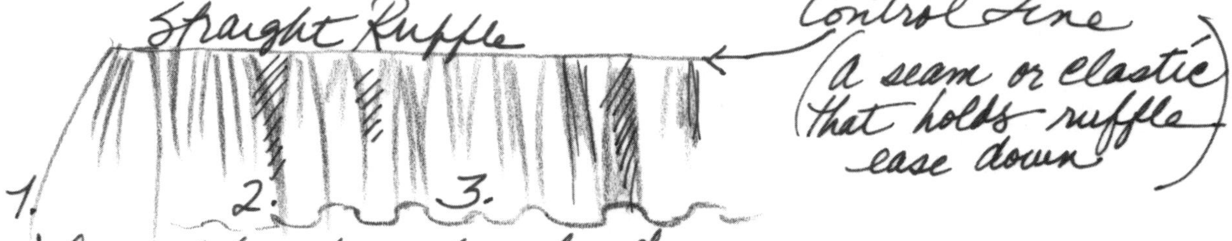

Straight Ruffle

Control Line
(a seam or elastic
that holds ruffle
ease down)

1.   2.   3.

1) Draw lines of varying lengths
2) Contour the bottom with curves as fabric falls
3) Shade and highlight contours

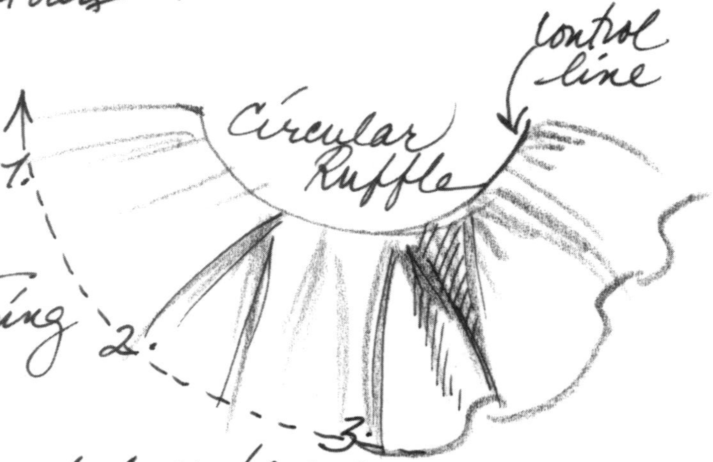

1) Draw guide line
equidistant from
control line
2) Draw uneven lines
from control line (bring
some lines out to
guide line)

control
line

Circular
Ruffle

1.

2.

3.

3) Contour bottom, shade & highlight

Cascade Ruffle

1) Draw control
line

2) Draw an
"S" curve
equally balanced
on both sides of
control line.

3) Detail curves
of fabric &
shade & Highlight

Control line

LIGHTWEIGHT FABRIC
Use a light, delicate line to draw ruffles in lightweight fabric.

MEDIUMWEIGHT FABRIC
A bold, loose line is effective for drawing a cotton sundress with a ruffle neckline. Capture the drape of the fabric.

RUFFLES

Ruffles are shaped in two ways: straight and circular. Straight ruffles tend to be crisper and fuller than circular ruffles. Cascading ruffles are continuous circles set into a vertical seam. All ruffles must be set into a controlling seam or elastic inset to regulate the amount of ease.

To draw ruffles, always establish the control line first. Then draft a guideline for the bottom of the ruffle. Uneven ease lines connected to the control line should be drawn next. Then contour the bottom of the ruffle and shade to add dimension.

Observe how different fabrics make ruffles. Limp soft fabrics will have smooth, flowing silhouettes when gathered. A crisp fabric like taffeta will have a bouffant, full ruffle. The smaller the ruffle, the crisper it will tend to drape. A gathered skirt is actually a long ruffle controlled by a waist band. Sketch many ruffles from photographs, observe how the fabric drapes.

99

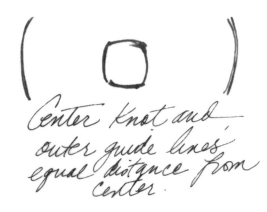

Center knot and outer guide lines equal distance from center.

Connect knot to guide lines

Draw gather lines from knot and ovals at top

Shade and detail

BOWS

Ties and bows are often found in fashion. They are feminine detailings added as a tie belt or softly bowed neckline. Bows can be made from self fabric or contrasting ribbon or lace trim. Whenever used, bows and ties should be drawn as if they were perfectly tied. They should have body. The streamers should flow gently, as if a soft breeze were blowing them. A limp, bedraggeled bow will make a garment look old and used. Cut a crisp piece of grosgrain or satin ribbon at least 2 inches wide, and tie it into a bow. Sketch it several ways and rearrange the ties each time. Capture the twists and turns of the ribbon. Apply this lesson to bows you see on garments.

self bow

Spaghetti ties

Self tie on shirt

Scarf

Cummerbund

Knotted Scarf

101

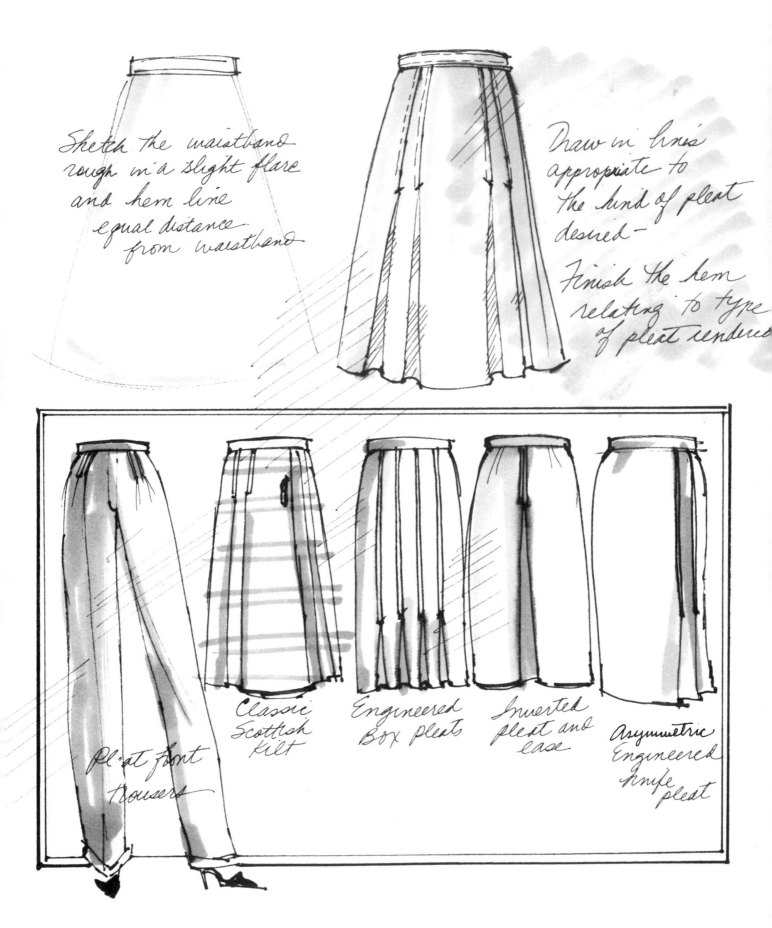

Sketch the waistband rough in a slight flare and hem line equal distance from waistband

Draw in lines appropriate to the kind of pleat desired —

Finish the hem relating to type of pleat rendered

Pleat front trousers

Classic Scottish Kilt

Engineered Box pleats

Inverted pleat and ease

Asymmetric Engineered knife pleat

PLEATS

Pleats are a way of adding fullness to a garment. Most pleats have a linear look, because they have been pressed into the fabric and set with heat so they are permanent. Pleats can be made in a great variety of sizes and styles. When left unpressed, a pleat looks like a soft fold in the fabric. The pleat can be emphasized with top-stitching. Pleats can be worked into tops and pants as well as skirts. A pleat that is stitched down or worked into a seam is called an engineered pleat.

Study the mechanics of these pleats. Observe a classic pleated skirt and render the precise execution of the crisp pleats. Notice how pleating in a soft delicate fabric like chiffon is different from pleats in a heavy-weight day-wear fabric like wool. Pleating in soft fabric is usually very small and has a gathered or ruffled effect.

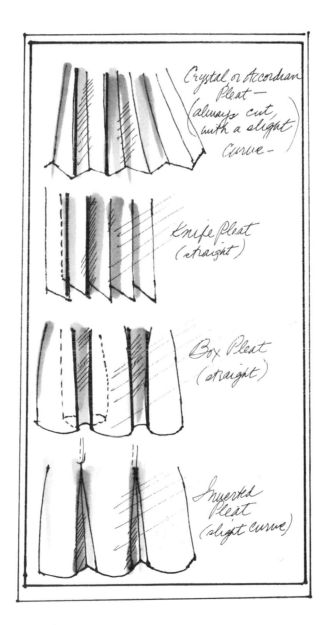

Crystal or Accordian Pleat — (always cut with a slight) Curve —

Knife Pleat (straight)

Box Pleat (straight)

Inverted Pleat (slight curve)

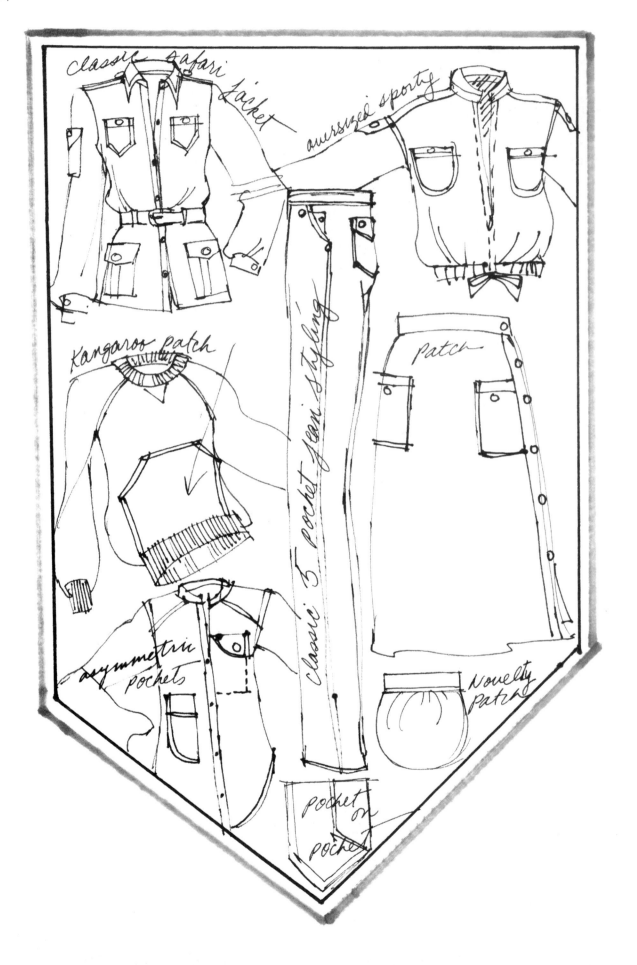

classic safari jacket

oversized sporty

Kangaroo patch

Classic 5 pocket jean styling

asymmetric pockets

patch

pocket on pocket

Novelty patch

POCKETS

Pockets are generally used in pairs evenly placed on either side of the median line of a garment. They look best when they are appropriately sized for the garment and the function they are to perform. Pockets are also used singly as in the traditional blazer breast pocket. Pockets may be used in mismatched pairs or singly for dramatic design impact. Patch pockets are extra pieces of shaped fabric sewn on the outside of the garment. Other pocket styles include upright flap, welt or buttonhole pockets, hidden and flap pockets. Many variations of these basic kinds are used. Observe pockets and their placement on photographs of garments. As with any small garment detail, sketch pockets precisely and place them carefully on the garment.

flap

open
welt or button hole pocket

open
upright flap

patch and flap

median

PANTS

Pants make a person seem taller because one expanse of fabric covers the body from the waist to the floor. High-heel shoes, hidden by long pants, extend the illusion of height even more. The illustrator enhances the illusion further by drawing pants or a long skirt on a longer than usual figure to emphasize the sweep of the long garment. Length is added to the figure in the leg. Be sure to keep the torso in proportion. Too low a crotch will look matronly. Extend the leg but take care not to make the figure look awkward.

Silhouette and fit of pants are their most important fashion aspects. Observe the subtleties of fit carefully before sketching. Always include seam and pleat lines because these strong vertical lines both enhance the long, slim appearance of the pants and detail the construction. Almost all pants have a center front seam line. Most pants have a zipper opening in the center front seam. Indicate this with a stitching line.

It is very important to sketch the entire figure when drawing pants, because the leg detailing and position must be accurate. There is no skirt to camouflage mistakes in balance or proportion. Sketch pants from life and photographs. Draw sporty and dressy pants in combination with a variety of tops.

▲

THREE MAJOR PANT SIL-HOUETTES
The flap on a pant fly may go right over left like a conventional woman's garment, or zip left over right like a man's jean.

▲

High heels or thick sole shoes increase the illusion of height, especially when hidden by the pant leg.

DRAMATIC PANTS
The full evening pant will drape gracefully, like a long skirt.

▶

Pants are worn for many occasions, dressy and casual. Novelty fabrics and details are popular ways of styling pants.

▼

► The bold silhouette line of this sketch emphasizes the full, soft shape of the pant and integrates the jacket into the outfit. (Courtesy of Steven Stipelman.)

108

Sketch in the general silhouette of the jacket — lightly indicate fall line of jacket lapel — relate it to waist line position.

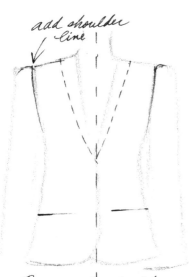

add shoulder line

Block in lapel guide lines equally on either side of the median. Correct length by relating to length of the sleeve. Indicate pockets — evenly balanced

JACKETS

Classic spectator sportswear and suit jackets are precision-tailored garments that depend on subtle differences of detail and fit to establish how fashionable they are. The size of a lapel can easily date a jacket. Subtleties of fit, the size of the shoulder pad, length, sleeve styling, and lapel and pocket details are the components of tailored jackets. Particular attention to these details is vital to capturing the fashion essence of this kind of garment.

Blazers are only one end of the jacket spectrum. A jacket is any outerweight garment that covers the torso. Study the casual and dressy jackets on page 107. Relate the image of the face and figure of the model to the activity and age of the person who would wear the outfit you are sketching. Hang several jackets on hangers and study their details. Meticulously sketch them very realistically as if they were on a body. Try the jacket on and compare your image in a mirror to your sketch. Make corrections and try to sketch other examples more accurately. Concentrate on making the details as clear and realistic as possible in the first drawings. As your sketching ability improves, you may wish to emphasize certain details and eliminate others to create an effect.

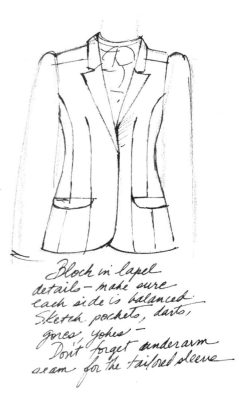

Block in lapel details — make sure each side is balanced. Sketch pockets, darts, gores, yokes — Don't forget underarm seam for the tailored sleeve

Detail, shadow, buttons and top-stitching. Clean up guide lines

Even
Stand

One leg
stand

Opposite Hip

SKIRTS

Skirt styles are characterized by four factors: shape, length, kind of fabric, and detailing. A skirt hangs from the waist, and the hem makes a downward arc that follows the same direction as the slant of the hip bones.

The length is determined by the relationship of the hemline to the knee. It is very important to not only place the hemline correctly, but to draw the leg shape accurately so the leg "reads" as the correct length for the skirt. During each fashion period study appropriate shoes — shoes that relate to the length and style of the skirt being illustrated.

Skirt shapes fall into four general categories: slim, straight skirts; dirndls (a gathered, full straight skirt); flared skirts; and pegged skirts. The shape, combined with the hand (crispness or softness of the fabrication), establishes the major silhouette characteristics of the skirt. Hang several skirts tautly on a clip skirt hanger. Observe how the fabric falls. Draw a skirt and carefully draw the the undulating shape of the hemline. The fuller the skirt, the more character the drape of the skirt will have.

Details, like the shape and width of the waistband, pockets, trims, and pleats, are the finishing touches. Observe skirts carefully and draw many. Put a powerful electric fan behind a model with a skirt on and draw the fabric as it blows in the breeze. Refer to page 103, on how to draw pleats, and apply these techniques to drawing pleated skirts.

SLIM SKIRTS

The slim skirt has little excess fabric so the body shape and motion is clearly visible. Slits and pleats are usually necessary for movement.

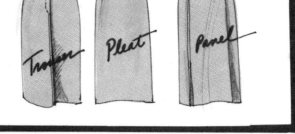

FLARED OR CIRCULAR SKIRTS

This silhouette is the most flattering and has the widest possible styling variations. The hip is slim, and ease is added with gores, flounces, pleats, or additional circles for a very full effect.

GATHERED OR DIRNDL SKIRTS

These skirts have straight sides and are gathered into a waistband. In a crisp fabric, they give the hips a full look.

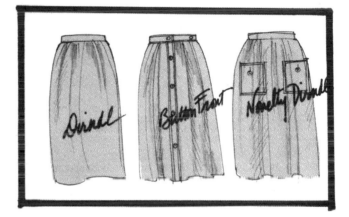

PEGGED SKIRTS

This skirt shape has a full hip and is tapered at the hemline. Pegged skirts are exaggerated and make the hips look large so they are used less often in fashion cycles.

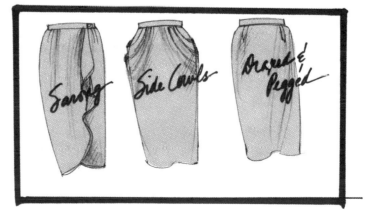

Mini Skirt

Short Skirts

Below Knee
(The knee is important in establishing the length of skirts)

Maxi Skirt

Ankle Length

Floor Length

DRESSES

Dresses combine blouse and skirt drawing techniques. When the dress has a waistline, or is belted, the drape of the fabric and the slant of the hemline are controlled by the angle of the hip, just as skirts are. A dress that has no belt and hangs from the shoulders is controlled by the angle and the size of the shoulders. The hemline of the chemise will be parallel to the shoulders.

Dresses are usually made in lighter fabrics than sportswear jackets and skirts. They have fewer traditional styling formulas than a classic blazer or shirt jacket. Variety and versatility characterize dress styling.

Dresses are often designed for a specific age. It is important to match the visual age of the model to the probable customer the dress was styled for. Hairstyle is a key factor in establishing visual age. Youthful, romantic dresses look appropriate on models with soft, flowing hairstyles. The more expensive dress is best carried off by a sophisticated model with a sleek, well-controlled hairstyle and well-defined makeup.

Dresses

THE ROMANTICS

FEMININE ALTERNATIVE
TO SUITS AND
TAILORED SPORTSWEAR

THE ROMANTIC BLOUSE /

BOWS BELT WAISTLINES / THE INNOCENT DRESS

JUNIOR DRESSES

To capture the essence of the perfect model for junior dresses, imagine a young, fresh high school girl with a shining face, going to her first prom. Use light, delicate lines when drawing the romantic dresses in lightweight fabrics.

▶

Young, carefree clothes are appropriately drawn with a loose, free style and a sense of humor. (Courtesy of Here and There, *Fashion Reporting Service.)*

◀

A fine, delicate pen-line sketch gives the dress a young look. The fabric looks light and lacy when handled in a fresh direct way.

115

DESIGNER AND EVENING DRESSES

The customer for this type of dress is sophisticated and an individualist. Consequently, the evening-dress model will usually reflect the most exaggerated of fashionable makeup and hairstyles.

MISSY DRESSES

This broad category refers to a woman's dress that comes in even-numbered sizes (6, 8, 10, 12, etc.). The model should have a youthful but sophisticated look and casual hairstyle. The shirt dress is a classic missy-dress silhouette.

SWEATERS

Sweaters are very versatile garments that can be worn for almost any occasion except the most formal. The yarn and stitch give the sweater its character. Bulky yarns can be knitted into intricately textured Irish fisherman's patterns for a casual garment. Fine shetland yarn is knit into jacquard patterns called Fair Isles. Knits can be sophisticated city suits or fluffy mohair novelty sweaters. Study the textures and patterns created by sweater knits. Gauge the volume of the sweater by imagining the body underneath. Block out the silhouette and then detail the pattern work.

Sweaters usually have very few seams or style lines. The sleeves can be set-in or raglan. Side seams are used but the clinging nature of the interlocking knit stitch makes a sweater naturally contour to the body's curves. Ribbing (a tight and low stitched banding) is used to finish the sleeves and bottom of many sweaters. This distinctive touch is typical of pattern changes used in sweater styling.

COATS

Outerwear is most often made in bulky fabrics for warmth. Camel's hair, melton, blanket-weight plaids, and fleeces are typical materials. Thicker fabric is best drawn with heavier lines. Round the corners of the silhouette and style details like pockets and collars to add to the illusion of bulk. Choose warm-looking accessories, like gloves, boots, scarves, and hats, as appropriate accents for coats. Balance the scale of buttons, belts, and style details to the enlarged volume of a coat. Fur collars and cuffs are popular accessories for coat styling.

Coats are essentially tailored garments, constructed in heavier fabrics than sportswear jackets. Seam and style details such as lapels, topstitching, pockets, and flaps are similar to the jacket details, but drawn in a larger scale.

use appropriate cold weather accessories

rounded corners

A Bolder shoulder

larger buttons

Bolder trim

gloves

Bulkier silhouette

larger details

Heavier line for heavier fabric

Hat is over dressed for outfit

Random fold lines make garment look used

Gather lines should be softer

Indicate zipper placket with dotted "stitching" line

Gloves inappropriate for outfit

A simple hair style would be more appropriate

Contour face

Draw the collar going around the neck

Emphasize the shape and contour of the jacket with a shadow and outline

Head size too large

Give form to the shoulder line

Smooth line and defined cuff

Raise crotch — Measure proportion of torso using head lengths

CHECK YOUR SKILLS

Collect the sketches you have made while doing the exercises. Compare them to the student work shown here. Analyze the strengths and weaknesses of your work. Refer back to the pages that teach lessons that you need more work on.

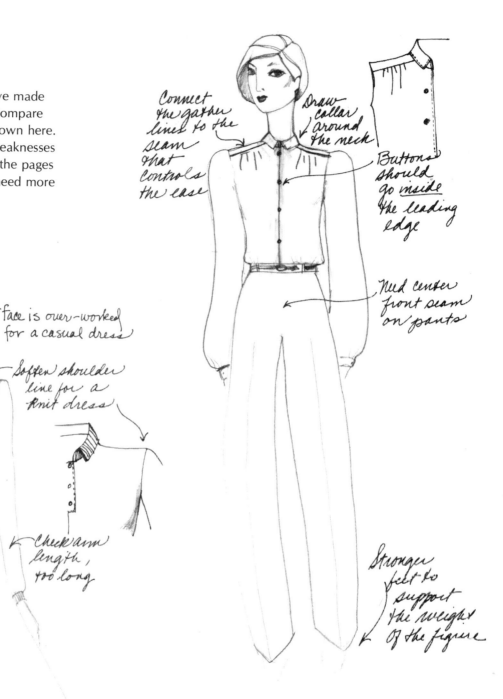

Connect the gather lines to the seam that controls the ease

Draw collar around the neck

Buttons should go inside the leading edge

Need center front seam on pants

Face is over-worked for a casual dress

Soften shoulder line for a knit dress

Shade bust line for a more natural look

Check arm length, too long

Stronger feet to support the weight of the figure

Draw dress to the hem line or draw feet, do not leave part of the leg

CHAPTER
SIX

RENDERING
FABRICS

Clothing is soft sculpture made from woven, knitted, or felted fabric. Clothing "sculpture" is supported and animated by the human body. Fabrics are made in a tremendous variety of textures, colors, patterns, and weights. *Hand* refers to the way the fabric feels.

Designers select fabrics and style them in the fashion look of the period. When fashion decrees tailored and shaped clothing, crisp-hand fabrics in medium weights are used to create geometric shapes. When bulky silhouettes are popular, large amounts of lightweight, soft- or crisp-hand fabrics can be styled with gathers and fullness to create a rectangular silhouette. Thick, soft-hand fabrics, often interfaced and cut in boxy or tent shapes, also give the effect of volume.

Drawing clothes requires keen observation of how different fabrics drape and fit the body. The fashion illustrator should know how different fabrics look when they are styled in garments. *Silhouette* means the outer form or shape of a garment. The character of a fabric is used to enhance the designer's concept of the garment.

Study the way fabric drapes on the body before beginning to draw a garment. The shoulders and hips support the garment, but the hand of the fabric will determine the silhouette of the garment. A soft fabric will flow and cling to the body. Draw it with smooth, downward-flowing lines. Crisp fabric has its own form and will stand away from the body when gathered or flared.

Get into the habit of feeling fabrics. As you touch a crisp, lightweight fabric, imagine how it will lightly puff when gathered into a full skirt. Feel the soft, fluid drape of a wool jersey, and visualize it clinging to a torso,

slipping sensuously over the hips, and falling into a soft fluid skirt.

Employ your senses in evaluating the way a fabric will perform on a body as a garment. Observe and feel fabrics. Collect your tactile and visual impressions to understand how to draw fabrics.

▲

FABRIC HAND
A soft fabric will drape from the shoulders and cling to the body's contour. A crisp fabric has inherent stiffness that makes it stand away from the body and creates a full silhouette.

123

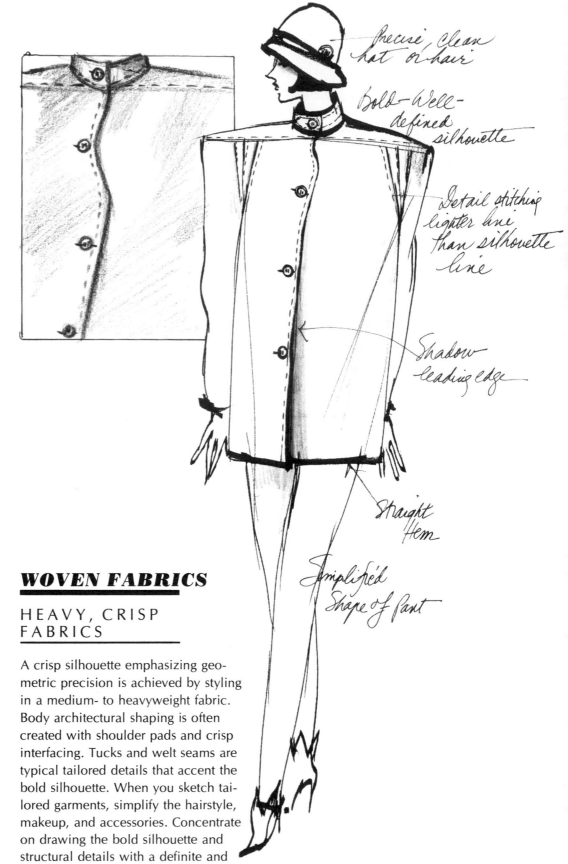

precise, clean
hat or hair

Bold-Well-
defined
silhouette

Detail stitching
lighter line
than silhouette
line

Shadow
leading edge

Straight
Hem

Simplified
Shape of Pant

WOVEN FABRICS

HEAVY, CRISP FABRICS

A crisp silhouette emphasizing geometric precision is achieved by styling in a medium- to heavyweight fabric. Body architectural shaping is often created with shoulder pads and crisp interfacing. Tucks and welt seams are typical tailored details that accent the bold silhouette. When you sketch tailored garments, simplify the hairstyle, makeup, and accessories. Concentrate on drawing the bold silhouette and structural details with a definite and bold line.

HEAVY, SOFT FABRICS

The heavy, soft fabric in this suit has a sensuous yet casual drape. The model's hair and slouchy pose emphasize the heavy texture of the wool basket weave. Use a bold line when drawing the silhouette and a finer detailing line for the lapel and topstitching. Wrinkles and folds should be well shadowed, suggesting the weight of the fabric. Round the edges of the hem boldly to emphasize the drape of the skirt.

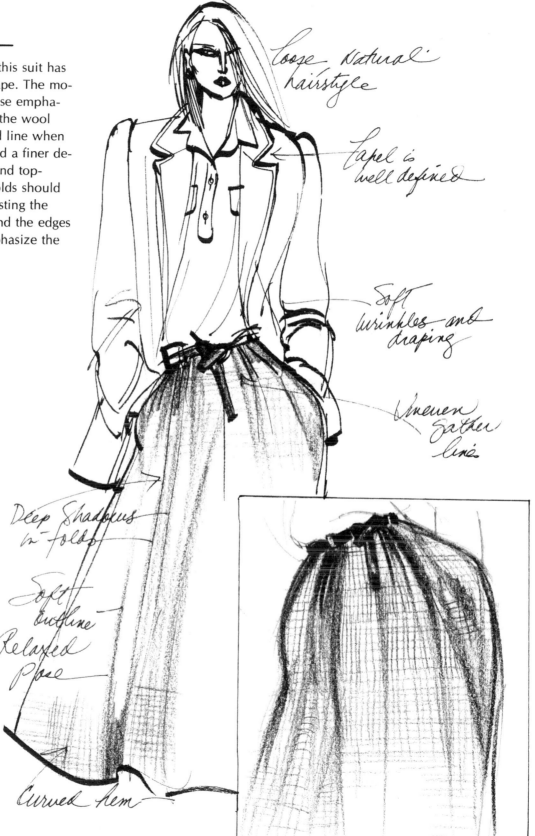

Loose natural hairstyle

Lapel is well defined

Soft wrinkles and draping

Uneven gather lines

Deep shadows in folds

Soft outline

Relaxed pose

Curved hem

Structured hairstyles

Bouffant puffy gathers

Crisp Bow

Silhouette has sharp line

Crisp hem

LIGHTWEIGHT, CRISP FABRICS

Lightweight, crisp woven fabrics can be styled in garments with a great deal of volume. Gathered, bouffant skirts and full sleeves are best in this type of material. Taffeta, organza, and moiré are typical lightweight, crisp fabrics. Use a light, smooth and precise line for rendering this silhouette. Gathers should be drawn with uneven lines and flow outward into puffy shapes. Bows curve upward with crisp precision. Avoid deep shadows that make the fabric look heavy. Emphasize highlights that are inherent in these fabrics.

LIGHTWEIGHT, SOFT FABRICS

Lightweight, clinging fabrics like chiffon, voile, georgette, and crepe follow the body's curves. These fabrics should be drawn with a smooth line for both the silhouette and details. A delicate pattern is most effective when it is loosely rendered with white space from the paper used as highlights. The model's casual hairstyle and S curve pose accent the flowing breeze-blown fabric. Avoid heavy shadows and too realistic rendering of the print or the fabric will look heavy.

Free Hairstyle

Softer bows

Delicate lines & ruffles

Breezy-flowing lines to emphasize light transparent fabric

Slim fit over hips

plaids or stripes can be awkward)

Crisp wedge shaped silhouette

Undulating Hem

Bias Pattern mitered at Center front

Hem has little movement

BIAS CUTS

Woven fabrics can be cut on the bias (the exact diagonal between the warp (lengthwise grain) and the filling (horizontal grain line). This diagonal is the most flexible part of most woven fabrics. When a garment is cut on the bias, it will fit the body with a soft clinging flare. Bias skirts have fluid hemline curves. Fewer seams or dart lines have to be used to style a bias-cut garment.

Bias garments are usually more ex-

Movement

pensive and sophisticated than garments routinely cut on the straight grain, because more fabric is used. When a pattern is cut on the bias, it should be carefully matched to compliment the garment. When a plaid or check is cut on the bias, the pattern becomes a diamond.

The master designer of the bias-cut dress is the Paris couture, Madam Grès. She made the bias dress her signature styling technique early in the twentieth century. The bias cut is still popular because it flatters the figure and gives wovens the drapability of soft knits.

CUT-AND-SEW SWEATERS
Rib bands are used to control the fit of sweaters cut from knit yardage to simulate a hand-knit look.

CUT-AND-SEW KNITS

STRETCH KNITS

Knit sweaters are distinctive garments, because banding, novelty yarns, and intricate stitches can create a great variety of styles. (See page 117.) Knit fabric is different from sweater knits, because it is made to be cut and sewn into garments. Knit fabrics are made in a great variety of weights and patterns and often look like wovens. Heavyweight, knit-base goods have the same styling requirements that wovens have. The great advantage in styling with knits is their comfort stretch and easy care characteristics. Most knits inherently stretch, because of their interlocking-loop construction.

Some knit fabrics are not made to simulate wovens but have a unique knit appearance and hand. Cotton, silk, or synthetic interlock has a smooth jersey face (surface of fabric) and clings to the body's curves. Knit jerseys stretch over 20 percent of their original size, so seams, darts, and fit ease can be eliminated. Garments

often fit snugly. Lycra spandex is added to knits when great stretch and recovery are required. Swimsuits, leotards, and active sportswear are often made from lycra spandex knits. These garments stretch to fit all the body's curves with no construction details other than side seams required.

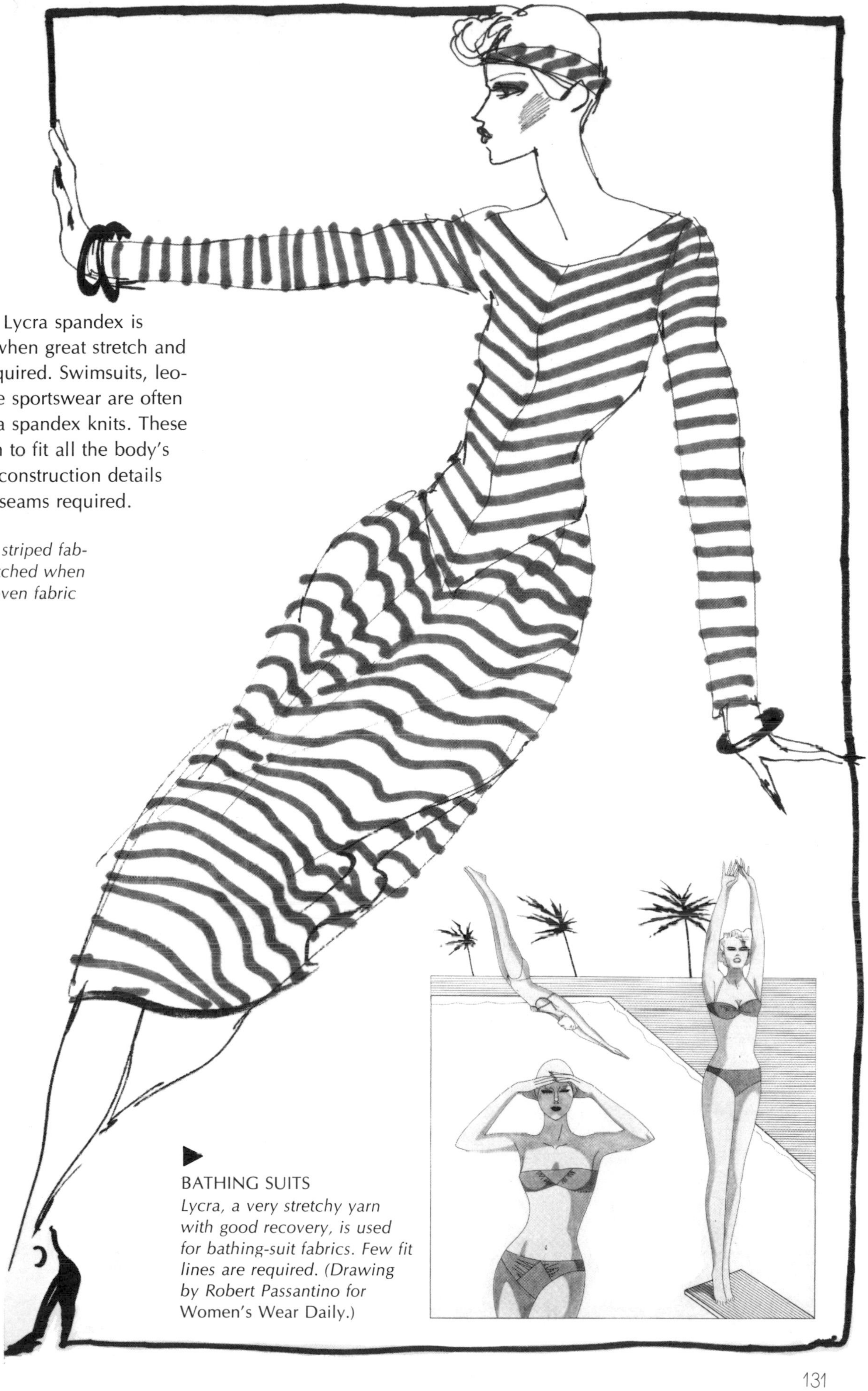

Cut-and-sew knit striped fabric should be matched when seamed like a woven fabric garment.

▶

▶
BATHING SUITS
Lycra, a very stretchy yarn with good recovery, is used for bathing-suit fabrics. Few fit lines are required. (Drawing by Robert Passantino for Women's Wear Daily.)

131

STYLED KNITS

Cut-and-sew knits are also styled as soft dresses, tops, skirts, and pants. They tend to have a lean, clinging line when gathered or pleated. The body shape is accented in even the fullest garments. Even though a soft knit is cut on the straight grain line, it will drape like a bias-cut woven garment. These soft garments often have more style details than stretch knits. Gathers, pleats, belts, tucks, and elastic shirring are typical ways to control cut-and-sew knits. Banding can be knit separately and sewn on cut-and-sew knits to imitate a sweater look.

Study the pictures of the knit dress shown here. Notice how the soft, sensuous flow of the fabric is captured in the bold, fluid line of the illustration. Sketch several cut-and-sew knit garments from photographs. Try to draw the fluid drape of the fabric.

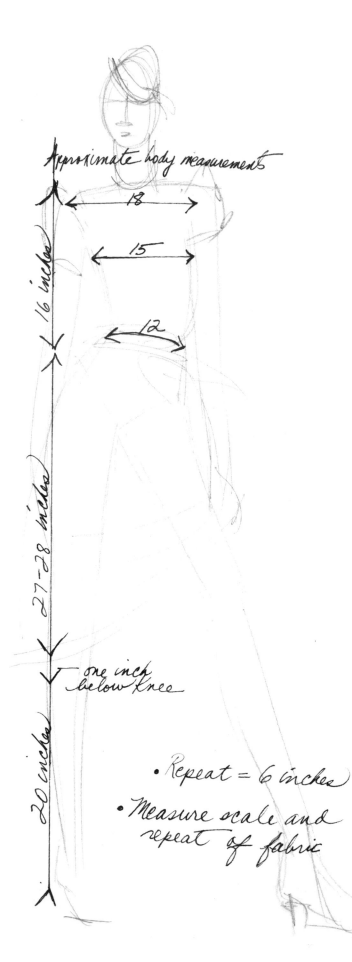

Approximate body measurement

18

15

12

16 inches

27–28 inches

20 inches

one inch
below knee

• Repeat = 6 inches
• Measure scale and repeat of fabric

PATTERNED FABRICS

SCALE

Patterned fabric presents an additional challenge to the illustrator, who now must sketch the figure and the garment plus rendering the pattern. The first consideration is to scale the size of the pattern to the size of the figure. Most artists draw a rather large figure, so they can render the print in a convenient size. The first figure has some body measurements to use as reference when scaling a print down to the size of the garment you are sketching. Measure the vertical and horizontal repeat of the pattern (where the single motif unit is repeated to form the overall pattern). Fit the repeat size to the body measurements. For example, a motif with a vertical repeat of 6 inches would be repeated in a knee-length skirt about four and one-half times.

Block the boldest parts of the pattern in with a light sketch line on the garment's silhouette. Sketch parts of the pattern that might be visible and loose the part that would be cut off at the edge of the garment. Render the pattern carefully, using pencils and felt pens.

A tight pattern indication shows an all-over pattern— tighter, crisper and more commercial

LOOSE RENDERING VERSUS TIGHT RENDERING

Realistic rendering of a motif is not necessarily the most effective way to illustrate a patterned garment. Often, the pattern can be rendered partially, using it to accent the silhouette of the garment rather than photographically reproducing it.

Compare these two illustrations of this

suit with a simple geometric pattern. The very realistic illustration is called a *tight* rendering. Every part of the print is carefully and realistically rendered.

The second illustration is loosely rendered. The print was suggested and large areas of the garment were left unrendered. Shadowed accent areas highlighted the pattern rendering.

The kind of rendering an illustrator should use depends on several factors:

A loose pattern indication is free, sporadically placed pattern, looser line

vision of how it should look when completed.

2. The skill of the artist—many illustrators gravitate towards one style that demands either a precise or a loose style compatible with their drawing skills. Good artists develop drawing skills to the level where they can easily use any style of illustration.

3. Time element—when an artist is rushed, a loose rendering is an effective way to quickly illustrate a print garment.

1. The personality of the garment—some prints look best carefully rendered. Experimentation and observation give an artist the ability to approach a finished rendering with a

Tighter rendering
of fabric pattern —
less editorial
more "salable"

loose
gives more
lively feeling
just a hint
of fabric
indication

Draw the garment
lightly in pencil on a
body with a hint of
tone

BUILDING THE FINISHED RENDERING

1. Lightly sketch the figure and block in the pattern in the correct scale.

2. Build up layers of color (or tone if you are rendering black and white).

3. Let each application of felt pen or paint dry thoroughly before working over it. Add the dark silhouette and detail lines with black pen or prisma pencil.

Render garment and
lines of the fabric with
felt pen and wash

Add darker
wash —
detail with
Ink and
felt pen

Stripes seem wider at the hem because they are gathered together at the top

Stripes are parallel to the hem line and are broken by gathers in the fabric

Flared skirts may be cut with the grain line making a design of the stripe.

Bias Three gore

Bias used as a design device

Darts distort stripes

Mitered bias - four gore

Stripes are effective when darts or seams don't interrupt the flow of the pattern.

Straight flare

STRIPES

Stripes are popular fabric designs. In woven fabrics, stripes are most often printed or woven in even parallel lines following the warp (or selvages) of the fabric. Knit stripes, especially T-shirt and sweater knits, are almost always knitted horizontally.

Before beginning your illustration, notice how the stripes are cut on each part of the garment. Stripes are often cut on a contrasting or bias grain line for design effect. As you block the pattern in, keep the stripes evenly spaced unless the garment is gathered.

Gathering will pull the stripes together at the gathering line. Darting will distort the stripe layout also. Scale the stripes approximately for the garment. Do not attempt to draw small stripes in exactly the correct amount, but keep the lines lightly rendered to approximate the scale.

Stripes are a unique challenge for the designer who may cut the fabric to

create a pattern from the stripes. Before you block in the pattern, estimate the size of the stripe in proportion to the garment.

Most knit stripes are horizontally constructed. Knit fabrics are often used on the basis for binding or as a styling detail.

Any fabric with a linear design should be treated as a stripe. Seersucker is a good example of a stripe pattern created by texture rather than contrasting colors.

CHECKS

Gingham and Shepherd's Checks
Checks conform to rules of geometric placement not unlike those applied to stripes. Straight garments are effective in checks because darts and seams alter the smooth grid of the fabric. Build a check by placing the vertical grid as you would a stripe on your rough sketch. Then fill in the grid with the horizontal stripe. Keep the check even in both directions. Accent the boldest part of the pattern as a final touch. Study how subtle design elements are accented by changing the direction of the check to a bias grain line. Remember to relate the size of the check to the size of the garment.

Houndstooth Checks Houndstooth checks are a variation on a gingham or shepherd's check; they are achieved by weaving a cross grid into a twill weave. From a distance, this pattern looks like a simple gingham.

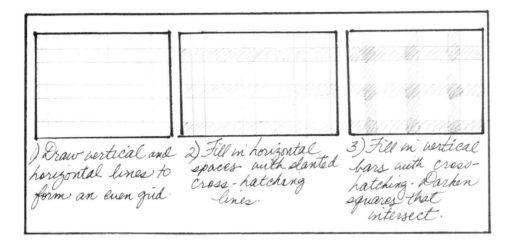

1) Draw vertical and horizontal lines to form an even grid.

2) Fill in horizontal spaces with slanted cross-hatching lines.

3) Fill in vertical bars with cross-hatching. Darken squares that intersect.

establish the size of the repeat of the plaid & relate it to the garment

← 18–20" →

Tone + Shadow The pattern

1) *Establish horizontal grid and shade lighter elements.*

2) *Add vertical elements of the plaid.*

3) *Detail the dark and light areas of the pattern.*

PLAIDS

Plaids are more complicated geometric patterns than checks. The most important things to analyze before beginning to draw a plaid garment are the special breakdown of the pattern and its scale.

A plaid is built when a horizontal stripe intersects a vertical stripe. The blending of yarns creates a wide variety of color and pattern possibilities, from bold tartans to subtle glen plaids. To analyze these complicated patterns, separate the two stripe directions and render the vertical repeat after you have drawn the horizontal stripe.

Measure the repeat of the plaid and block in the pattern on a light sketch of the garment. Notice how a bias grain line alters the direction of the plaid on various parts of the garment. Felt pens in different colors or tones of grey are very good for rendering plaids, because they are easy to control and the intersecting lines build in tone intensity when they cross, just as the actual fabric pattern does.

BIAS PLAIDS

Cutting the entire garment on the bias is an interesting design device. Measure the block of the plaid on the diagonal and scale it to the garment as you did the straight plaid.

A plaid is complicated to work out. Draw a rough sketch and work out the scale and placement of the plaid. Then trace over the rough sketch on vellum. The finished drawing will be cleaner and easier to render accurately, because the preliminary sketch acts as a guide.

147

2) Detail with a fine line marker – cross hatching details

1) Block in tonal stripes with a felt pen.

3) Shadow and emphasize the silhouette with soft pencil

TEXTURED FABRICS

MEN'S WEAR SUITING PATTERNS

Herringbone The herringbone pattern is created when a twill is reversed in narrow stripes. Two or more colored yarns define the weave. Essentially this pattern is a stripe. Herringbones are often cut on the bias and alternate grain. Lay out the direction of the stripe with a light-tone felt pen on all parts of the garment. Detail the reverse twill pattern with a fine-line marker or sharp pencil. Overplaids are often used with herringbone ground.

Tweed Contrasting yarns define the basket weave of a typical tweed. Accent-colored nubs are often used to spark tweeds. Use an undertone of broad-nib felt pen or a light wash to begin your rendering. Work over the base tone with prisma pencils or felt pens in a cross-weave texture. Leave open space in your pencil work so the toned ground looks like a subtle highlight. Paper with a rough surface is particularly effective for rendering a tweed. The paper aids in creating highs and lows of color. Detail the pockets, lapels, and other style details with a black fine-line marker.

1) Tone garment with felt pen

2) sharpen details & outline with fine pen

3) Shadow with soft pencil

① Define the direction of the wales with a light toned marker

② Leave some white space as highlights

③ Shadow the details

④ Detail the silhouette with a fine line marker

TAILORED SUITINGS

Corduroy   Corduroy is a linear plush fabric that conforms to the layout rules of striped fabrics. Corduroy's pile (called wales) gives the fabric a soft luster. Begin your rendering by laying out a linear pattern in a light-toned felt pen. Leave highlights on parts of the garment. Study real corduroy fabric or a garment to see how it reflects the light. Shadow the lapels and folds in the fabric with a soft pencil. Use deep shadows. Reinforce the linear quality of the fabric with pencil or fine-line marker. Detail the style elements of the garment with a dark fine-line marking pen.

Linen Linen has a slightly glazed surface, which reflects light. Leave highlights of untoned paper to capture the glaze. A slub yarn is characteristic of linen and best rendered over the light wash and highlights with a fine-line pencil or pen in a slightly darker tone than the ground. Keep the style details and silhouette crisp and precise. Topstitching is very visible on linen's smooth surface.

Hop Sacking, Raw Silk Tone the garment with a light color wash or felt pen. Study the fabric and leave untoned areas as highlights where appropriate. Detail the texture with a pencil on rough paper to accent the heavy, nubby yarns used to construct this fabric.

Brush or felt pens in several tones for base

Pencil in textures for dark detail

Fine line pen for details and patterns

leave white space for soft highlights —

Then add white paint for "pop-up" sharp highlights

LUSTER FABRICS

Lamé Luster fabrics reflect a great deal of light because they are woven with smooth, shiny yarns. Metallic yarn called lurex is the most lustrous yarn available and is woven with other yarns to create lamé. Notice the highly reflective areas occur in the top folds of the fabric. Random glints highlight the mid-tone and deep shadow areas in the folds of the garment. In addition to usual highlights, accent the most brilliant areas of the garment with a highly concentrated mixture of opaque white paint. Use metallic paints or pencils when working in color.

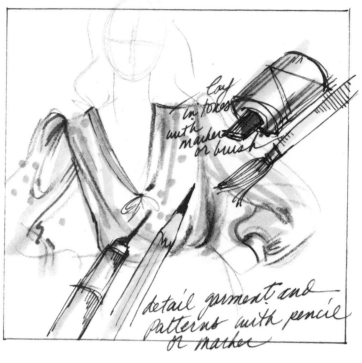

lay in tones with marker or brush

detail garment and patterns with pencil or marker

Satin and Crepe de Chine Crepe de chine, satin, taffeta, and other smooth, reflective surface fabrics have highlights in broad areas of the garment. There is no metallic ''super'' highlight as in lamé. Study the illustration for a typical shadow and highlight pattern for this kind of fabric. A small dot can be woven in the fabric. Satins and crepe de chine can be printed also. Begin with a wash or tone with a light-color felt pen. Build up the color with several overlays of color. Leave original paper highlights on a loose rendering. Shadow with smooth, flowing darker tones of the same cast as the base color. When you render the silhouette and details, keep the line smooth, light, and crisp.

Sequins and Rhinestones Sequins (also called palettes) are small disks of reflective metal or plastic sewn on a carrier fabric. They form a dot pattern of highlights on a medium tone when reflecting the light. Begin rendering a toned ground with wash or broad-nib felt pen. Highlight the most reflective area of the pattern with dots in a dense white paint. If your illustration is in color, tint the white slightly to tone into the ground color. Study the pattern sequins make when highlighted from a photograph or real garment. Rhinestones react like sequins in reflecting light and can be rendered with the same technique.

Moiré Moiré is taffeta with a characteristic pattern that looks like a watermark. This motif is best rendered over a light tone with a fine-line pen in a darker tone. This fabric reflects light like satin, so many areas of the illustration should be highlighted. Notice

how a medium-tone area can have accented light highlights that form the moiré pattern.

Velvet, Velveteen, Velour Velvet-type fabrics absorb light because of their deep, rich pile. The highlights occur around the edges of the garment. A wet water-color wash applied several times is an effective way to render pile fabrics. Build the densest color at the center of the garment and allow highlights where the fabric is gathered and at the edges of the garment. Velvet is effective when rendered in dark, rich colors. Light tones are difficult to render convincingly, because deep contrasts cannot be built up. Render style lines and details in dark velvets with opaque white paint and a fine brush, after the wash has completely dried. Round the corners of collars, pockets, trims, and the general silhouette so the bulky nature of these fabrics is captured.

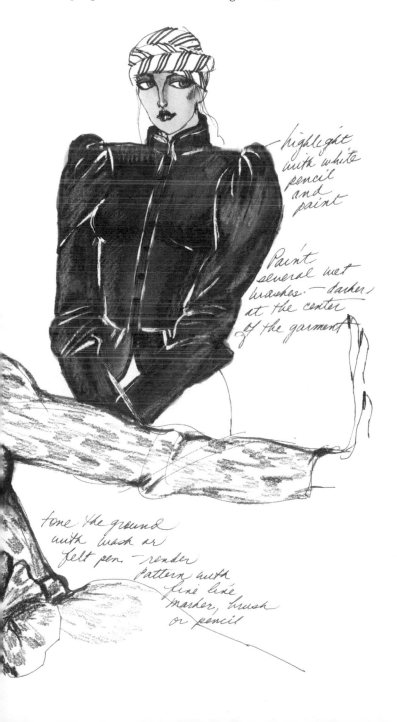

highlight with white pencil and paint

Paint several wet washes. — darker at the center of the garment

tone the ground with wash or felt pen. — render pattern with fine line marker, brush or pencil

Shadow with felt pen or pencil

③

②

Reinforce tone with mottled texture of tone

④

Detail with fine line marker

① With brush or light felt pen build up basic tone

Suede has a softer feel— shading is not too harsh

LEATHERS

Suede Suede surfaces have an uneven pile that catches and reflects light. This "mottled" surface is characteristic of this sporty leather. Render suedes by interpreting the texture with different tones of the base color, building in varying grades of color. A transparent broad-nib felt pen does this particularly well, because the uneven texture is rendered by randomly clotting the basic tone repeatedly with the marker. Shadow with marker or prisma pencil. Detail with fine-line marker or a sharp prisma pencil.

Smooth Leather, Kid   Smooth leathers are finished with a reflective surface that is rendered like a satin or crepe de chine. Kid leather usually forms stylized highlights when it is a medium or heavy weight. Reinforce the natural paper highlights with opaque white accents. Try to feel the leather before rendering it. Many fine leathers are as thin and pliable as fine fabrics. Less expensive smooth leathers may be quite stiff and bulky. Many variations of leather surfaces are available. They may be stamped with an overprinted or hand-painted pattern. Before beginning your illustration, study the hide and analyze the weight and surface.

① Tone with wash or pen
② Leave white space for highlights
Detail, Tone & shadow

To get shiny feeling of leather — use a stronger technique — leaving ample white space for highlights

QUILTING

Quilting is joining two pieces of fabric together with a stitched pattern. A filling of fiber or down can be added as insulation to keep in the body's heat. Quilting is an age-old method of creating a heavy outer-weight fabric from two lightweight fabrics.

Many geometric quilts are popular for robes. These are done on large machines that make a variety of patterns. Outerwear jackets and coats, especially active ski wear, often feature quilt details. Hand sewn quilting motifs are creative and flexible means of detailing all kinds of apparel. Contrast color stitching, patterned fabrics, colorful backings, and reversible and puffy fillings are variations that make quilting a unique design device.

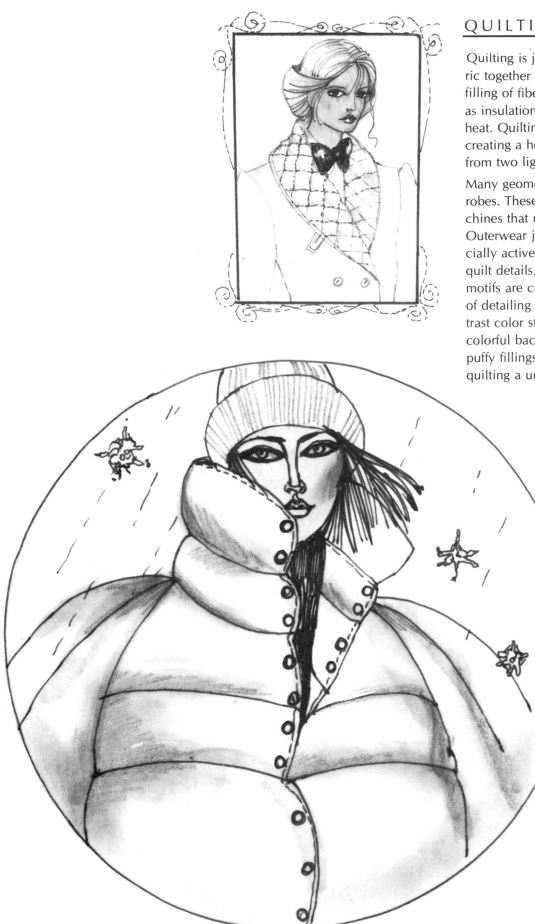

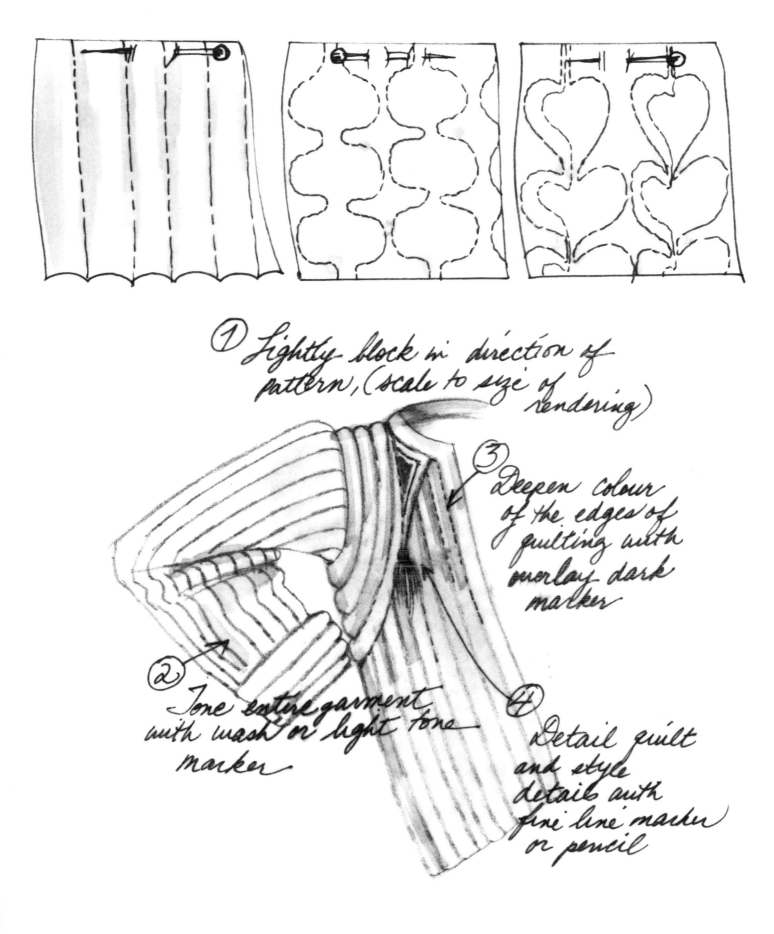

① Lightly block in direction of pattern, (scale to size of rendering)

③ Deepen colour of the edges of quilting with overlay dark marker

② Tone entire garment with wash or light tone marker

④ Detail quilt and style details with fine line marker or pencil

1) Draw the garment lightly in pencil on a body with a hint of undergarment.

2) Render body and garment in a light tone of wash or felt pen

3) Render a darker tone over face and exposed hand, to indicate a light coloured sheer garment

4) Shadow and detail sketch with white pencil and fine tip pen

SHEERS

Sheer fabrics are transparent. The body contour is visible through the garment. Undergarments and linings are designed to be seen. Both knits and wovens are sheer, and can have a crisp or soft hand. Chiffon and georgette are two typical soft-hand sheers. They are often used in draped garments, because they cling to the body. Organdy, dotted swiss, and eyelet are crisp bouncy sheers.

The body shape should be lightly drawn first with the silhouette of the sheer garment sketched over it. As you render the fabric, subtly reinforce the body contours with a flesh tone or darker shade of the fabric color. The details and silhouette should be rendered with a fine light line.

Sheers are natural fabrications for evening wear. Sheer cover ups may be worn over swimwear; they reveal the bathing suits underneath.

LACES

Lace has a transparent quality similar to a sheer. Lace has an additional motif to be rendered over the transparent fabric tone. There are many kinds of laces. Varieties include wildly spaced motifs on a net ground, lace edgings and ruffles, dense heavy cotton laces used in suits, and stretch laces that are used for foundation garments. Lace can be dyed in a range of colors. Dark colors are best rendered with a fine-line marker over a flesh-toned body. White lace is most effective when rendered on a colored board. Tan or shades of taupe or grey are neutral colors that will not detract from the finished illustration. Use a fine brush and a dense opaque white point to detail white lace.

Begin the illustration of a specific lace by analyzing the predominant pattern from a swatch or photograph. Lightly sketch it on the basic figure, scaling it to the garment as you did with fabric patterns. Work on a fairly large figure, so that the motif is large enough to render easily. Tone the body and undergarments or lining with felt pen or wash. Let this base color dry completely before working over the sketch with the fine-line marker or white paint for the actual lace pattern.

Expensive lace garments are sewn so darts and seam lines are invisible. The pattern is cut out where the garment has to be shaped and then hand sewn back together with a seam that conforms to the motif. Style and fit details in the lace should be minimal, even in less expensive garments.

RENDERING WHITE LACE
A contrasting illustration board sets off the pattern of white lace because of the contrast. A neutral-color board is most effective.

FURS

In the past, traditional furs were limited to natural colors and a limited variety. Mink was the most common fashion fur. Beaver, rabbit, seal, sable, chinchilla, and broadtail were novelties. Today many fashion designers have entered the fur market and innovated with artificial colors and new methods of styling furs. Fashion dictates the way furs look, and, at this time, the conservative ''little fur piece'' is out. Fun furs, casual outerwear, and fake furs add to the variety of garments available. New kinds of furs have become popular. When endangered species have limited a specific kind of fur, illustrators use novel methods of stenciling or clipping available pelts to imitate the real thing.

Each fur garment is styled around pelts with unique markings. Illustrators should work from actual garments or good photographs. Instead of attempting to render every hair, a bold loose style is the most effective approach to capturing the rich and varied texture of furs.

Charcoal or a soft conté crayon worked over a paper with a toothy (textured) surface is a very effective way of rendering the plush depths and highlights of furs.

Mink pelts have a characteristic dark stripe down the center of each strip or

pelt. A fine line indicates the direction the pelts have been worked. Use bright highlights to accent the dark richly toned areas of mink by leaving white paper unworked. Be guided by an actual garment or photograph when you render the shadows and highlights.

Draw the edges and collar details of bulky furs with thick, rounded corners. The longer furs will have greater volume. Lynx and spotted long hairs should be rendered with a great deal of white paper left open. Detail the fine hair lines with charcoal, a dry brush, or a fine-line marker. Keep the illustration loose and open. Soften the spots in a long-hair fur and give them an unprecise quality.

MINK

Smudge some areas of the charcoal and deeply shadow others to capture the depth of the fur. White highlights painted over dark areas with opaque watercolor are very effective.

Pen

Wash

Charcoal

SABLE, SEAL, BEAVER

Sable, seal, and beaver are such deep, rich pelts that—very much like velvet—they absorb rather than reflect light. Highlights tend to occur around the outer edges of these plush furs. Render these with deep, dark tones near the center of the garment, and highlight and feather the soft silhouette of the fur with a fine marker.

BROADTAIL, PERSIAN LAMB

Broadtail is much less bulky than other furs, because the fur is curled close to the hide. Corners of the silhouette and collars should be slimmer than other furs. The pattern resembles a natural moiré. Work over a lightly toned ground with a sharp charcoal or soft pencil, imitating the intricate pattern of the curly lamb fur.

SPOTTED, FLAT FURS

Spotted patterns are most effective on a light ground. Keep the spots irregularly rendered. The spots are well defined on a flat fur. Light shadows are typical of the edges of the large smooth pelts.

Draw collar with a firm rendering of its shape

thick neck

review faces and hair

redraw collar

Buttons

foreshorten arm as it recedes

line up pockets with the bottom level of the jacket

Slant of jacket bottom makes it awkward

rendering looks murky because of lack of good contrast areas

Give pants a smooth flowing line and a crisp front crease

hair too fussy— detracts from image

Shape the silhouette of the sleeve with more distinction

Scale of torso and waistline is too narrow to balance the full skirt details are too large to work with dress

Enhance the folds with darker tones

Shading of fabric has no character

Even up hemline so it has a smooth flow

#1 Block in the body first so the proportions are not over extended

#2 Block in body line of clothes next

Use hatch lines rendered in a marker to render elastic

Let the shape of the body form the garment

Study the highlights in an actual piece of satin to know how to render them

Shoulder line sags

Wash technique becomes murky here

head too low

use dark contrast lines for details

A "spaghetti" person shows no preliminary consideration of the pose and figure lines made

the quality of satin is lost because of one tone in the wash

Practice washes to get a clean line — Cover mistakes with white, opaque paint!

how crotch looks matronly

Knees too low!

Study faces and draw the eyes with a softer gaze — feather the eyebrow

Take the startled look away by using the eyelid to cover the top third of the eye

Blouse would be enhanced with highlighting

Details of the shirt are difficult to see — use a contrast line

Skirt is effectively rendered with shadow and a wash and screen

CHECK YOUR SKILLS

Collect the sketches you have made while doing the exercises on rendering fabric. Compare them to the student work shown here. Analyze the strengths and weaknesses of your work. Refer back to the pages that teach lessons that you need more work on.

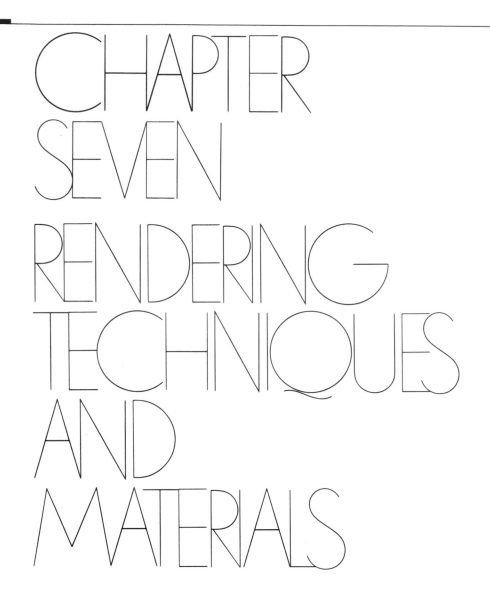

CHAPTER
SEVEN

RENDERING
TECHNIQUES
AND
MATERIALS

Learning to draw in a clear and easy manner, without gimmicks, should be the primary goal of a fashion illustrator or designer. Knowledge of what the figure is and how the body moves is the essence of fashion illustration. A visual concept of the way garments are constructed and the way fabric drapes as it surrounds and enhances the body is the second key to illustrating fashions. When you have developed this knowledge and transformed it into a high level of skill with easily controlled media like pencils, felt pens, and prisma pencils, then explore and master more complicated media.

A good art-supply store will have a wide range of papers and materials. Trained sales personnel can explain and demonstrate media. New innovations are found here. Illustrators should shop art-supply stores frequently. Often catalogues can be requested for ordering by phone.

Several quality ranges are offered in each kind of product. Price will vary, depending on quality. Serious students should buy the best materials they can afford. "Artist" quality brushes, paint, and paper will be easier to handle and will produce professional results easier than inexpensive products. "Student" quality art supplies are less expensive but often produce inferior results. Inexpensive paper may not accept paint as well as an artist quality paper. Brushes that shed their hair spoil a painted surface. Weigh the cost of art supplies against the quality of the product you wish to produce.

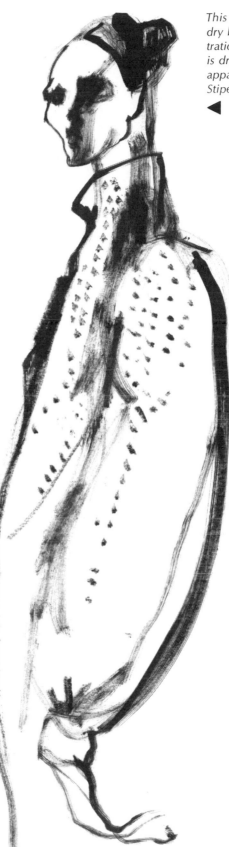

This skilled artist uses a bold, dry brush line to give his illustration a painterly quality that is dramatic for high-fashion apparel. (Courtesy of Steven Stipelman.)

DRAWING PAPERS

Papers range widely in weight, use, quality, size, color surface characteristics, and price. The list of basic paper terms that follows will give you a clue to basic varieties and their uses. Nothing substitutes for experimentation and experience in selecting a specific paper for a special effect. Begin to purchase a variety of papers and experiment with colors and quality. It is always best to buy extra sheets to cover the mistake that might happen. Keep odd paper scraps for working out future ideas.

Illustration board is the ''work horse'' paper for drawn and painted illustrations. It is a good quality watercolor paper mounted on cardboard for greater stability. A cold-pressed or slightly ''toothy'' surface is preferred, because it withstands repeated erasures and reworking without destroying the surface. Illustration board is available in several weights and surface patterns and a wide range of colors. Illustration board is fairly expensive and, as a beginner, you will want to work out a rough soft-pencil sketch on a less expensive bond paper. To transfer this image to the illustration board, use a soft lead pencil to cover the back of your rough sketch where you have pencil lines. Use two small pieces of masking tape to secure the drawing to the illustration board. Then use a sharp, hard (#3) pencil to draw over your sketch. Remove the rough drawing and clean any carbon smudges off with an eraser before working further into the illustration.

Professional illustrators often draw directly on the illustration board. Sure drawing skills produce a looser, more

Patterned Screens

Heavy drawing Paper

Instant Landscape

Textured Paper

9

Vellum

Screens

Overlay

Heavy Watercolour Paper

Press type

Construction Paper

Watercolour

AA Charcoal Paper

interesting sketch than the transfer technique. Strive to build your drawing skills so you feel comfortable lightly sketching your rough drawing directly on illustration board.

Collect several subtly colored illustration boards and novelty papers. Buff, ecru, grey, and taupe are good neutral tones that will not detract from your illustration. Colored paper is very effective for rendering white garments.

Use a very toothy surfaced paper when sketching with charcoal or pastels. The rough surface enhances the soft sensuous charcoal line. Smooth surface papers take fine pen lines and delicate line drawings best.

Build a supply of different papers so you can select the appropriate vehicle for any drawing or medium you wish to attempt. Add several hot press illustration boards (they have a smooth, slick surface) so you can mount or mat your best work for a truly professional presentation.

BASIC DRAWING PAPER TERMS

☐ Tooth (also called bite)—in a good paper, a textured surface is created by the arrangement of fibers. These little peaks and valleys are visible as a textured line when drawn on with a lead pencil, crayon, or charcoal. More tooth makes the surface bulkier, more absorbent, and more reflective.

☐ Feel—this refers to the comparative bulk, finish, snap, and feel of the paper. Similar to the hand of a fabric.

☐ Grain—the direction the paper fibers run as it is made. Grain line affects the folding ability of paper and how it tears.

☐ Hard, high surface, hot press, smooth, slick, or plate finish—these terms all describe a smooth, hard surface paper that is appropriate for a delicate line drawing. This finish is difficult to erase and paint on because the fibers absorb less media and feather easily when erased or dampened.

☐ Medium surface, vellum, kid, or cold press finish—these terms describe a toothy surface with a slight texture that accepts almost any technique, from air brush and paints to marking pens and pencils.

☐ Rag content—a paper which contains 25–100 percent rag or cotton pulp. The greater the rag content, the more erasing and wetting the paper can take.

☐ "Pound" substance—the weight of a paper in pounds is determined by the weight of a ream (500 sheets) in the paper's basic size. For example, one ream of bond paper, size 17-by-22 inches, weighs 16 pounds and is called a 16-pound bond paper. Ledger bond weighs 32 pounds in the basic bond paper size of 17-by-22 inches, so it is designated as 32-pound ledger bond.

☐ Point—the thickness of illustration, matt or mount boards, and papers are measured by the point. A point is .001 inch (a thousandth of an inch).

☐ ST—single thickness illustration board is approximately $\frac{1}{16}$ or 60 points thick.

☐ DT—double thickness board is approximately $\frac{1}{8}$ inch or 110 points thick.

☐ TT—triple thickness board is approximately $\frac{3}{16}$ inch or 165 points thick.

☐ Bond paper (16 pounds) is about 3 points thick.

□ Ledger bond (32 pounds) is about 6 points thick.

APPLIED PAPERS

□ Color screens—these are pressure-applied, transparent acetate sheets in a wide range of colors that are often used in professional illustrations. These overlays are transparent and may be used over a drawing and then reworked with paints, pencils, or marking pens. The colors are available in many graduated tints of each color.

□ Printed color sheets—opaque printed color that may be used in a collage. Must be applied with glue.

□ Shaded screens—many kinds of patterns are available in black, printed on transparent acetate screens that are applied to paper by pressure. The basic range is a dotted surface that ranges from a light grey to a dense grey surface. These patterns are helpful devices for doing black-and-white camera-ready artwork.

□ Typeface—pressure-applied screens with alphabets and numerals are available in a great variety of styles and sizes. They are applied like the color and tonal screens.

□ Tissue paper, book end paper, novelty papers—a great variety of novelty papers are available for collage illustrations. Usually they may be purchased by the piece.

APPLIED PAPER TECHNIQUES

Acetate Screens   Machine-made screens of transparent paper, over-printed with a color or pattern, can be purchased at most art stores. They are easily applied to tone an area on a sketch. The finished illustration has a smooth, professional look.

Sketch the basic illustration on a smooth piece of paper or illustration board. You may shadow the illustration before applying the screen. The screen can be painted, or reworked with pencils or markers. Carefully place the full sheet over the illustration and cut a piece slightly larger than the area you wish to cover. Be careful not to apply any pressure to the screen. When the shape is cut, place it on the illustration and cut out the exact contour with a matt knife. Be careful only to cut the film and not the paper the illustration is on. Lightly press the sheet to "tack" it in place, and then burnish it firmly with a smoothing tool. Be sure to securely press down the edges of the screen. Detail shadows, highlights, and style lines with paint, pen, or pencils.

Because of their transparency, several color screens can be applied over the same area, creating blended colors. Experiment with scraps of colored screens to see how colors mix and other media work with the blends you create.

The geometric screen focuses the eye on the face and enhances the strong graphic quality and bold line of Passantino's work. (Courtesy of Robert Passantino for Women's Wear Daily.)

▼

Screens give a clean even tone on Fashion Figures

Cut section of screen of approximate size you will need

"Cut with sharp blade"

Press down Cut around area to be shaded — lift off...gently!

The glory of Summer. Brassy light dry wind and sparkling waters. Sea breezes; mists dissolving into the heat. Childrens' laughter, kites and balloons float to the sun.

Tissue Paper and Novelty Collage Materials Colored tissue paper can be used as a collage (pictures created by assemblies of paper and objects). Brilliant colors are available in single sheets or as packages at most art stores. To apply with liquid starch carefully paint the area to be covered with starch. Press down the precut piece of tissue paper and repaint the

The end of the year, goals accomplished or left to rest. The deathly silence with rains and minute white doilies falling softly to paint the earth a stark white. Die only to be reborn, the seasons rush in and hesitate to leave.

area with another coat of starch. The tissue color will bleed, so wash the brush after each application and let the piece dry before applying paint or additional tissue layers. The tissue will often wrinkle, forming an interesting texture. The double application of starch makes the tissue look glazed. A different effect is achieved when the tissue is mounted on paper with rubber cement. Precut the shape you want. Apply a thin, even coat of rubber cement to the back of the tissue and where it is to be applied. Let both sides dry completely. Carefully place the precut shape, and smooth the tissue into place. This application gives the tissue a matt surface.

Any kind of paper can be used as collage material. Paper can make a distinctive color or texture area, and then your illustration can be finished with paint, felt pens, and pencils. Collage is a versatile and quick method of illustrating. Collect scraps of interesting paper, and experiment with several collage approaches to illustration.

PASTELS AND CHARCOALS

Pastels are dry color. When applied to paper, the colors may be blended with the fingers or with a paper-blending stump. To fix the colors to the paper permanently, a spray fixative must be applied over the finished illustration.

This technique is difficult to use for fashion illustrations for several reasons: (1) it is most effective applied directly to the page, with no under-drawing requiring advanced drawing skills; (2) it tends to be messy and imprecise; and (3) special papers with a very toothy surface are most effective.

Pastels and charcoals lend themselves to rendering of furs, despite the care needed to master this media. An accomplished artist can achieve fresh, spontaneous drawings in charcoal. Conté crayons are stick drawing pastels from France, available in black-and-white and sepia tones that are fine traditional drawing pastels.

Draw quickly and boldly directly on a toothy drawing paper. Concentrate on drawing the silhouette and shadows instead of the tiny details of the garment. Do not overwork the sketch, because it will tend to become dirty and muddy. Enhance the spontaneous drawing style by using color boldly and directly. Preserve the drawing with a coat of spray fixative, available at any good art-supply store.

PAINTS AND PAINTING EQUIPMENT

PAINTS

Paint is a pigment mixed with binder, a "glue" which makes the color adhere to a receptive surface. Binders are dissolved and extended by water or mineral spirits (turpentine). The vast majority of color fashion illustration is done with water-base paints, because they dry rapidly, are relatively inexpensive, are easy to work with, and dry with a matt surface for camera-ready art.

Water-base paints are available in two main kinds: transparent and opaque (also called gouache). These two kinds of paint may be mixed. They are compatible with dyes and acrylic (polymer emulsion) paints—in fact, with all paints that use water as an extender. Water-base paints are not compatible with oil-base paints.

Transparent watercolors are available in individual tubes, in bottles as liquid watercolor, and in solid cakes contained in palette sets. Palettes usually have 12 or more colored cakes and are very economical and portable. These solid colors should have a drop of water added to each cake several minutes before using. The water will

break down the binder, and intense color will be readily available. When either cake or tube watercolor is mixed with enough white paint, an opaque surface results. This is gouache, or opaque watercolor. To paint a light, transparent color, thin the pure color with water, not white paint.

Dyes are extremely concentrated liquid pigments. When painted full strength on a white surface, dyes produce a billiant, transparent tone. Dyes come in bottles with eye-dropper tops, so a small amount can be dropped onto a palette or into white paint and then brushed on paper. A great variety of colors are available.

Liquid watercolor is available in eye-dropper-top bottles very similar to dyes. They are usually more costly than liquid dyes or cake watercolors.

Transparent watercolor paint tends to produce a looser, more painterly illustration than the opaque techniques. Opaque surfaces are most effective when they are applied as tight color areas within an illustration and reworked with a well-defined outline and precise detailing.

Gouache or "designer colors" are most frequently used in fashion and commercial illustration. These are good quality paints that can be easily mixed to produce a smooth, even surface. A high degree of color control and density of paint is possible. Designer colors are available in tubes. A wide variety of colors plus black and white are an asset to any beginner. The medium-sized tubes are most practical, because they will not dry out before they are used up. Many tones of grey are available premixed to facilitate rendering black-and-white camera-ready art for commercial illustration purposes.

Acrylic paints produce a dense opaque surface with a slight gloss. Acrylic paints can be extended with water and used to tint white designer color paint like dyes and watercolors. Experiment with this paint medium to determine if it adds a unique dimension to your illustration.

BRUSHES

Brushes are offered in many qualities. Red sable watercolor brushes are the finest quality. Brushes are numbered to define the size. The smaller the number, the finer the brush size. The beginner should buy a range of brush sizes in the best quality brush the budget will allow. Several fine brushes for detail work are important (select an 000, 0, and a #1). Medium sizes are #2 through #5; select a #3 and a #5 for a beginning. Buy a #7 or #8 for larger washes and one medium-sized blunt "sky" brush (named for fine artists' background "sky" washes) for painting larger areas.

Nylon brushes are preferred when painting with acrylics, because the polymer binder produces a texture that is quite thick and oil paint effects can be achieved with these slightly firmer brushes, which have a natural "snap."

Clean and store your brushes carefully. Never leave brushes in water for extended periods of time, because the glue that holds the hairs into the ferrule will loosen, and the points will blend. Wash your brushes with a mild hand soap, flush with clear warm water, and let them dry naturally. With care, good brushes will last many years.

The following list may help you in your selection and use of brushes:

☐ Japanese (sumié) brush — a long, pointed brush often made with a bamboo handle that is used for painting Japanese characters and brush painting.

☐ Nylon bristle brushes — used for acrylic paints because of the large amount of paint they can hold and because of their "snap," or resiliency. Available in flat, round, and chisel shapes, and in a range of sizes.

☐ One-stroke, lettering brushes — flat, broad-tipped sable (or mixed-hair) brushes designed for lettering.

☐ Oval, "sky" brushes — blunt-end brushes used for broad washes, especially sky tones in fine art painting.

☐ Pointed brush — needle-sharp pointed hairs with which you can paint fine line. To paint washes with this brush, load it with paint and use it on its side.

☐ Red sable — the best quality hair for a watercolor brush. The hair is obtained from kolinsky (red tarter martin) foxtails. These brushes are soft, resilient, and durable.

☐ Student quality brushes — less costly hair from black sables, squirrel, ponies, and oxen are used to make these less expensive brushes. Though they often resemble the red sable quality, these brushes rarely perform or last as well. They are less expensive, however.

MISCELLANEOUS EQUIPMENT

Buy a plastic palette for mixing colors, or save clean white styrafoam egg cartons. Blotters or absorbent paper towels are an important painting aid; use them for cleaning brushes or lifting excess paint from an illustration. Use a large glass or jar for fresh water to rinse an unwanted color from your brush.

A smooth drawing board made from a soft wood or masonite board is important. To make painting easier, raise the board in the back and draw on a slanted surface. Buy a clip or push pins to secure your paper or illustration board to the drawing board.

BASIC COLOR TERMS

☐ Primary colors—red, blue, and yellow. The foundation colors that can be combined to form all the others.

☐ Secondary colors—combinations of two of the primary colors: orange = red + yellow; purple = blue + red; green = yellow + blue.

☐ Tertiary colors—colors created by the combination of three colors: for example, red + yellow + blue = brown.

☐ Black and white—colors at the opposite end of the grey scale that combine with pure colors to create shades (black + color) and tints (white + color).

☐ Chroma—the intensity of a particular hue.

☐ Color wheel—an arrangement of colors radiating out from the primary and secondary colors.

☐ Complimentary colors—colors across the color wheel.

☐ Hue—pure color.

☐ Saturated colors—pure, full strength, intense color with no black or white to alter the tint.

☐ Shade—color + black, which gives a darker tone to the hue.

☐ Tint—color + white, or transparent color diluted with water.

☐ Value—the amount of light or dark in a color (luminosity scale).

PAINTING TECHNIQUES

Experimentation and practice are the key ingredients to mastering mixing colors and handling brushes and watercolors. Nothing substitutes for the trial-and-error process of mixing a color or developing a technique by trying to duplicate an illustration you admire or envision.

Begin painting by doing the following exercises to master transparent and opaque washes. Repeat the exercises several times, first using black and white, then substituting a color. Then begin to experiment with color mixes. Duplicate illustration and painting techniques from this book and your scrap collection. Experiment with paint without expecting to produce a finished illustration. Painting experi-

ments and "doodling" will help develop your techniques of mixing color accurately.

Learn from your mistakes, as well as from the successful illustrations you produce. Hold a finished illustration up to a mirror for a new perspective on your fresh work. Put a finished piece of art away for a day or so, and then reevaluate your achievements and analyze how your work could be improved.

Watch professional illustrators whenever possible and imitate their work methods. Attend fine arts classes for tips that may improve your technique. Ask an illustrator or instructor to critique your work. Rework past pieces, using their directions.

There is no substitute for experimenting and doing to learn how to paint and mix colors.

This superb gouache rendering is accented and highlighted with pencil and pen. (Courtesy of Catherine Clayton Purnell.)

▶

FALL NEWCOMERS

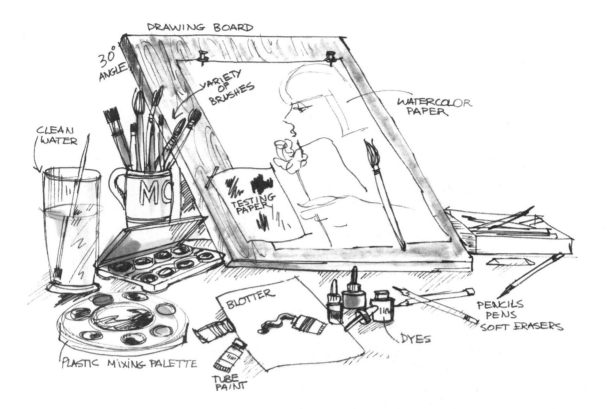

WORKING SPACE SETUP

1. Store brushes in a container with the points up in the air. The size and kind of point will then be easily visable, and the hairs will not bend. After using, always clean brushes with a mild soap and flush with warm water.

2. A palette of 12 or more color cakes is a good basic investment. Before using, add a drop of water to each cake to break down the binder, so the color is in solution and ready to use. After a number of uses, the palette may be cleaned by rinsing with a gentle flow of warm water.

3. Use a plastic palette for mixing paint for washes. Premix the colors thoroughly in one of the wells before painting for the smoothest coverage.

4. Clear water is necessary for mixing paints and rinsing brushes between colors. Change frequently to keep colors brilliant.

5. Dyes and tubes of paint are additional aids that should be added to your supplies as your budget allows. A tube of white designer color is a must for a beginner.

6. A paper towel or blotter is used to mop up excess water and excess color and to dry brushes.

7. Drawing pencils and felt pens should be handy. Use them to work into the illustration when the washes are completely dry.

8. Before you apply paint to an illustration, test a dab for color and consistency on a spare piece of paper.

9. Elevate your drawing board to a 20- or 30-degree angle, so the paint can flow down the area you want to cover.

TRANSPARENT WASH TECHNIQUE

Grey-scale Washes

1.   Draw a series of 2-inch squares on illustration board or a good quality watercolor paper.

2.   Paint two or three squares with a small amount of clear water, and wait until the paper absorbs most of the water. This priming makes the paper accept the paint smoothly.

3.   Put a small amount of water in a well of the palette. Tint it with a dab of black paint from your black watercolor tube or cake. Mix the pigment and water well. Paint the first square with a medium-sized (#7 or #8) brush.

4.   Paint from the top of the square downward. Work one stripe after another, overlapping them slightly and blending the overlap area with your brush so you have a smooth, even wash.

5.   Add more black paint to your palette and paint successively darker squares. Paint at least 20 squares. Cut the squares out of the paper, and select 10 grey tones that are evenly graduated from a pale grey tint to a deep shade of charcoal.

6.   Paste the squares in the center of a 7-by-14-inch white board. Use rubber cement. Make sure the 10 squares are arranged in two rows, with an even distribution of space around the grouping.

Rendering with a Transparent Wash

1.   Lightly sketch a figure on good watercolor paper or illustration board. Mix a light grey tint, and paint it as the flesh tone of the figure (did you remember to prime the area with water before painting?). Let this wash dry completely before continuing.

2.   Mix a medium grey tint, and paint the garment in your sketch. Let some of the paper remain white where the highlights of the garment would fall. Work the shadows and folds of the fabric with a deeper shade of grey. Let this wash dry.

3.   Build shadows in the folds and edges of the garment. Tone the hair, again leaving highlights of white paper. Shadow the cheekbones and eyelids with one of the grey tones on your palette. Allow the washes to dry completely.

4.   Detail your finished sketch with silhouette and style lines done with a very fine brush and black paint or a fine-line marking pen.

Practice several figures. Notice how the transparent wash technique can create a dramatic, loosely rendered illustration. Render some garments from photographs. Instead of grey tones, use tints of pure color from your palette. Dilute brown paint and tint with a touch of red and yellow to paint a skin tone.

Lay in sketch with pencil—erase guide lines and float a wash over skin tones and tone over garments

OPAQUE WASH TECHNIQUE

Grey-scale Opaque Washes

1. Draw 2-inch squares on a piece of good watercolor paper or illustration board, and prime with water as you did in the last grey-scale exercise.

2. Squeeze an aspirin-sized dab of white designer color into a bowl in your palette.

3. Dilute the white paint with several brushfuls of water (use a #7 brush). Mix the water and paint thoroughly until it is of brushing consistency.

4. Add a drop of black paint to the white mixture, and mix it again (use the brush for mixing). Completely blend the black paint and the white paint until no streaks are visible.

5. Paint the first square from top to bottom with slightly overlapping strokes. Smooth out any streaks with your brush.

6. Continue mixing deeper tones of grey from white and black paint extended with water. The secret to streakless washes is to thoroughly premix the paint in the palette before painting it on the paper. Paint 20 squares in graduated grey tones. Cut them out. Select 10 squares that are evenly

Build up illustration with darker grey washes – begin to highlight light and dark areas of sketch – add black ink for blackest tones, and white gouache for highlighting. Use fine line pen or pencil for rendering facial features

RUFFLES TIERS
BOWS
FACE FRAMING BLOUSES

graded steps from a grey tint to a deep charcoal shade. Mount as you did the transparent wash examples.

Compare the two kinds of paint. Notice how the dense opaque washes cover pencil lines and kill most of the quality of the paper. Opaque paint lends itself to tightly rendered illustrations; transparent washes have a looser, more painterly feeling.

Rendering with an Opaque Wash

1. Lightly sketch a simple figure on watercolor paper or illustration board. Mix an opaque light-grey wash with black and white, and paint the garment.

2. Mix a grey wash several tones lighter, and paint the garment. Allow each painted area to completely dry before beginning the next. Remember to prime your paper with water before painting each area.

3. Work back into the basic wash with deeper tints of grey to accent the folds and shadows of the garment. Use an opaque white paint for highlighting the basic wash.

4. Detail the silhouette lines and style lines and features with a fine brush and black paint or a fine-line marker.

Work out several more illustrations using the opaque-wash technique. Use a fashion photograph to guide you to the way the fabric falls and reflects light. Observe the shadows and highlights in garments and hair. Duplicate them with your grey tone paints.

Experiment with a combination of transparent and opaque washes in one illustration. For example, render the skin tones with an opaque wash, and paint the garment with a loose, transparent wash, emphasizing paper highlights and brush strokes.

COLOR RENDERING

The majority of professional fashion illustration is done as black-and-white art for newsprint advertising purposes. Colored fashion illustrations are used for color-print-media camera-ready art, design plates (especially for theater costume design), and commercial design presentations. Color work is also extensively used in print fabric designing.

A basic knowledge of painting and mixing a wide range of colors from the three primary colors is helpful to any artist. In practice, most professional artists use a great variety of premixed paints, dyes, and marking pens to cut down the elaborate mixing necessary to create colors from scratch.

Experimenting with this range of artists' aids is essential to developing an eye for color matching. Begin to learn how to mix colors by substituting a primary color for black. Develop a range of tints from the pure hue to a pale pastel shade of the color. Deepen the pure color in steps to achieve near black. Select ten equal steps of these tints and shades plus the saturated color, and mount as you did the grey scales.

To improve your color-matching ability, mix paint to match several fabric swatches. Remember, watercolor drys slightly lighter than when wet. Refer back to the chapter on rendering fabrics and repeat several exercises for each fashion problem presented.

Paint

Marker

Using a variety of materials gives more life to your sketch!

pencil

kim ann

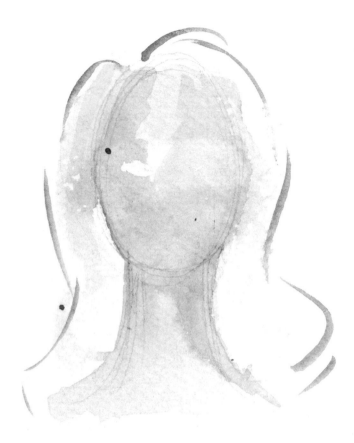

Color Rendering of the Head

1. Mix an opaque skin tone by extending a drop of white paint with water, in a well of your mixing palette. Tint this to a skin tone by adding dabs of red, brown, and yellow. Mix thoroughly and test on your trial paper. Correct with additional dabs of color until you are satisfied with the shade.

2. Paint the basic skin tone on the face. Leave the eyes white. Tint the remaining skin tone in your palette several shades darker with brown paint. Shadow the cheekbones, nose, and top edges of the forehead with this deeper tone. Allow to dry.

3. Paint the iris with an appropriate color. Use the eye color to tint a small amount of flesh tone and paint the eyelid with a complementary shadow. Use a red, coral, or pink to

color the lips. Do not overemphasize these colors; keep them looking natural.

4. Mix a hair color. Paint the hair with a transparent wash with loose brush strokes. Leave white paper highlights. Let the basic hair tone dry thoroughly. Mix a darker color of the hair shade and detail the flow of the hairstyle with a fine brush.

5. Detail the whole drawing by outlining the features, blackening the pupil, finishing the eyebrows and eyelids, and so on. Reinforce the hairstyle lines with black paint, unless it contrasts too strongly with a light hair shade.

6. Mix a pure, dense white and apply to the whites of the eyes and teeth, if visible. Highlight the tip of the nose, the black pupil, and perhaps a touch at the bottom lip.

CHAPTER EIGHT

DESIGNING THE ILLUSTRATION

Skillfully drawing a fashion figure is only one phase of fashion illustration and design-style presentation. The figure should relate to the space of the total composition. A well-drawn figure—the positive image—is enhanced by the design of the setting or the negative space that surrounds the image. In addition, an illustrator or designer usually has to arrange several elements on one page. The fashion layout artist who plans print media has to integrate these elements for a typical newspaper ad: several fashion figures, a headline, the body of copy, the store logo, and miscellaneous print information. A designer usually illustrates several figures or a group of garments, and adds swatches of fabric and colors and handwritten instructions on a typical fashion presentation plate.

The total space must be planned so the eye focuses on the main point of interest and flows logically through the subordinate elements. Design means the planned pattern of the whole subject. A visual atmosphere that enhances the subject matter is essential to successfully designing a good fashion illustration. A limited drawing ability can be camouflaged by a well-designed presentation that stresses the positive skills of the artist.

The successfully designed page should do the following:

1. Capture the interest of the viewer.

2. Direct the eye toward the most important element on the page.

3. Support the center of interest with explanatory print areas or descriptive materials.

4. Reinforce the subject matter with an appropriate format.

5. Avoid the opposing excesses of monotony and confusion through careful planning of the positive images and the negative space that surrounds them.

The creative application of the principles (guidelines) to the elements (components) of design results in a successful page. Think of baking a cake. The recipe tells a cook how to combine the ingredients and at what temperature to bake them to produce a delicious cake. To an artist, the principles of design govern the way the elements or ingredients should be combined to create a successful illustration.

▲
This delicate air-brush rendering of a face for a cosmetic product is effective because of the range of light and dark tones that contour with no hard edge line. (Courtesy of David Horii.)

▲

Contrasting areas of line and mechanical screened tones move the eye through this complicated layout. Notice how the car frames the figures and directs attention to them. (Courtesy of Mia Carpenter.)

CONTRAST

Contrast creates the focal point and the subordinate elements by varying value, line, and form.

VALUE

Value creates emphasis by drawing the eye to high contrast areas of an illustration. A bold dark area is most effectively seen against a lighter value or white background. A white circle on a black ground rivets the eye because of high contrast. Equal areas of light and dark are monotonous. To maintain interest, vary the size of each value area in a composition.

LINE

Line creates interest because of direction, weight, and character. A bold, crisply drawn line has an interesting character even before it describes a specific object. A light, smooth line suggests light fabric, delicate details, or sleek limbs. A bold, heavy line best describes a bulky fabric, the silhouette of a garment, or a bold, masculine face. Compositions that have strong linear directions assume a definite personality based on traditional perceptions of directional lines.

☐ *Horizontal lines* are restful and tranquil.

☐ *Diagonal lines* are exciting and express action. Avoid using diagnonal composition lines as a beginner. Undisciplined use of angles can be confusing.

☐ *Vertical lines* seem to reach or climb. They represent power and growth.

☐ *Curved lines* remind the eye of natural forms. The eye takes longer to

The contrast of light, generalized lines and detailed tonal rendering focuses the eye on the product. The gesture and attention of the models directs the viewer to the copy area. (Courtesy of Gregory Weir-Quiton for The Broadway.)

▼

perceive a curve than a straight line. Curved lines seem lyrical and tranquil.

FORM

Form creates a contrast when large bold areas are accented with small details or crisp smaller shapes. This is a contrast of scale, large compared to small. A small dark space can "read" (seem to the eye) more important than a lightly outlined larger shape.

▲

The bold central focal point of this layout dramatizes the silhouette of the garment. A wide range of grey tones moves the eye quickly from the top to the bottom of this illustration. (Courtesy of Paul Lowe for The Broadway.)

RHYTHM

Rhythm is the repeated use of a similar value area, shape, or line technique, in order to create a unified whole. Repeating the same form creates a repeated rhythm that can be successfully accented by changing the shape, line quality, color, or value of the accent unit. The one black sheep is immediately seen in a herd of white sheep.

UNITY

Unity or harmony is the logical emphasis of the focal point and the subordination of less important elements of the composition. Harmony unifies the elements of design to fulfill the visual goals of an illustration.

Unplanned use of color, line, value, and form will detract from the impact of the focal point. Picture an advertisement for a discount drug store or market. These ads are composed to cover every part of the newspaper page with a jumble of copy and unrelated illustrations. Almost no negative space is left. The eye has no place to pause. Confusion results. The purpose of the ad might be to sell inexpensive merchandise, but no image is projected for the goods or the store except one of seller of bargains. More sophisticated merchandise is sold by developing an exclusive image for the selective customer. A successful fashion ad uses well-designed images to enhance the consumer's perception of the styles illustrated. The personality of a fashion store should integrate

◀

These figures, arranged rhythmically on a slightly asymmetrical axis, break up the space beautifully and direct the eye through the illustration. The wide variety of lights contrasting with black and medium tones adds more excitement to the layout. (Courtesy of Mia Carpenter.)

with the visual message given by the merchandise, so the store image gains prestige from the advertisements.

BALANCE

Balance is the way forms are arranged on a page.

Formal or symmetrical balance is an equal distribution of shapes on either side of a median line. The human body is symmetrical. Formal balance seems strong, dignified, restful, and static.

Informal balance is the placement of dissimilar shapes in a pleasing arrangement on the page. Asymmetry creates a more dynamic illustration than a symmetrical arrangement. Asymmetrical formats can easily seem unbalanced or random. They must be carefully designed to fully exploit the exciting composition potentials of asymmetrical pages.

Complicated subject matter requires careful planning to avoid confusion and allow the eye to logically follow the figures through the illustration. The consistent style and line accented by dark areas unifies this complicated illustration (see pages 200–201). (Courtesy of Here and There, Fashion Reporting Service.)

▶

This bold asymmetrical layout balances the headline with the central figure. The subordinate figure is well integrated into the positive space. Consequently, the negative space highlights the elements of the illustration. (Courtesy of Steve Bieck for J. W. Robinson's.)

▼

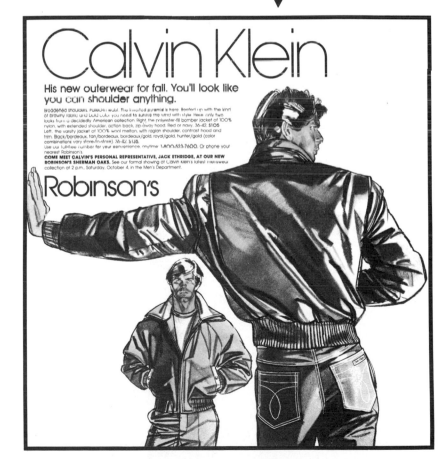

1. Color

(Brights with Black)

(Classic Spectators)

(Directional Muted Tones — Spring '80)

(Directional Sweets — Spring '80)

2. Fabrics & Patterns

Resource: Gartex

Resource: Scacchi

Resource: Gartex

Resource: Gartex

Resource: Braghenti

Resource: Etro

(swatch shown ½ actual size)

5. Jackets & Coats

YAMAMOTO
SLIDE #62

MONTANA
SLIDE #64

KRIZIA
SLIDE #61

MONTANA
SLIDE #65

DE LUCA
SLIDE #49

MONTANA
SLIDE #41

6. Sportswear

TER ET BANTINE
SLIDE #74

DE LUCA
SLIDE #26

MUGLER
SLIDE #77

ALVEAR
SLIDE #78

KRIZIA
SLIDE #12

CHLOE
SLIDE #21

PABLO ET DELIA
SLIDE #6

KRIZIA
SLIDE #75

Themes
(Hollywood Glamour from the 40's and 50's)

MONTANA
SLIDE #28

CHLOE
SLIDE #35

BANTINE
SLIDE #46

CHLOE
SLIDE #31

ANDREVIE
SLIDE #37

YAMAMOTO
SLIDE #39

CHLOE
SLIDE #22

ALBINI
SLIDE #44

(Sailors and Sirens)

4. Suits

ERREUNO
SLIDE #56

KRIZIA
SLIDE #48

CHLOE
SLIDE #1

ANDREVIE
SLIDE #19

HECHTER
SLIDE #53

KRIZIA
SLIDE #47

ANDREVIE
SLIDE #50

MUGLER
SLIDE #16

7. Knits

MUGLER
SLIDE #75

ARMANI
SLIDE #55

TER ET BANTINE
SLIDE #60

BERETTA
SLIDE #68

ARMANI
SLIDE #54

KRIZIA
SLIDE #76

ST. LAURENT
SLIDE #66

MUGLER
SLIDE #85

YAMAMOTO
SLIDE #72

CHLOE
SLIDE #79

KRIZIA
SLIDE #83

BASILE
SLIDE #80

YAMAMOTO
SLIDE #89

YAMAMOTO
SLIDE #81

8. Dresses
(Day into Evening)

CHLOE
SLIDE #96

MUGLER
SLIDE #100

BIS
SLIDE #80

KRIZIA
SLIDE #91

DE LUCA
SLIDE #97

TER ET BANTINE
SLIDE #99

BASILE
SLIDE #32

LAYOUT SKILLS

The layout sketch is a plan for the organization or *make* of the page. The way the page should look is governed by these factors:

1. The slant of personality of the subject matter

2. The size of the page

3. The size and number of elements (figures, swatches, body copy, headline, logo, etc.) that must be incorporated into the layout

4. The image of the store

These conditions establish the *problem,* or the limitations of the page's make. The limitations of a problem do not hinder the artist's creativity. Rather, they focus attention on the specific requirements of the project and eliminate many possible solutions to designing an illustration. Layout artists specialize in planning the visual composition of an ad. They usually do not render the finished artwork. Many finished artists must do their own layouts in addition to the camera-ready art. The layout plan must carefully follow all the instructions for a specific page make. If a specification is missed or ignored, the artwork may be unusable, resulting in a loss of valuable time and money.

A design presentation should be planned like a good retail store advertisement. The designer must consider the subject matter and the audience who will see the presentation. If a designer is sketching for a boss or patternmaker, a simple pencil sketch of the front and back of the garment with sewing instructions and a swatch will be enough. If the presentation is for a store buyer, the illustration will have to have figures, well rendered in color, and a complete set of swatches, trims, and price notations. The designer plate is a selling tool just like a store ad. The designer should set up specific requirements that will govern the graphic presentation of the garments. Besides the basic layout criteria, some additional considerations for a design presentation are the drawing skills of the designer and the time element allotted for the project.

The beginning designer or illustrator should list the requirements of a particular project first, so they are clearly in focus and not forgotten during the execution of the project. Establish a realistic deadline and time yourself so you know how long each phase of the project takes.

The second step to executing a project is the thumb-nail, or layout, sketch. A thumb-nail sketch is a rough drawing that shows the position of all the elements on the page. The size and position of the figures and other elements are roughly indicated on bond paper or vellum in pencil or felt marker.

The Western eye tends to read a page from left to right and top to bottom out of habit. (Japanese perception is opposite to the Western tradition and their print media reverses these rules.) A figure on the left-hand side of the page looking to the right seems to be entering the illustration. A figure on the right seems to be leaving the field of interest. For this reason, the dominant focal point usually is on the left-hand axis of a composition.

The principles and elements of design discussed in the first part of this chapter strongly influence good layout design. Negative space is as important as positive space. The white area guides the eye to the focal point of

Axial   Band   Formal   Group

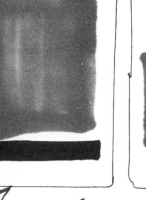

Path

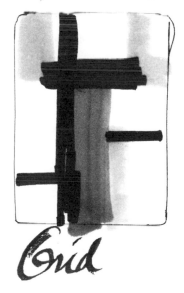

Grid

the page and should be as carefully planned as the positive images on the page. Lavish use of negative space implies the advertiser does not have to cover every inch of space with a copy or an image of his or her product. The prestigious object can be surrounded with space that enhances it. Avoid using equal amounts of light and dark. Vary the line and value of the page to focus the eye's attention on the focal point of the illustration. Avoid using strong diagonal elements in early compositions; they can be confusing.

The beginner should work the layout sketch the same size as the finished illustration. The figures may be sketched freehand, redrawn from photographs or scrap, or traced from earlier sketches. Make several layout sketches and select the best one for the finished artwork.

BASIC LAYOUT FORMATS

Above all, remember there are no set rules governing how to lay out a page or which format is most acceptable for a given subject matter. There are typical layout formats that can be adapted to a great variety of subject matter and requirements. Six typical formats are:

1. Axial
2. Band
3. Formal
4. Grid
5. Group
6. Path

Study these layout formats, their descriptions, and the fashion examples of each. Use these examples for future reference when you tackle complicated layout projects. Realize these are guidelines and not dogmatic formulas that govern the layout of a page. Go through a good glossy fashion magazine and identify as many typical layouts as possible. Experiment with the layout problem at the end of this series.

Axial

Dadmy Geneve

AXIAL COMPOSITION

Think of a tree trunk and branches forming a pleasing breakup of space. The subordinate elements should balance off the central axis. Make sure the positive space results in an uneven distribution of negative areas, so the composition is an interesting and dynamic one.

Band

BAND COMPOSITION

The elements in this format are tightly placed on a vertical or horizontal band. Avoid leaving arbitrary space between the figures in the band. The figures should touch and overlap in interesting relationships. Mix the values and patterns in the band to keep the eye reading through the composition. The negative space at the sides of a band looks best if it is asymmetrical.

Formal

Gloves by 7th Avenue

HUNTINGTON'S INC.

FORMAL COMPOSITION

Formal composition is the identical grouping of the same elements on either side of the axial line. This format gives the illustration a static simplicity. The negative areas on either sides of the blocks should be divided with uneven spaces to make the elements in the composition most interesting.

GRID COMPOSITION

A grid composition fills the whole area of the page with a pleasing mix of elements. To be effective, this composition should have a variety of large and small images rendered in a range of values that emphasize the most important area of the composition. This format gives a rich feeling of abundance to the items illustrated. Great care must be taken so the grid format does not get too cluttered or confusing. The grid format is effective when illustrating a group of accessory items.

Group

TEXTILES

GROUP COMPOSITION

The group format is a cluster of tightly grouped elements that forms an interesting overall contour. The positive images should be grouped to make the contour crisp and well defined. The elements must interact within the grid so there is no confusion about the central element and the subordinate themes.

Path

PATH COMPOSITION

The path format should lead the eye on a "walk" across stepping stones in a stream. There should be a natural flow through the composition. Remember the eye will tend to read down the page from left to right, so organize the elements accordingly. Vary the negative areas, and connect the elements of the page with interesting value, line, and form variations. In this way you will make sure that the eye doesn't "fall off" the stepping stones.

LAYOUT PROBLEMS

GENERAL CRITERIA

1. Size is an 8-by-11-inch rectangle, which can be used vertically or horizontally. Draw a bold, sharp outline on layout bond paper with precisely drawn 90-degree corners.

2. Render in pencil and grey-tone felt pens.

3. Use two of the typical formats for each set of criteria, and do not use a format more than once.

Too stiff - too expected a layout

More animated - more movement - headline is important - copy leads the eye around the ad

SPECIFIC PROBLEMS

Problem 1

1. Three figures

2. Three geometric shapes representing fabric swatches

3. Two-word headline, handwritten or printed

4. Handwritten copy

Problem 2

1. Five figures with one dominant figure

2. Two- to three-word headline

3. Copy area indicated by greytone lines

4. Store logo

O.K.—but stiff—doesn't get the viewer involved

Leads the eye into and through the ad—creates more of an atmosphere.

Problem 3

   1. Two figures within a geometric shape rendered in a half-tone grey

   2. Store logo

   3. Copy area indicated by grey-tone lines

   4. Three-word headline

METHODS

   1. Study each problem, and visualize a possible format that will effectively arrange the elements. Refer to fashion illustrations for additional ideas.

   2. Collect scrap of store logos of varying sizes, and use a print copy book or instant type book to trace off headline copy.

   3. Trace or draw some of the elements on bond or tracing paper, and cut them out so you can move them around the basic 8-by-11-inch rectangle to experiment with positioning.

   4. Work out rough layouts and label each format used.

   5. Discuss with an instructor or designer, and select one layout for each problem to render as finished artwork in tones of grey.

Good use of space —

This headline indication is more important as a design element —

(Many times you will like two layouts equally —) .... The problems of being creative...

STYLIZING YOUR DRAWINGS

CONTOUR DRAWING

Contour drawing teaches your hand to draw a bold dramatic line with no "stuttering" (no sketchy, interrupted lines). Save your first contour drawing to compare it with the drawings you can produce after several days of practice. Notice how dramatically your ability increases. Use these techniques to loosen up your drawings every so often when you get tight.

Start with a large, clean sheet of bond paper. Draw with a #2 soft lead pencil. Sketch a partner, or sketch yourself by facing a large mirror. Do not look at the paper as you draw.

Imagine your eyes are directly connected to the pencil in your hand. Look at every detail of the subject.

Force your eyes to explore every part of the head you are drawing, and imagine the vision flowing through your body and out of your pencil. Move the pencil as fast as your eyes. Travel over each part of the subject slowly and carefully. Concentrate on really looking at every detail.

Empathize with the subject. Some areas should be drawn with a different line. The smooth planes of the face require a lighter, smoother line than the texture of the hair or clothing. To emphasize the definite contours of the face, vary the pressure you put on the pencil. Make your pencil line match the surface your eyes are seeing.

The initial results are often very disoriented. Concentrate on capturing volume and proportion and soon your powers of observation will develop so you can produce a dynamic image.

ABSTRACT DRAWING

Abstraction requires that the artist observe the subject carefully and analyze the strongest and most important structural elements. These are reduced to their simplest form and carefully stylized to produce the desired effects.

The abstraction is usually influenced greatly by the apparel styles of the period. When fashion features a slim silhouette with strong vertical style lines, the abstract figure will naturally be simplified to simple vertical shapes. During periods when full, rounded silhouettes are fashionable, the curved flowing line and rounded oval shapes will be exaggerated to emphasize the fashionable shape.

Successful abstractions depend on good final concept. Begin by sketching a realistic face. Gradually eliminate and simplify the features. Bold use of geometric shapes can replace the hair, mouth, and eyes. Eliminate some of the features and test the effect. Keep the proportion and layout of the features fairly realistic.

A beginning illustrator or designer can develop a simplified figure and face that is effective for presenting quick sketches while working on improving his or her drawing skills.

EXAGGERATING THE FIGURE

High-fashion illustrations can be enhanced by subtly altering the proportion of the figure and simplifying the realistic details. Emphasize the main theme of the fashion silhouette by exaggerating the shape. The proportion of the body between the neck and the hips should remain realistic, so the clothes do not look awkward. The head may be drawn smaller and stylized for effect. Length should be added in the neck, thighs, and lower legs.

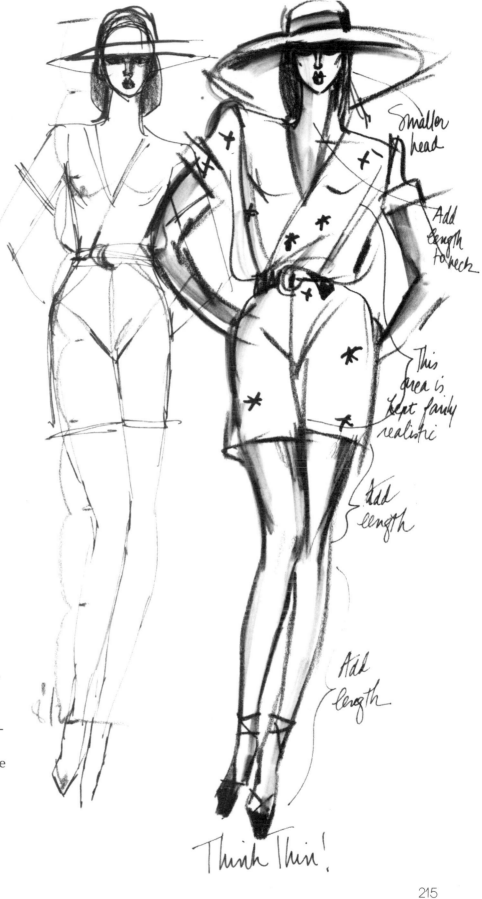

Smaller head

Add length to neck

This area is kept fairly realistic

Add length

Add length

Think Thin!

(BEFORE)

(DURING)

Too much
linework—
too sweet—

Broken and
looserline.
eliminate some
detail

(AFTER)

Leave just enough
detail to describe
the garment —
let minds' eye
complete broken
lines

Unique Concepts for Blousons

Rococco
*Note: Oversized jacquard.
Elongated cardigan.
Roses in pastel colors.*

Vava
*Note: Texture mix —
mohair/chenille.
Ombred blue.*

La Squadra
Note: Ombred jacquard.

ELIMINATION DRAWING

Elimination drawing reduces a fashion figure to the most dramatic essentials. This is a very effective method for illustrating high-fashion apparel. The artist should consider the audience before abstracting a drawing. When the drawing is supposed to sell the garment, a realistic rendering is the best choice. The customer is interested in the silhouette and a faithful drawing of the details. Abstract drawing is effective for editorial coverage, because there the newspaper or magazine selects the garment for an editorial to illustrate a fashion point. A direct sale is not the desired result. The editorial illustration is designed to stimulate a sophisticated audience with a new fashion trend.

A professional artist knows intuitively what to emphasize and what to underplay or delete in an illustration. The beginner can gain this knowledge by experimentation. Here's one way to go about it: Work from a tightly rendered sketch of a fashionable outfit. Place tracing paper over the illustration, and trace the most dramatic part of the silhouette and pertinent details of the garment. Simplify the figure and face. Do several tracings, eliminating more details and emphasizing the important fashion elements of the garment with a heavier line or exaggerated shape. Use various media and experiment with the results. Compare all the sketches with the original. Evaluate the most effective illustration.

Study the examples of elimination illustrations shown here. Experiment with garments and subjects that lend themselves to editorial illustration.

▲ *A simple stylized face and hairstyle allow the viewer to focus on what is most important in the garments. Legs and accessories are minimal to accent the patterns of the tops. (Courtesy of* Here and There, Fashion Reporting Service.)

CAMERA-READY ARTWORK

Camera-ready art, photo-ready art, and the *mechanical* are all terms for illustrations that can be photographed for print reproduction. The fashion illustrator works from a layout sketch and the actual garment to produce a crisp line and tone illustration. When the artwork is done to size, a paste-up artist pastes it on the mechanical with the appropriate headline type, copy, and logo. When the artwork is not done to size, it is photographed, sized up or down by the camera, and then integrated into the mechanical by the printer. In a large department store art department, three phases—layout, finished art, and paste-up—are usually done by specialists. The freelance finished artist often gets an illustration job for a small client and must lay out the ad, illustrate the garment, and prepare the art for printing with color overlay work. The newspaper or printer will then add the headline and copy area to the specifications of the artist.

The black-line and tone drawing should be prepared first. The illustration will print clearly if rendered with clear black line, wash, pressure screens, or other matt media that can be photographed with no reflective shine. The camera will "forgive" the artist many corrections. If the finished art needs correction—a redrawn head, for example—paste the new head over the mistake with rubber cement. The outline of the corrected paper will not photograph and will save the artist hours of rework time. Line up artwork and type with a light-blue pencil, which does not photograph.

A line drawing with no tones of grey is the easiest and least expensive kind of art to reproduce. This is effective on newsprint, because the poor paper quality reproduces grey tones with less clarity than does better paper. Grey tones do add dimension and complicity to an illustration. Camera-ready art is usually rendered in black-and-grey tones. When a special color job is desired, the press is inked with a colored ink instead of black.

A two-or-more-color job requires color overlays that work with the black-line art. After the black-line art is done, a clear acetate or vellum sheet is placed over the illustration for each color desired. The areas to be colored are outlined with a sharp, light pencil line. A registration mark is placed in two areas outside the art-work border on the black illustration, and in exactly the same place on all subsequent color overlay sheets, to guide the printer in lining up the ace-tate screens with the black-line art. The color areas are filled in with opaque gouache, ink, or transparent pressure screens. Ruby-red artist's aid may be used instead of a dense black screen, because it photographs as black, yet the artist can see through it to cut out a complicated shape. Each color requires a separate overlay sheet.

This method is inefficient for compli-cated color work, but excellent for low-cost, two-or-three-color jobs. Each acetate screen should have the color ink indicated by name and number or a smoothly painted 2-by-2-inch color swatch for the printer to match. The press is cleaned and reinked for each color that is

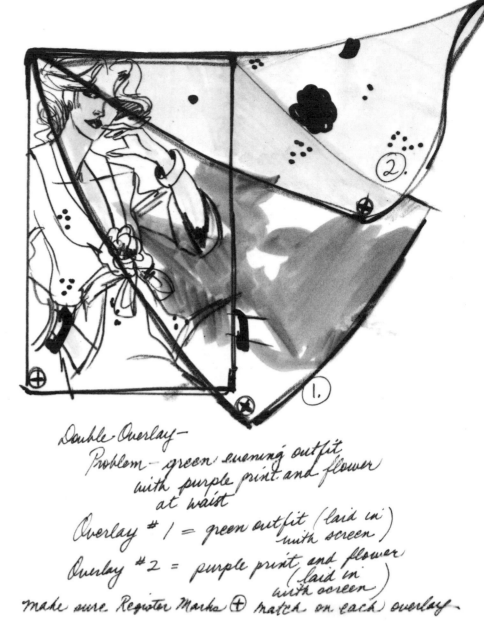

Double-Overlay—
Problem — green evening outfit with purple print and flower at waist
Overlay # 1 = green outfit (laid in with screen)
Overlay # 2 = purple print and flower (laid in with screen)
make sure Register Marks ⊕ match on each overlay.

required. The print job is run through the press for each color used.

Evaluate your camera-ready art jobs. Analyze how much darker a grey tone has to be rendered to print well on each kind of print stock. Remember which wash or line technique is most effective. Save all your printed art-work for reference. Include the best pieces in your portfolio.

Groove for mat knife

A good mat is cut at an angle allowing a bevel of the board's core to show

PRESENTING YOUR ILLUSTRATIONS

MATTING

A matt is a frame cut from illustration board. To make a matt:

1. Select a medium-to-dark neutral tone, single-ply illustration board that complements the color of your illustration. White or cream matt gets dirty and offers little contrast to most plates. Limit the matt size so it can be easily carried in your portfolio.

2. Measure the board with a T square to insure 90-degree angles at all corners. To insure smooth outer edges, use a paper cutter to cut the overall size down from the 30-by-40-inch board size. Draw the size of the window with your T square and a sharp pencil on the front side of the board. Sides should be an inch or wider for strength.

3. Use a very sharp matt knife with

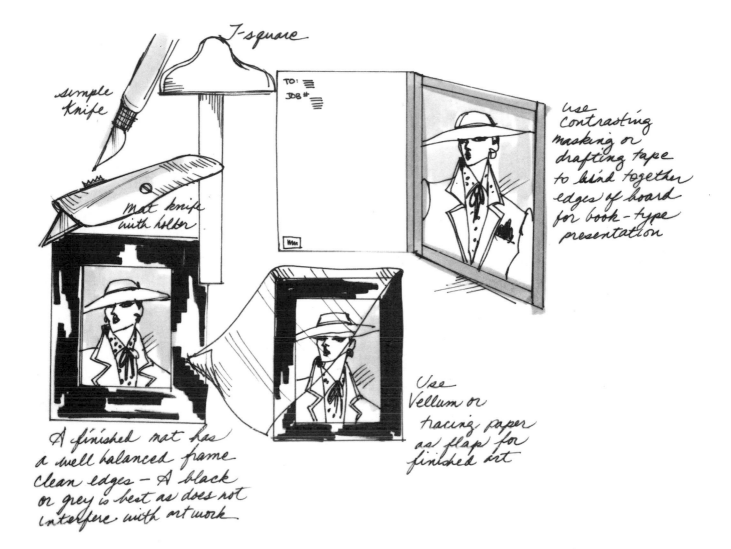

T-square

simple knife

matt knife with holder

TO: JOB #

use contrasting masking or drafting tape to bind together edges of board for book-type presentation

A finished matt has a well balanced frame clean edges — A black or grey is best as does not interfere with art work

Use Vellum or tracing paper as flap for finished art

a large handle. Hold it at an angle facing the window to form a bevel. Use a braced T square as a guide to cutting a straight line. Several passes with the knife are sometimes necessary. A mechanical matt knife may be set at a bevel angle and guided with greater ease. Cut completely through the board until the window falls out. Save the window and recut the edges for a smaller matt.

4. Attach the illustration with masking tape from the back of the board.

MULTISECTION ARTWORK

Designer presentations are often done in several sections and joined with colored art tape. This allows the presentations to be portable, for easy displaying and mailing. Make sure the boards have been carefully cut to a good size relationship. Tape the hinge with a contrasting color tape that complements the art, and finish outlining the edges of both boards with the same color tape.

MOUNTED ARTWORK

An illustration can be front mounted on board with rubber cement or dry mount paper. A vellum overlay paper, cut to the exact size of the matt board, will protect the art and allow correction notes to be written over pertinent parts of the illustration.

INTERVIEWING FOR A JOB

PORTFOLIO AND RESUMÉ

A portfolio is a representative collection of an artist's best work. The material should represent the kind of work the artist wants to be hired for, but not be so narrow that more general jobs are eliminated in the eyes of the interviewer.

A resumé is a brief summary of work experience and education. The resumé is headed with name, address, and phone number. Work experience should be listed by date and employer. List the most recent job first. Include a brief description of the job and specific duties. List the schools attended and the degrees received. Type neatly on one page. Professional resumé services will write and print a resumé for a fee.

The student should collect school projects and artwork which has been printed. Before graduation, review this work with an instructor, to evaluate your strengths and weaknesses. Ask for suggestions for filling gaps in your work. Students are wise not to be too specific about the type of design they want to do after leaving school. A period of apprenticeship to gain a concrete idea of the requirements of a specific job will enable a person to develop more realistic career goals.

Research a company before an employment interview. Shop a manufacturer's line, and then select designs or illustrations from your pool of work that are suitable or slightly more fashionable than the apparel produced by the interviewing company. Study the advertisements and catalogues of a retail store before interviewing for the job. Shop the store, and have a firm grasp of the kind of customer and merchandise the store is dealing with so you can relate your experience to the image of the retailer or agency.

Select consistent material from your artwork so it looks as though it was done by one person. Make sure to show enough variety to emphasize your strengths. A portfolio is often judged by its weakest example, not the strongest. Show from 12 to 15 pieces of work. Make sure the illustrations are clean and neatly mounted or matted. Published material is especially effective, because it shows that other people thought enough of your work to buy it.

The job seeker is evaluated in many ways. The total package is important. Dress in a businesslike manner for the interview. Stress your desire to participate in the team effort needed to make the company a success. A huge portfolio is awkward to look at and spoils the image of the person carrying it. A portfolio should be a neat, flat case of a reasonable size, containing your well-edited material. Three-dimensional or oversize examples of work can be photographed, printed in a 5-by-7-inch or 8-by-10-inch format and mounted on illustration board.

Occasionally, a design applicant will be asked to do sketches appropriate for a specific line or job. A limited number of these assignments are reasonable for a beginning applicant to do. The designer should never leave any sketches with an interviewer without receiving remuneration or a concrete job offer.

PREPARATION FOR THE INTERVIEW

To avoid excessive nervousness, prepare carefully for the interview. Some important tips are:

1. Know the exact time and place of the interview. Arrive on time or a few minutes early. Know the interviewer's full name (and how to pronounce it) and title.

2. Investigate the specific facts about the company. A retail store is easy to shop, but also check the public library for annual reports or other information. Research the clients of an advertising agency. Look for advertisements and evaluate the image a manufacturer is trying to achieve through illustrated ads.

3. Prepare questions to ask the interviewer. Accepting a job is a two-way street. Ask about growth potential, training programs, and advancement possibilities.

4. Fill out an employment application neatly (in pen) and completely. Bring two copies of your resumé, and leave one with the application. Give the other to the interviewer.

5. Greet the interviewer by name. Shake hands firmly. Smile and be as relaxed as possible. Listen and respond alertly to questions. Look the interviewer in the eye.

6. Do not chew gum or smoke.

7. Ask about the requirements of the job as early in the interview as possible. Then you will be able to relate your skills and abilities to those requirements. Be prepared to answer questions about your goals and abilities. Show your portfolio as reinforcement for your career goals.

8. Answer questions truthfully and as to the point as possible. Do not overanswer questions. Do not make derogatory remarks about your present or former employers.

9. Ask for the job if you are interested in accepting the position. Accept an offer on the spot if you want the job. If necessary, arrange a specific time to think it over. Call the interviewer with a response even if you have decided not to take the job.

10. Thank the interviewer for his or her time and consideration. In several days, follow up with a note summarizing your interest in the job.

CHAPTER NINE
SOURCES OF INSPIRATION

Fashion illustration is a synthesis of two abilities, fashion awareness and graphic skills. The fashion illustrator must develop an eye for current style details and cultivate an interest in fashion trends. Fashion trends traditionally originate in European prêt-à-porter (ready to wear) and Paris couture. Several times each year the American fashion press, fabric designers, store buyers, manufacturers, and designers cross the Atlantic to absorb the European fashion predictions for the coming year. They edit, copy, and export the creative European fashions for the American consumer. A fashion illustrator should read as many foreign and domestic fashion magazines and reports as possible. Often slide and fashion shows are presented in major cities in America. See these shows and sketch to record the fashion trends. Develop your fashion taste level to enhance your graphic skills.

COLLECTING SCRAP

Cut out any picture or photograph that captures your imagination. Keep these clippings (scrap) in a folder and refer to it often. Check Chapter Five for a list of influential foreign and domestic fashion magazines.

SKETCH BOOK

Select a handy-sized book with plain pages. Cover the book with a decorative fabric or paper so it is inconspicuous. Carry your sketch book with you when you shop the stores, attend a show, or travel. Fill your book with quick, informative sketches to be worked into future finished illustrations. Get into the sketching habit to record memorable images.

A scrap collection and a well-used sketch book unite fashion exposure with drawing skills, the inseparable tools of the fashion illustrator.

Awareness of lifestyles and interest and participation in current trends is one of the joyful requisites of a fashion illustrator. A creative artist has the ability to combine things in a unique way to produce a new visual image. Artists have a keenly developed sense or awareness of familiar things that are seen from their unique perspective. An artist is curious to experiment and take advantage of accidental events to create a new visual order or a new arrangement of design elements. The artist tries to solve problems with no guarantee of success— the artist is an experimenter.

The fashion illustrator is an artist who focuses skills and perceptions on presenting the decorative human form. A fashion artist must also be sensitive to the demands of the commercial world so the high-fashion message is interpreted for a specific customer without becoming so diluted it becomes dull. The commercial image must generate excitement and enthusiasm for a garment without seeming too radical.

The illustrator often works closely with apparel designers and store buyers to convey their fashion message visually to the consumer. These professionals can provide some fashion expertise but rely on the illustrator's graphic and layout skills to enhance the original concept of the garment. To develop a graphic taste level, the illustrator should constantly refer to the following things.

MUSEUMS AND FINE ART BOOKS

Museums are invaluable sources of inspiration. Attend special shows devoted to a specific artist, period, or craft. Explore the general collections of period fine art and take courses in art history. Frequent museum book stores and purchase books and postcards of paintings or drawings that you admire. Sketch directly from works that you see in museums and save for future reference.

CONTEMPORARY FINE ART

Galleries and museums featuring current artists offer the illustrator many inspirational techniques and themes. Fine artists are often more experimental than commercial graphic artists and tend to preview trends and techniques that flow into commercial illustrations years later.

COMMERCIAL ARTS

Commercial illustrators and photographers produce a constant innovative body of work—often with very advanced rendering skills that are easily incorporated into fashion illustration. Read *Grafix*, a quarterly magazine devoted to republishing outstanding international examples of innovative commercial illustrations.

Read children's books for specialized illustration techniques in juvenile graphic trends.

MOVIES

Influential films may start a fashion trend. Truly original and timely films often influence lifestyle and fashion trends.

HOME FURNISHINGS

Trends in interior decoration often influence fashion trends. The way people style their homes often reflects the way they decorate their bodies. Stylish interiors provide an appropriate setting for a garment. Observe the trends published in the interior design magazines, *House Beautiful, House and Garden, Casa Vogue,* and *Architectural Digest.* Collect scrap of accessories and setups that can be used to enhance a fashion figure.

Artists are guided by the people and things they see and emulate. They must be sensitive to the visual images that surround them. Constant exposure to a wide variety of visual stimuli will enhance your taste and enlarge your store of possible solutions for specific illustration problems.

USING PERIOD ART AS INSPIRATION

Art from the past is used by the artists of a new age as a foundation for their creativity. Students of fine arts often

▲

Two Women *by Utamaro Kitagawa, Japanese, 1750–1806. Japanese wood block prints depicting scenes of everyday life are called ukiyo-é. They had a tremendous influence on nineteenth-century European art. The novel treatment of space and perspective was widely imitated. Utamaro was a leading artist who specialized in portraying beautiful women. These two women capture the viewer's attention because of the contrast of the white skin to the dark hair and the intricate pattern of the kimonos. (Courtesy of the Collection of the Grunwald Center for the Graphic Arts, UCLA.)*

▲

The modern interpretation focuses on the interplay of textures in the hair, robes, and faces.

The expressive pose and vigorous line inspired the modern fashion illustration.

▼

copy paintings and drawings to absorb the techniques of the master. The true artist is a synthesizer—a person who creates a new visual order out of existing things. Creative fashion illustrators can be inspired by period artists and can integrate their work with appropriate current fashions.

A knowledge of art history is valuable to focus on artists and periods that are rich with inspiration. Perhaps the serendipitous (accidental) discovery of an artist that appeals to you is more inspirational than a methodical search for historical sources. Exposure to as many visual stimuli as possible is the

Henri de Toulouse-Lautrec, French, 1864–1901. This familiar artist worked in Paris during the late nineteenth century. His realistic posters of dancers and entertainers of the Montmartre district showed a gripping insight into the personalities of his subjects. Lautrec's posters were not decorative collector's items like those of his contemporaries Mucha and Chèret. The modern viewer appreciates Lautrec's bold style and fine artist's eye for reality. (Yvette Guibert Lithograph, Courtesy of the Collection of the Grunwald Center for the Graphic Arts, UCLA.)

▼

key to collecting a body of inspirational references.

Decorative art periods are valuable sources of inspiration. Art nouveau and art deco trends offer a rich source of visual inspiration. Japanese woodblock prints (ukiyo-é) have unique arrangements and colorations. Poster art from the last half of the nineteenth century is a rich source of decorative human forms.

The inspirational art should suggest a technique, color scheme, layout, or perspective that can enhance modern fashions. Combine the elements of the period piece with the modern styles to create a new visual order.

▲

Erté (Romain de Tirtoff), Russian, born 1897, detail of the poster, 1979. Romain de Tirtoff adopted the name Erté. He emigrated from his native Russia and worked briefly as a designer for the house of Poiret. He became a major contributing artist to Harper's Bazar, Vogue, *and* La Gazette du Bon Ton. *His drawings and designs are noteworthy because of their precision, imagination, humor, and superb drawing technique. Erté has produced a continuous body of fashion illustrations throughout the twentieth century. His fashion and theater design work was most popular during the 1910s and 1920s. (Courtesy of the Collection of the Grunwald Center for the Graphic Arts, UCLA.)*

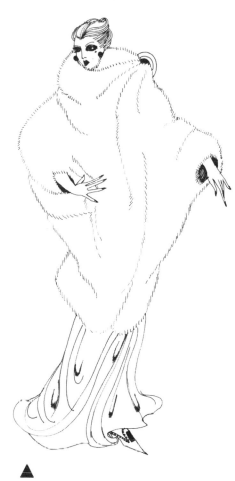

▲

The delicate rendering and flowing line of the Erté drawing was emulated in this illustration.

Alphonse Mucha, Bohemian, 1860–1939, Monaco-Monte Carlo Poster. Alphonse Mucha designed art nouveau posters during the last half of the nineteenth century. Sarah Bernhardt was so pleased with a poster Mucha did for the play Ghismonda she contracted Mucha to create all her posters. He designed commercial posters for many products from beer to bicycles. Mucha's posters were widely collected by contemporaries and have remained popular during the twentieth century. (Courtesy of the Collection of the Grunwald Center for the Graphic Arts, UCLA.)

▼

Collage areas build up intricate pattern layers on this illustration that has an art nouveau flavor.

▼

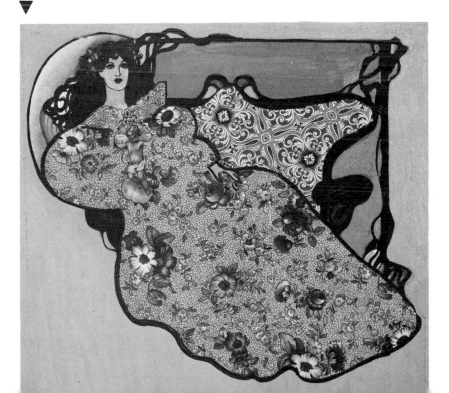

Howard Chandler Christy illustrated many short stories and fashion "situation illustrations" and this typical romanticized illustration of Western life for Harper's Bazar. *(Courtesy of* Harper's Bazaar.*)*

PERIOD FASHION ILLUSTRATION

Fashion art has paralleled style trends through the twentieth century, with echos of fine art influencing form and content. Museum costume departments and larger libraries often have copies of *Vogue* and *Harper's Bazaar* from the early 1900s. *La Gazette du Bon Ton* and *Delineator* are two out-of-print magazines from early in the century which have high quality illustrations. These valuable periodicals contain a wealth of information for the fashion designer and illustrator.

1900–1930

Fashion emerged from the cumbersome, overblown costumes of the nineteenth century to a slimmer yet mature silhouette, which finally evolved into the flapper silhouette of the 1920s. Women became more active, and their clothing was gradually streamlined and pared down to accommodate the new lifestyle of the twentieth century, but this evolution took almost 25 years.

▲

Charles Dana Gibson illustrated a series of society cartoons for Harper's Bazar. His definitive rendering technique makes his sketches of fashionable women of the period the prototype of beauty called the "Gibson Girl." (Courtesy of Harper's Bazaar.)

◄

Drian worked exclusively for Harper's Bazar during 1913 and 1914, illustrating covers and fashion articles in this monthly woman's magazine. (Courtesy of Harper's Bazaar.)

Soulie regularly illustrated basic fashion articles for Harper's Bazar. *The vigorous line technique gives these figures movement and character. (Courtesy of Harper's Bazaar.)*

Paris couture directed fashion. Early couture designers like the House of Worth, Paquin, Poiret, Vionnet, Chanel, and Lanvin began to design costumes that could be worn by ordinary women, as well as their royal counterparts, and for everyday events, not just grand occasions. These in turn were copied by seamstresses all over the world from illustrations in the new fashion magazines.

This fanciful rendering by Sarah Stilwell Weber integrates a figure in a garden setting. The natural forms and flowing lines show a distinct art nouveau influence. (Courtesy of Harper's Bazaar.)

Wealth was taken for granted by many women who faithfully supported custom dressmakers and the couture. The masses emulated handcrafted fashions by sewing for themselves or ordering ready-made garments from the newly emerging catalogues like Sears and Roebuck. Illustration during these early decades ranged from the fantasy creations of Erté, the famous Russian costume designer and illustrator, to the practical catalogue illustrations produced to sell garments to the masses. Theatrical posters advertised famous plays and movies of the period and equally publicized the star's costumes and individual style. Other artists of note during this period were Valentine Gross, Barbier, Sem, Vuillard, Pierre Brissard, George Lepape, Helen Dryden, Drian, Ruth Eastman, Marie Laurencin, John Martin, Howard Chandler Christy, and Charles Dana Gibson.

After World War I the first youth-oriented decade of the twentieth century emerged. The shape of garments was a slim rectangle with no hint of a natural waistline. Hemlines rose to their highest point in 1927. Makeup, especially lipstick—a new innovation—was an important accessory. Hair was bobbed short and styled like a man's. As an alternative to formal dress, spectator and active sportswear were developed for resort wear. Art greatly influenced the designers and illustrators of the 1920s.

The fashion world was shaken by the crash of the New York Stock Market in 1929, and the repercussions were widespread. Forty years were to pass before the carefree, irreverant, youthful fashions that characterized the 1920s again were in vogue.

This typical fashion reporting illustration uses a stylized background to set off the models. (Courtesy of Harper's Bazaar.)

Erté was a regular contributing artist to Harper's Bazaar *after it was purchased by William Randolph Hearst (he changed the spelling of Bazaar to the double a). Erté illustrations have spanned 60 years of fashion history. His early fame and exposure peeked during the 1920s. [Courtesy of the Los Angeles County Museum of Art, Mille Fleurs, Erté (Romain de Tirtoff.)]*

1930–1950

Fashion from the 1930s reflected the depression mentality of America and the world. Dresses in dull, safe styles and somber colors were the rule. Photography was popular during this period. Illustrations grew more frequent as the decade matured and moved into the 1940s.

American fashion emerged late in the 1930s, and by 1940 *Vogue* covered the American ready-to-wear market for the first time. Design direction still emanated from European couture. Motion pictures were popular during the depression, because they offered an inexpensive way to escape the worries of everyday life. Movie fashions were glamorous, and movie stars were widely emulated. Many designers started costuming stars and developed ready-to-wear businesses after their names had become fashionable on the screen.

▲

*Vértès' quick sketches and fantasy illustra-
tions were popular during the 1930s and
1940s. (Courtesy of Harper's Bazaar.)*

◄ ►

*The variety of texture and delicate han-
dling of the fluid line of the furs creates a
delightful, informal illustration. (Courtesy
of Harper's Bazaar.)*

▶ The distinctive line carves this silhouette out of the negative space of the page. (Courtesy of Harper's Bazaar.)

PIGUET
BERGDORF GOODMAN

LELONG

MOLYNEUX

LELONG
HENRI BENDEL

▲ These quick pen, ink, and wash sketches have a good flow and movement because they have not been overworked. Note the influence of Dior's "New Look." (Courtesy of Harper's Bazaar.)

▶ This artist interpreted a poster of Toulouse-Lautrec to advertise fabrics. (Courtesy of Harper's Bazaar.)

This fresh wash and contrasting line illustration by St. Johns captures the fluid flow of the fabrics swatched. (Courtesy of Harper's Bazaar.)
▼

▶
Bouché was often called upon to illustrate the fashion face during his career. This example captures the elegant, sophisticated model perfectly. (Courtesy Vogue. Copyright © 1959 by The Condé Nast Publications Inc.)

Accessories, especially hats, were popular during the thirties and forties. The suit and little fur piece were important trends that developed into the uniform-influenced severe suit. World War II imposed restrictions on the amount of fabric that could be used in apparel. Until after the war, a slim silhouette prevailed out of necessity.

In 1947 Dior began his "New Look": long, bouffant skirts with a nipped-in waistline. A return to femininity and more exaggerated apparel that was to carry over into the first years of the 1950s began. Fashion changes became more rapid from this point on.

This was a period of rich fashion illustration inspiration. Look for the work of René Bouché, Marcel Vértès, Carl Erickson (Eric), Ruth Sigrid Grafstrom, Bernard Boutet de Monvel, Dorothy Hood, Christian Berard, and R. B. W. (Count René Bouët-Willaumez).

1950-1970

The apparel mood in the 1950s in America developed from the bouffant "New Look" to the sack dress or chemise late in the decade. The waistline was "lost" for 10 years, while women wore simple, slim dresses. The fashion mood moved from conservative, feminine apparel to the youth revolution that characterized the 1960s.

American lifestyle was profoundly changed by technological advances during the 1950s. Affluence and abundant power allowed the suburbs to grow. Two automobiles and a television set became the symbols of the upwardly mobile, better educated American middle class. Airplane travel and improved mass communication made the world smaller. Synthetic fiber production was implemented, and mass production of inexpensive, easy care textiles greatly enlarged the source of materials available for producing apparel.

Dotted chiffon shirt
+
dotted surah skirt
or
red jersey suit

VOGUE, FEBRUARY 15, 1959

VOGUE PATTERN 9485
VOGUE PATTERN 9654

Eva Larsen's free, vigorous style suited this full skirt dress typical of the 1950s. (Courtesy Vogue. Copyright © 1959 by The Condé Nast Publications Inc.)

▶ *This stylish illustration on a toned board uses highlights and line very effectively. (Courtesy of Saks Fifth Avenue.)*

René Bouché had an active illustration career spanning several decades. His work was published consistently in Vogue. These exuberant contour drawings were done at the Dublin Horse Show in 1959. The sketches effectively capture the excitement of the spectators and participants, as well as the formal evening apparel. (Courtesy Vogue. Copyright © 1959 by The Condé Nast Publications Inc.

▼

▶ *J. Hyde Crawford's dramatic charcoal illustration has a simple elegance. (Courtesy of Bonwit Teller.)*

SHEPARD COLLECTIONS
designed by
Marina Victor
&
FRENCH
RIVER
MILLS
create for
THE TREVIRA ERA

B ALTMAN & CO. (ALL STORES) JULIUS GARFINCKEL (ALL STORES) JOSEPH HORNE—PITTSBURGH HARZFELD'S—KANSAS CITY BULLOCK'S (ALL STORES)

BY
GINALA
&
FRENCH
RIVER
MILLS
create for
THE TREVIRA ERA

LORD & TAYLOR—NEW YORK HALLE BROS.—CLEVELAND JACOBSON'S—ALL STORES I. MAGNIN—ALL STORES NEIMAN-MARCUS—ALL STORES

◄◄ ▲

Kenneth Paul Block is the dean of modern illustrators. His versatile style has illustrated fashion for over two decades. These illustrations capture the youthful sophistication of the mini during the 1960s. (Courtesy of Hoechst Fibers.)

◄

Dorothy Hood's signature style for Lord & Taylor captures the image of their chic yet casual suburban customer of the 1960s. (Courtesy of Lord & Taylor.)

The 1960s was a revolutionary period, when change was accelerated by the new passions of the youthful population majority. Fashion responded slowly—the youthquake and fashion from the streets coexisted with the structured space-age dressing designed so well by Courrèges and the typical ladylike look of celebrities like Jacqueline Kennedy.

The fashion magazines of the 1960s featured a great deal of photographic editorial art. The illustrators of the day flourished in retail store advertisements and trade papers. Newcomers to the fashion illustration scene during these decades include Kenneth Paul Block, Antonio, Dorothy Hood, Eva Larsen, Barbara Pearlman, Laslo, and J. Hyde Crawford.

1970–PRESENT

The "me generation" of the 1970s was clothed with a new conservatism. Fashion for the masses—as opposed to fashion as the privilege of the wealthy—became the rule. Both in Europe and America RTW became the common fashion denominator. European and American designer apparel were the status symbols—available in many price ranges and apparel categories, from jeans to luxe apparel and fine furs.

A fit and active body became the fashion ideal. There was no longer an easily defined manifesto. Fashions ranged from fantasy costumes to establishment uniforms, hanging side by side in the same wardrobe, to take a person from a conservative business day through an evening of dining and disco dancing. Modern life created many optional activities that demanded specialized dressing and enlarged the typical wardrobe.

Versatility of apparel offered an opportunity for many styles of fashion illustration to flourish. The illustrator today is supported by trade papers, retail store advertisements, catalogues, manufacturer's ads, and the glossy domestic and foreign fashion publications. These contemporary illustrators are a constant fresh source of inspiration for the fashion student.

The beginner should clip and save illustrations that are appealing. Try to emulate the style and techniques of an artist that you admire; be like the apprentice fine artist copying a masterpiece. Copy to learn how to incorporate the best of another artist's tech-

niques into your own skills. Once you master the technique, use it to create your own unique image. Follow the style of favorite contemporary illustrators as they evolve into greater and greater proficiency. Emulate and adapt, practice and experiment. In this way you are likely to develop a style that is unique and continuously improving.

Laslo's distinctive style integrates a subtle blending of tone, wash, and line. (Courtesy of Hattie Inc.)

▼

SONIA RYKIEL
EN RESIDENCE AT
HATTIE
INC

555 SOUTH WOODWARD AVENUE BIRMINGHAM, MICHIGAN 48011 (313) 645-5755

▲

Sandra Leichman's drawing has a sophisticated femininity (Sandra Leichman for Martha. Courtesy of C. J. Herrick, Assoc.)

▲

The painterly quality of Barbara Pearlman's illustrations creates an interesting interplay of line and texture. (Courtesy of Burlington Industries.)

▶

The bold line contrasts with the simple border and copy area of this illustration by Sandra Leichman. (Sandra Leichman for Martha. Courtesy of C. J. Herrick, Assoc.)

▶

Stavrinos' illustrations create a rich pattern of line and tone interaction. (Courtesy of Barney's.)

"The Tango" by Holly's Harp. Barney's, New York.

Lord & Taylor is spirited American fashion

For romantic evenings
—frothy separates in a dance
of point d'esprit

Meant for each other— our airy
white peplum camisole with a light frivolity of organza ruffles,
the slenderest of straps, 80.00
And breath-taking full skirt of navy point d'esprit,
made even fuller by underlayers of organza and taffeta, 130.00
By Jeri in polyester and acetate, 4 to 14.
Evening Collections, Third Floor, Lord & Taylor,
Fifth Avenue at 39th Street—call (212) 391-3300.
Open daily 10 to 6, Thursday 10 to 8. And at Manhasset,
Westchester, Garden City, Millburn, Ridgewood-Paramus and Stamford
Shop Sundays 12 to 5 at our Manhasset,
Westchester, Garden City, Millburn and Stamford stores.

Lord & Taylor artist Fred
Greenhill's casually elegant illustrations have a painterly
quality. Notice how the shadow area lends drama to
the negative space surround-
ing the figure. The visible
brush stroke adds dimension
to the fabric. The vigorous
line accents the swingy fashion figures. (Courtesy of Lord
& Taylor.)

Lord & Taylor is spirited American fashion

Calvin Klein turns your
favorite sweatshirt
into a dress

Our hooded sweatshirt dress is in the pink
(a vibrant duck pink) with all the easy comfort you love—
dropped shoulders, roll up sleeves and roomy pockets
(great to pull over your bikini—or for lazy, lounging days).
All cotton, in sizes 4 to 12, 90.00. The Calvin Klein Shop,
Third Floor, Lord & Taylor, Fifth Avenue at 39th Street—call (212) 391-3300.
Open daily 10 to 6, Thursdays 10 to 8. And at Lord & Taylor, Manhasset,
Westchester, Garden City, Ridgewood-Paramus and Stamford
Shop Sundays 12 to 3 at our Manhasset, Westchester, Garden City and Stamford stores.

This Stavrinos illustration uses
a selective light source to
highlight and shadow the style
of the garment. (Courtesy of
Barney's.)

248

FERNANDO SANCHEZ'
NEW QUILT COLLECTION
(TOO BAD THIS PAGE
ISN'T IN COLOR!)

A mischievous mix of vivids: cozy, comfortable quilts...softer and lighter on than a feather.

Fernando has brought home the aura of the Orient and spiced it with the chic delight of moiré satin in nylon, polyester and cotton.

The black kimono spiked with magenta cuff and lining, petite or average, 124.00.
The cummerbund, 13.00.

The red jacket cuffed with magenta, petite or average, 94.00.
The ivory satin top, P-S-M-L, 38.00.
The black roll-up pants with magenta cuffs, P-S-M-L, 56.00.

New York.

◀ ▼ ▶

Antonio is a virtuoso draftsman with a superb control of form and technique. His experience as a fashion photographer enhances his layout concepts. (Courtesy of Bloomingdale's, illustration by Antonio, art direction by John C. Jay.)

CONTEMPORARY ILLUSTRATORS

249

Meet Jean Cacharel

Saturday, September 13, in Beverly Hills, see our special showings of his fall menswear collection, with a personal appearance by the designer himself.

The minute you see this collection you'll be struck by something uniquely different. A finely honed sense of color. A particular attention to line. The hallmarks of Jean Cacharel's justly famous designs. Join us, Saturday, when we present this remarkable collection, modeled from 2 to 3 p.m. Here, shown from the left, the cotton glen plaid shirt, $40; abstract intarsia v-neck sweater in black or gold wool with contrast stripe, $65; cotton velvet jean in chocolate, wine or grey, $65. Cotton windowpane plaid shirt, $40; 5-pocket cotton denim jean, $40. Cotton tartan plaid shirt, $40; teal/gold/berry stripe crewneck wool sweater, $65; cotton corduroy jean in saddle, teal or black, $55. Robinson's Men's Collection, 36, Beverly Hills, Los Angeles, Newport, San Diego, Santa Barbara, University Towne Centre, Westminster, Woodland Hills. Use our toll-free number for your convenience, anytime: 1-800-523-7600. Or phone your nearest Robinson's.

Robinson's

Calvin Klein

HIS NEW TAPERED SWEATERS PUT THE EMPHASIS ON YOUR SHOULDERS
The optical illusion of the raglan sleeve, chest stripe and drop-shouldered armband. Combined with the very real effect of a smaller waist. And you're going to be looking a lot healthier come fall. From his all-new, all-American collection, inspired by the American Navajo Indian penchant for graphics and design. Translated into pure merino wool for sizes S-M-L-XL. Left, crewneck armband sweater in black/bordeaux, natural/bottle or red/black $60. Middle, hooded sweater self-faced with contrast color: Bordeaux/bottle, natural/bottle, navy/bordeaux. $75. Right, serape-stripe crewneck in black/navy/red/bordeaux. $65. Robinson's Men's Collections, 36, all stores except Palm Springs. Use our toll-free number for your convenience, anytime 1-800-523-7600. Or phone Robinson's.

Robinson's

◄ ▲
◄

Steve Bieck specializes in illustrating men's wear. He illustrates for retail stores and manufacturers. He is challenged by the unlimited potential for growth and interpretation in fashion illustration. (Courtesy of Steve Bieck for J. W. Robinson's.)

Gianni Versace

HIS NEW SPORTSWEAR IS AN ITALIAN VERSION OF SOMETHING YOU KNOW QUITE WELL: AMERICAN CLASSICS
Gianni Versace is an important new voice in men's fashion melds the contemporary with the classic. Simplifying shape. Refining texture. And achieving a masculinity more compelling than ever. Come discover Gianni Versace Design first at Robinson's. Left, Shetland wool argyle sweater, $95. Brushed cotton button-down sportshirt, $50. Charcoal stripe polyester/wool pant with double pockets, $80.

Right, lambswool tee-shirt sweater, $55. Cotton corduroy pant with velvet leg stripe, $60. Just part of the overall collection in Robinson's Collections, 36, Beverly Hills, Newport, Woodland Hills only.
Use our toll-free number for your convenience, anytime: 1-800-523-7600. Or phone your nearest Robinson's.

Robinson's

Mia Carpenter has worked for manufacturers, retailers, and publications for many
years. She loves to draw and feels that
each time the pen or pencil touches the
paper it alters the surface with exciting potential. Carpenter loves fashion, and illustration gives her the ability to exaggerate

252

the form of the clothes and the body in order to heighten the original fashion concepts. See also page 251. (Courtesy of Mia Carpenter.)

▼

Now you can get into
Studio 54 … jeans.
You'll find them
exclusively
in our Junior World.

It's the most famous disco
in the world. And you'd love to go there.
Well, we've brought Studio 54 to the west
coast. Their jeans in heavy blue denim
or medium wale corduroy, with a signature
pocket that lets everyone know you're in
touch with New York. Both in waist sizes 26-33.
Denim, **$38.** Corduroy, **$40.**
You'll receive Casablanca's Studio 54
album when you purchase any Studio 54
jean (while supply lasts; limit one
to a customer). Junior World, 236.

We're giving away a Studio 54 trip for two.
Come in and enter our special drawing
for a chance to win. Trip includes: airfare to
and from New York, an evening at Studio 54,
one night paid hotel stay (with dinner and
breakfast), limousine service to and from
Studio 54 and $250 in cash. You must be
18 years or older to be eligible. But no purchase
is necessary to win. Contest runs today
through October 6.

Meet Casablanca recording artists
Love and Kisses at our Century City store
on Saturday, September 29 from 12-3 p.m.
Also in our Junior World.

▲▲▶
David Horii is a versatile illustrator and superb draftsman. When he is commissioned to illustrate merchandise that is very basic, he depends on lighting and detail to create a dramatic or romantic effect. He is inspired by films and photographs from the thirties and forties. (Courtesy of David Horii.)

256

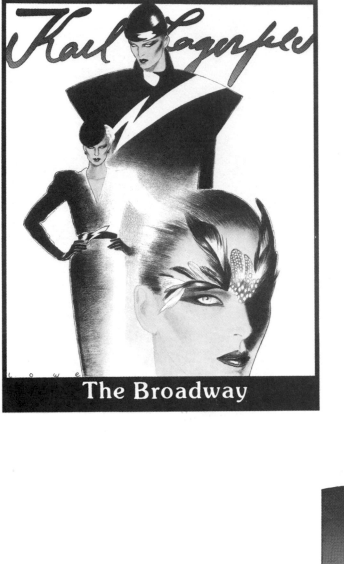

The Broadway

Control of the image and the media characterize Paul Lowe's versatile style. Lowe uses a light source to focus on the subject's most dramatic point of view. High-fashion illustrations and men's wear are Lowe's particular specialties. (Courtesy of Paul Lowe.)

◀ ▼ ▶

Catherine Clayton Purnell is a staff artist for Women's Wear Daily. *Her versatile style and superb control of the human figure enable her to illustrate many categories of fashion. Children are her favorite subject, and she relishes an assignment in children's wear.* (Courtesy of Catherine Clayton Purnell.)

◀ ▼ ▶

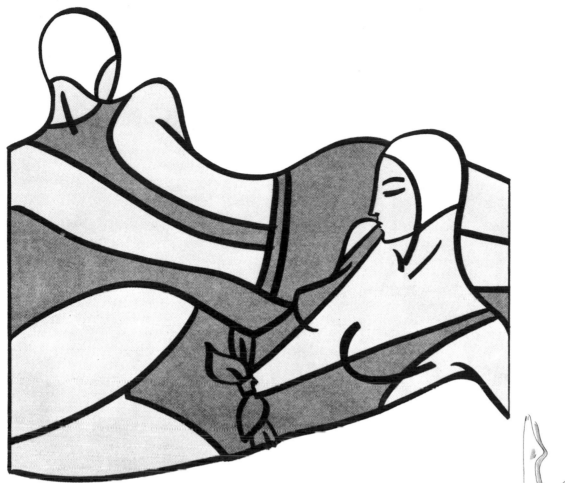

SEA-ing Stars

◄ ▲ ►

*A designer's control of space and form
characterize Robert Passantino's high-tech
graphic style. He feels a designer should
have a strong sense of graphic design, dynamic use of space, individuality, honesty,
and clarity. Passantino's work is widely
seen in* Women's Wear Daily *and in the
ads for fashion-oriented department stores.
(Drawings by Robert Passantino for*
Women's Wear Daily.*)*

This illustrator uses a bold, painterly line to create high-contrast figures. Steven Stipelman works as a teacher, staff artist at Women's Wear Daily, and illustrator for fashion-oriented retailers. He believes fashion illustration encompasses more than drawing skills. Illustration has to relate the body to the clothes. When he plans an illustration, one of two things happens — the clothes dictate the body or the body dictates the clothes. This relationship is the start of a fashion drawing. (Courtesy of Steven Stipelman.)

263

it's spring again!
patti cappalli / california
patti cappalli's men

© WEIR-QUITON 1980

◀▲▶

Gregory Weir-Quiton is an active and versatile illustrator and teacher. He encourages his students to practice, because many will be late bloomers. He heads the local chapter of the Graphic Artist's Guild. This national association helps independent illustrators to market and profit from their commercial graphic work. (Courtesy of Gregory Weir-Quiton.)

CHAPTER TEN

DRAWING MEN

The male fashion figure is usually drawn with less exaggerated proportions than the fashion female. Realistic facial and apparel details are typical of men's wear illustrations. A male figure is drawn eight to eight and one-half heads long. The torso length is slightly longer than the middle of the body (line 4½). Length is added in the legs, not in the neck.

A man's body is broader than a woman's even though the vertical proportion is similar. Muscle structure has more definition and bulk. A youthful male fashion figure should have a lithe, active, natural look. When an illustration requires a more mature man, slightly more bulk should be added to the torso and shoulders. The features show maturity when they are more boldly defined. A higher hairline and a touch of grey hair at the temples adds a final note of distinction for an older fashion model.

Styles influence fashion types. Fashion sketches of casual, active apparel will usually look best on a more youthful figure with a slim torso and shoulder muscle definition. A European-cut suit will also be most appropriate on a well-developed figure.

Fashions that emphasize classic tailoring with natural shoulders and a relaxed fit require a more mature, less muscled figure.

Men's fashions change slowly and subtly. Adept male illustrators have a keen eye for apparel details and fit. The exact width of a shoulder, lapel, or tie is important when illustrating a man's suit. The silhouette and correct fit of men's wear must be very close to reality or the subtle styling will be misinterpreted. Attention to details and small variations in style and fabric is essential for successfully illustrating men's wear.

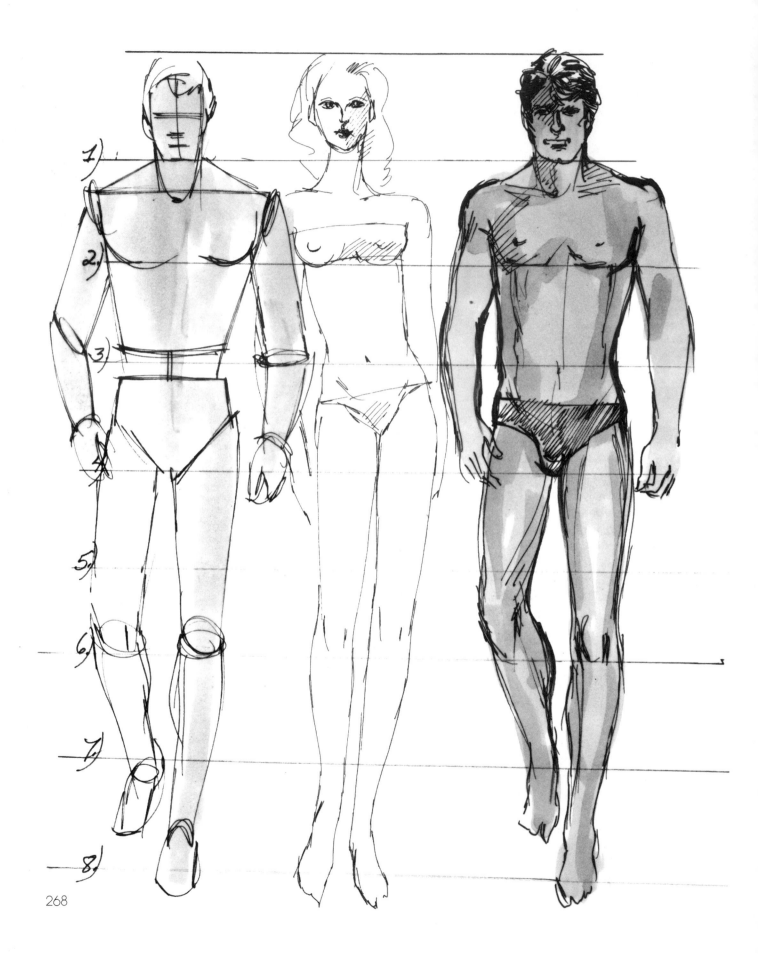

1)

2)

3)

4

5

6

7

8

MALE MUSCLE STRUCTURE

Shoulder and neck muscle structure should be well defined in a male fashion model. The torso is slim. Leg and arm muscle structure should be defined, but not developed to the point clothing is distorted.

The axial line determines the weight balance of the male figure just as it does in women's movement. The axial line must drop from the base of the neck to the heel of the support foot when a man stands primarily with the weight on one foot. The balance point falls between the legs when the weight is evenly distributed.

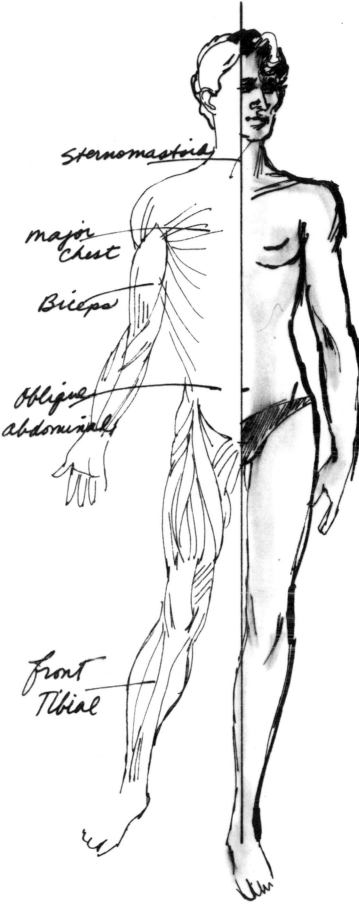

sternomastoid

major chest

Biceps

oblique abdominals

front Tibial

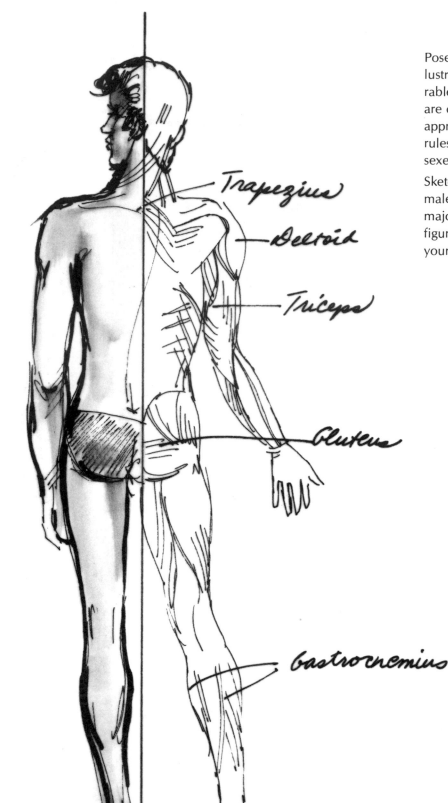

Trapezius

Deltoid

Triceps

Gluteus

Gastrocnemius

Poses are much more static when illustrating men's suits than for comparable women's wear. Active clothes are often sketched on men playing an appropriate sport. The same action rules pertain to movement in both sexes.

Sketch the muscle structure of the male figure several times. Label the major muscles. Draw a fleshed-out figure on tracing paper placed over your drawing of the muscles.

DRAWING MEN, STEP BY STEP

Men's clothes are a series of layers that interact to form a total look. Draw from this example for your first effort. Then sketch several outfits from life or detailed photographs. Carefully compare your drawing to the source to correct any missing or inaccurate details.

1. Sketch the body in a relaxed pose.

2. Block in the shirt and neck line details. Draw the lapel line. Draw the silhouette. Be sure the jacket is the correct length. Relate the size of the lapel to the size of the shoulder. Draw the trousers. Render the face and hair with a wash or a tone.

3. Paint or tone the sketch with paint, felt pen, or pencils. Interpret the subtle fabric pattern in the jacket, pants, and shirt.

4. Detail the drawing with bold silhouette lines and render the details with a fine-line pen or pencil. Render the features and hair.

fairly low hairline

wider forehead

heavier brows
eyes at 1/2 point

stronger nostrils
and nose
upper lip
more developed
stronger facial
lines
angular, strong
jaw
and chin

MEN'S FACES

Feature placement is the same for both men and women. A man's face differs in contour and bulk from a woman's. Study the diagrams of the face and the profile head. Notice that the forehead and jaw line are fuller. The eyebrows are heavier and well defined. No eye makeup enhances the eyes or emphasizes the lashes. Placement of the eyes is at the horizontal median of the guide rectangle. One eye space is allowed between the eyes.

The nose is prominent, with a strong bridge and well-defined nostrils. Laugh lines are often drawn. The upper lip is more muscular than a woman's. Do not give special emphasis to the lips, because there is no artificial contrast. The chin and jaw line are strong.

Draw these diagram faces several times on overlay paper, and make corrections by placing them over the drawings. Sketch a number of men from life or photographs.

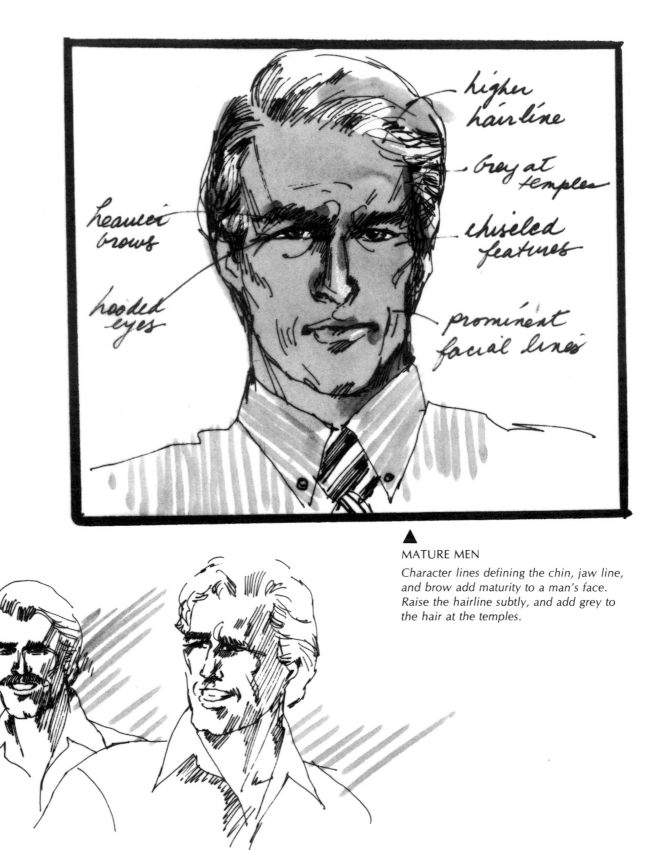

higher hairline

grey at temples

chiseled features

prominent facial lines

heavier brows

hooded eyes

MATURE MEN

Character lines defining the chin, jaw line, and brow add maturity to a man's face. Raise the hairline subtly, and add grey to the hair at the temples.

lower
hairline

lighter
brow

soften
point of
nose

Full
hair

more
open eyes

Fuller
lips

YOUTHFUL MEN

Fewer character lines, a lower hairline, and a thinner face are typical characteristics of the young male fashion model.

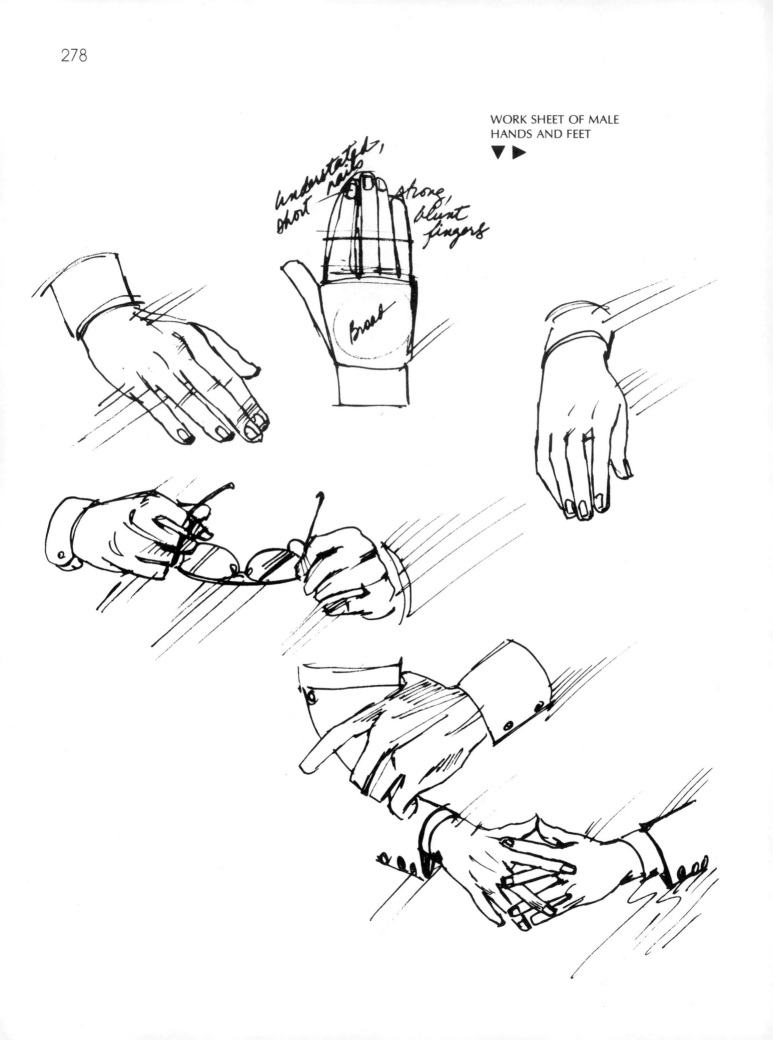

understated, short nails

strong, blunt fingers

Broad

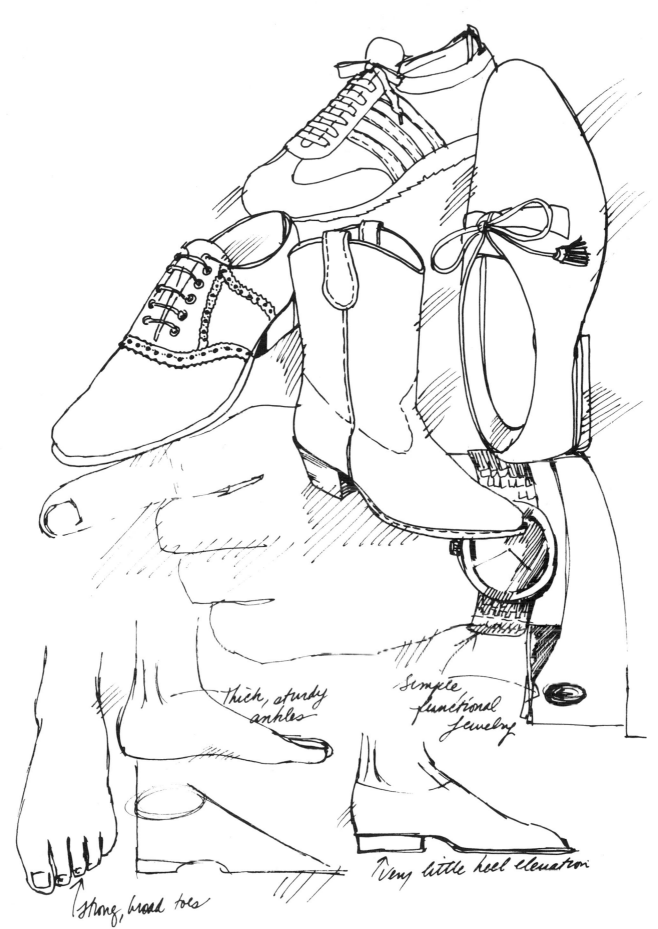

thick, sturdy ankles

simple functional jewelry

strong, broad toes

Very little heel elevation

279

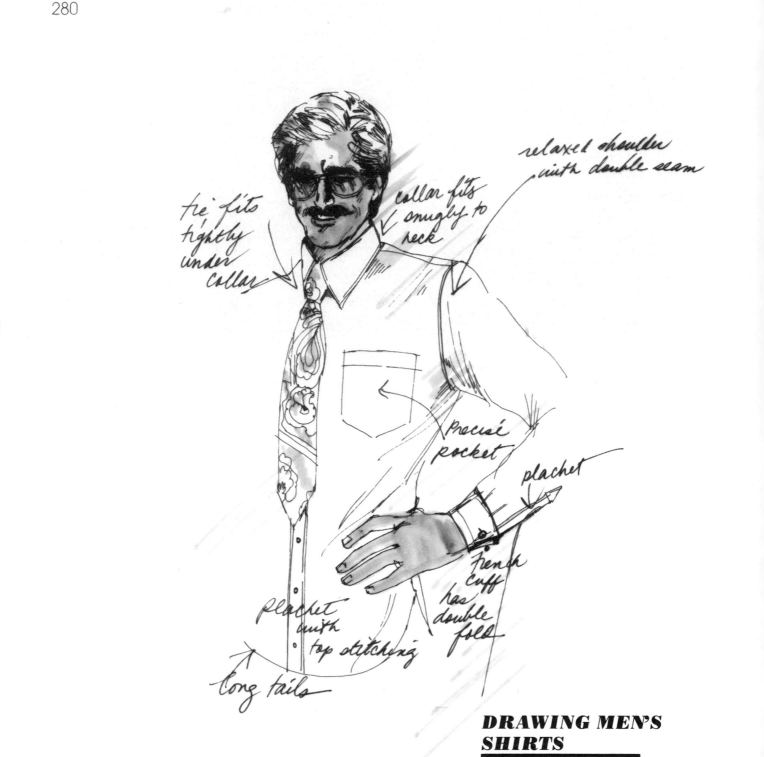

tie fits tightly under collar

collar fits snugly to neck

relaxed shoulder with double seam

Precise pocket

placket

French cuff has double fold

placket with top stitching

long tails

DRAWING MEN'S SHIRTS

Men's shirts have a typical fit. Dress shirts are designed as underlayers for a suit, and this dictates the styling. The shoulder seam extends slightly beyond the point of shoulder to allow for free movement. This style device also makes the shoulders seem wider.

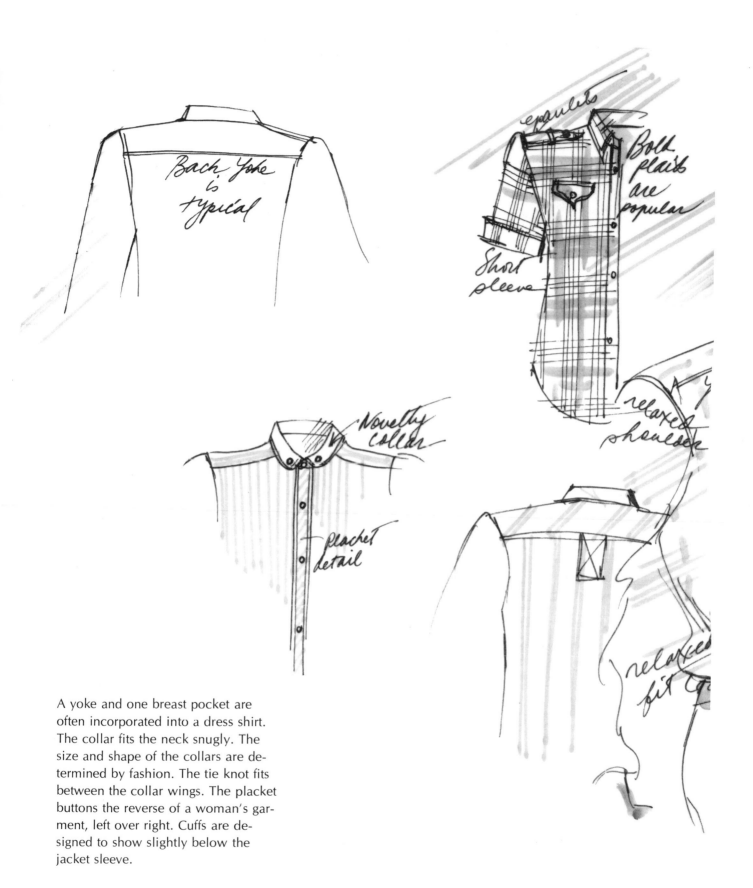

Back Yoke is typical

epaulets

Bold plaids are popular

Short sleeve

Novelty collar

placket detail

relaxed shoulder

relaxed fit

A yoke and one breast pocket are often incorporated into a dress shirt. The collar fits the neck snugly. The size and shape of the collars are determined by fashion. The tie knot fits between the collar wings. The placket buttons the reverse of a woman's garment, left over right. Cuffs are designed to show slightly below the jacket sleeve.

DRAWING MEN'S CASUAL TOPS

A casual shirt is designed to be worn solo, as well as under a jacket. More style details are usually added for this reason. The collar can be worn open or closed. Double pockets are a styling option. Bold prints and plaids are popular. Sleeves can be long or short. Pleats at the back yoke or shoulders give additional mobility.

Knit tops are casual alternatives to woven shirts. Rib trim often finishes the sleeves, necklines, and hem. The shoulders are usually extended beyond the point of shoulder. Raglan sleeves are popular for casual knit tops. Cut-and-sew knits have seams like woven shirts. Full fashion sweaters have the bodies and sleeves knit to a specific shape before they are sewn together. The full-fashion seams have a characteristic pattern illustrated here.

Sweater tops are made in a wide range of styles. Some are designed to be worn under a jacket and others are heavy enough to be outer wear. The most classic styles are illustrated here. They can be colored and patterned in a great variety of knits.

▶

The vigorous lines in this spontaneous sketch by Richard Rosenfeld dramatize the ribs of the bulky outer-weight sweater. (Courtesy of Richard Rosenfeld.)

knit collar

rib to finish sleeve

short Placket Buttons left over right

Polo Shirt

saddle shoulder

Fall bulky ribbed sweater

Rugby shirt

Pant Placket Buys to Left

raglan sleeve

Cardigan

subtle pattern

Shoulder line softly padded

contrasting material

show cuff

Exact lapel size

placket detail

Vest is fitted

well fitted but not tight

Crisp lines

Side Vents

Understated shoes

DRAWING MEN'S SUITS

Men's suits have two main style divisions, the natural shoulder or classic suit, and the European fitted suit. The natural shoulder category has less shoulder definition and a looser, more conservative fit. Traditional fabrics like tweed, corduroy, plaids, and flannels are popular. Lapels and style details are very subtle and change little from season to season. A more mature model is appropriate in this style, but it can also be worn by a younger man.

Double Breasted Jacket

Exaggerated fit

fitted body

Back Vent

more hipped-in waist

Slim pant leg

fancier shoe

The European-cut fitted suit has a built-up, well-defined shoulder line. The body is usually fitted with several style lines. The lapels are often exaggerated. To emphasize the cut of the suit, fabrics tend to be solid gaberdine, linen, or other hard-faced, smooth fabrics in solid colors. A slim, youthful model is appropriate wearing this cut.

Sport coats—jackets meant to be worn with contrasting pants—are styled in both cuts. Accessory pieces, vests, and pants complement the styling and fabric of suits in both categories.

▲
ACTION SKETCHES

Active sportswear is most ef-
fective on an active model.
Sketch from life and photo-
graphs. Block in the basic fig-
ure first. Check the axial
line so the figure is standing
straight. Detail the clothing
and render the fine details
and fabric.

DRAWING CASUAL
MEN'S WEAR

Casual apparel is often "spun off," or
derived, from active sportswear. Styling is influenced by ski wear, Western
apparel, hunting and fishing gear,
swim and surf wear, and tennis apparel. Pieces of active sportswear are
often incorporated into spectator day
wear.

These styles should be illustrated on
vigorous, active men of all ages.
Sports props that relate to the specific
apparel are effective to set the stage
for casual wear.

military shirt

windbreaker

straight cut jeans

Swimsuits ride low on waist

Papa drilles

Bomber or Eisenhower jacket

falls just below the waist

287

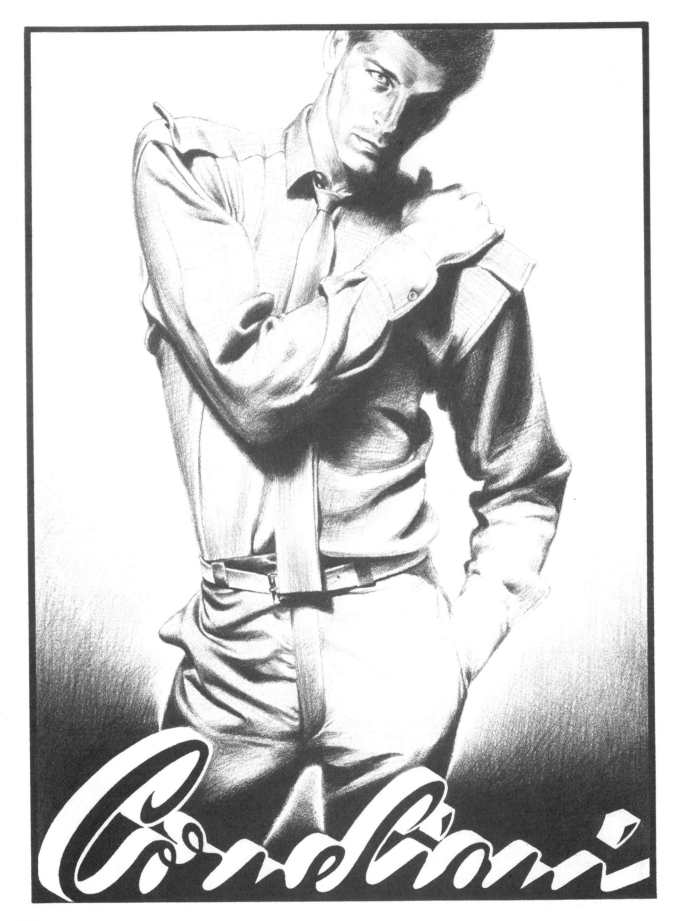

SOURCES OF MEN'S WEAR INSPIRATION

Men's wear is featured in a number of trade, foreign, and consumer publications. Fairchild, publishers of *Women's Wear Daily,* also print the *Daily News Record (DNR)* covering men's wear. This is a very influential trade journal. Men's wear merchandising is also covered by *Retail Week,* a monthly trade magazine widely read by manufacturers and retailers.

Foreign publications of importance are:

☐ *Arbiter* — an Italian publication featuring men's suits and formal wear.

☐ *L'Homme Vogue* — the French fashion magazine covering fashion men's wear.

☐ *L'Uomo Vogue* — ten issues a year cover general men's fashions in the Italian edition of *Vogue's* speciality publication. Each country has unique issues.

☐ *Preview* — a German publication that covers conservative European men's wear. Available quarterly.

☐ *Sir, Men's International Fashion Journal* — published quarterly, featuring men's fashion apparel.

☐ *Uomo* — published by Linia Italia quarterly, this glossy features fashion men's wear and accessories.

Some foreign consumer magazines focus on a particular sport and have spot editorials on appropriate clothing for that sport. They include:

☐ *Uomo Mare* — published every two months in Italy. Features men's nautical apparel.

The distinctive high tech grid gives the bold, graphic face a modern look. (Drawing by Robert Passantino for Wo-men's Wear Daily.)

High contrast emphasizes the dramatic, masculine character of this illustration. (Courtesy of Paul Lowe.)

Line, pattern, and tone variety gives this sketch by Richard Rosenfeld a dramatic masculinity. (Courtesy of Richard Rosenfeld.)

▼

☐ *Linia Italia Sport*—focuses on sports apparel of all kinds. Published three times a year.

Domestic men's wear consumer publications are lead by *Gentlemen's Quarterly (GQ)*. This magazine offers superior fashion coverage of domestic and foreign men's wear and is published 12 times a year. Often domestic men's periodicals which often have fashion articles are *Esquire* and *Playboy*. *Sports Illustrated* covers general sports. Specialized sports like surfing *(Surfer),* horsemanship *(Equis),* and skiing *(Skiing),* have specialized publications featuring specific apparel for the sport.

Men's wear catalogues from prestigious men's wear stores like Brooks Brothers and Cable Car Clothiers and fashion-oriented department stores are important style arbitrators. Many sports-oriented catalogues like L. L. Beane, Land's End, Chris Craft, and Cutter Bill's carry active sportswear for men.

The illustrators and photographers found in these publications offer the fashion artist a wealth of ideas for illustrating men's wear. Painters and illustrators who specialize in sports illustrations for posters and features often have a style easily adapted to fashion. Le Roy Neiman's bold illustrations have influenced men's wear fashion illustration greatly.

A bold, vigorous line quality gives an illustration a masculine tone. The settings should be appropriate to the style and formality of the apparel. Experimentation and observation are the keys to developing a definitive men's wear illustrating style.

CHAPTER
ELEVEN

DRAWING
CHILDREN

Bringing
up
baby

Children's body proportions differ radically from adult proportions. The toddler's head is about one-fourth of the total body length. As the child grows, the head becomes smaller in proportion to the lengthening body. A young child has a curved spine which is so weak it throws the tummy out. Limbs are plump and bone structure is covered with baby fat. The child evolves a mature figure in slow stages.

A toddler (ages 1 to 3) has small features with soft, undefined facial bone structure in the rather large head. As the child grows and baby fat disappears, the features slowly sharpen and become more defined. A natural look is important when drawing a child's face. Hairstyles should be simple and uncontrived. Bangs are worn by both boys and girls, because the hair tends to grow forward. Children move differently from adults. Their poses are active and less formal. Children's poses do follow the same movement and balance-line rules as adult.

Each age has inherent figure problems that require special design solutions. Style details like collars, cuffs, and plackets and trims should be smaller to complement the child's size. Clothing proportions are usually uneven to emphasize height and create a slender line.

◀▶

Catherine Clayton Purnell specializes in children. Her work with toddlers is exceptional because each personality is captured through gesture and features. She makes use of a fantasy setup in the illustration on page 292, turning her babies into fairies. (Courtesy of Catherine Clayton Purnell.)

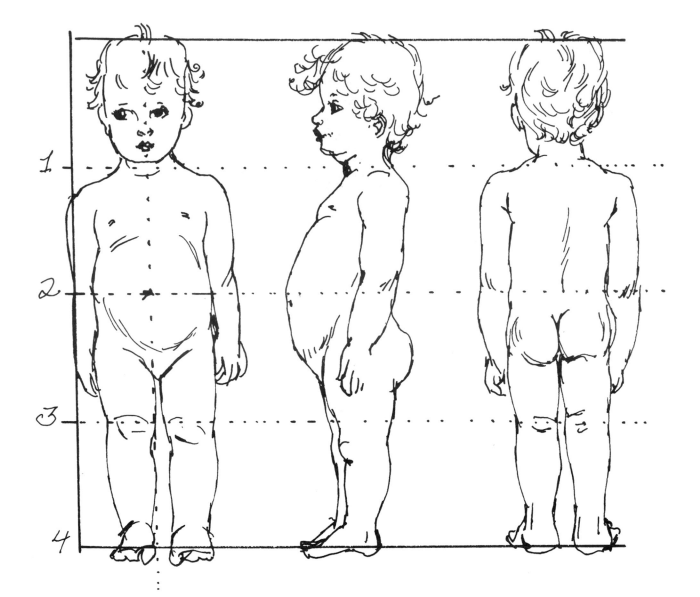

TODDLER PROPORTION

1-YEAR-OLD

The 1-year-old has a body length of four heads. Boys and girls are undistinguishable at this age. Even fashions are often unisex. Most children do not walk until they are 16 to 18 months old, so at 1 year the baby is usually drawn lying down, sitting, or crawling.

Study the proportion sketch. Notice that the neck is not developed and the head seems to sit on the shoulders. The shoulders are rounded and have almost no width. The spine is weak and cannot hold the back erect. This throws the tummy out making it a prominent feature of any pose.

Dressed, the 1-year-old is well padded with diapers. Often no shoes are worn and the feet have a relaxed curve. The foot will flatten out and begin to develop an arch as the child learns to walk.

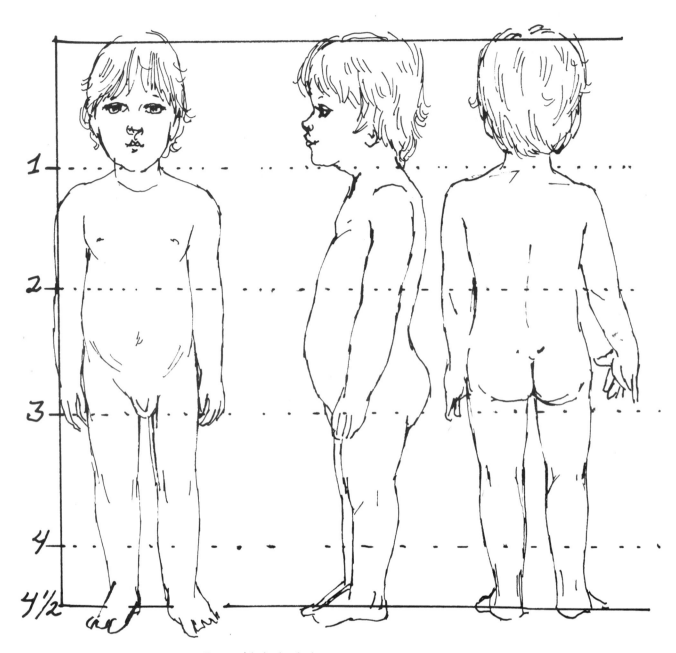

1

2

3

4

4½

To establish the baby's proportion in your mind, practice drawing the basic figure in all the views shown here. To master drawing the baby, sketch from photographs and life.

2- TO 3-YEAR-OLDS

A dramatic difference occurs between the ages of 1 year and 2. The child walks, which makes the legs stronger and more defined. The typical 2-year-old has a body length of four and one-half heads. Most of the length is added in the legs, but the torso is still very long in comparison. Boys and girls have the same body proportions and figures at 2 years old, but hair and clothing styles are more clearly masculine and feminine. The neck is stronger and now appears to support the head. The shoulders are still narrow. The tummy protrudes because of the natural curve of the spine. Diapers are often worn until 2½ years, so the bottom has a padded look for the younger toddler.

Sketch the proportion drawings several times. Draw both boys and girls from life or photographs.

When drawing very young children in action, use the same axial line to keep the figure from tipping off balance that you used when drawing adult figures in action. Block in the proportion and action lines. Draw the body silhouette and then the details. For realistic poses, draw from life.

▼ ▶

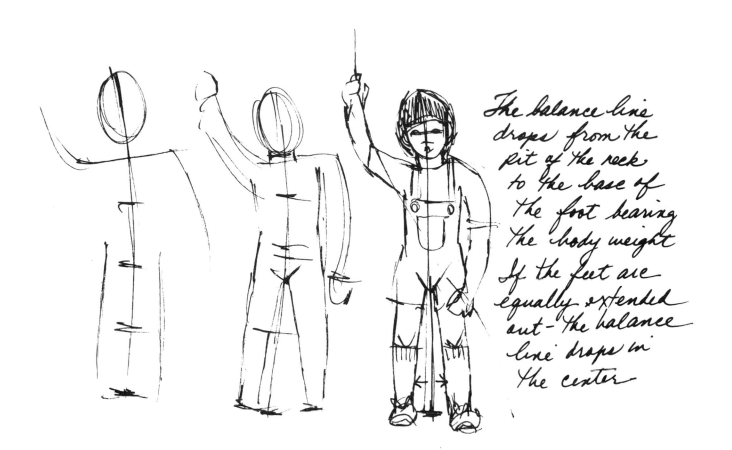

The balance line drops from the pit of the neck to the base of the foot bearing the body weight If the feet are equally extended out — the balance line drops in the center

THE BABY'S FACE

The baby's head is about half the size of the adult head, but most of the size is concentrated in the skull above the forehead. The features are placed in the lower half of the head. The face does not have a well-developed bone structure and is fleshed out with baby fat. The nose has a soft, rounded shape because the bridge has not developed. The nostrils are small.

A baby's eyes are often quite large. Place them equal distance from the median line with about one and one-half eye lengths in between. The eyebrows are very light. Because the child is so small, the eyes are often looking up. They should have a wide-eyed innocent look. The upper eyelid almost disappears when the eyes are wide open.

The lips are soft and small. Because few teeth develop until the second year, the mouth seems narrow. The jaw is undefined and the chin small. The ears are placed below the level of the eyes and are small and delicate.

Sketch several faces from life or photographs, and compare them to the facial proportions shown here. Draw the features and hair with a light line and soft tones, or your drawing will look too mature and heavy. Hairstyles should be soft, natural, and rather short for this age.

Young children's hands and feet are plump and have a soft silhouette. Practice drawing from these step-by-step sketches.

▼ ▶

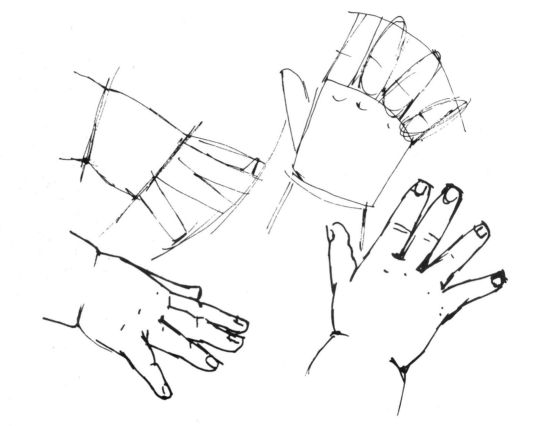

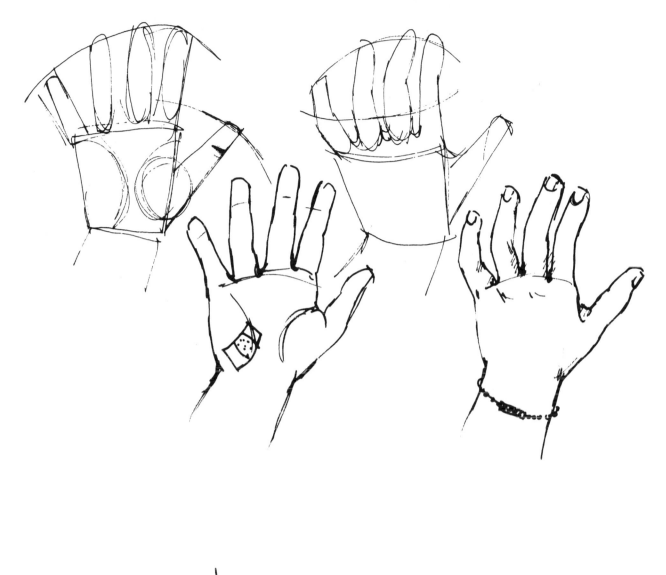

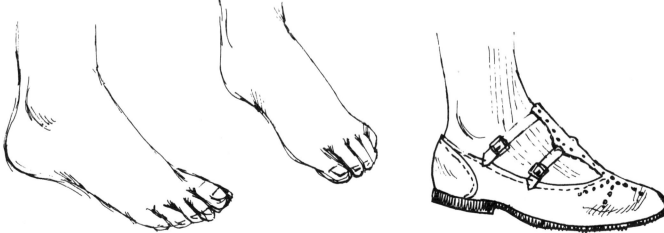

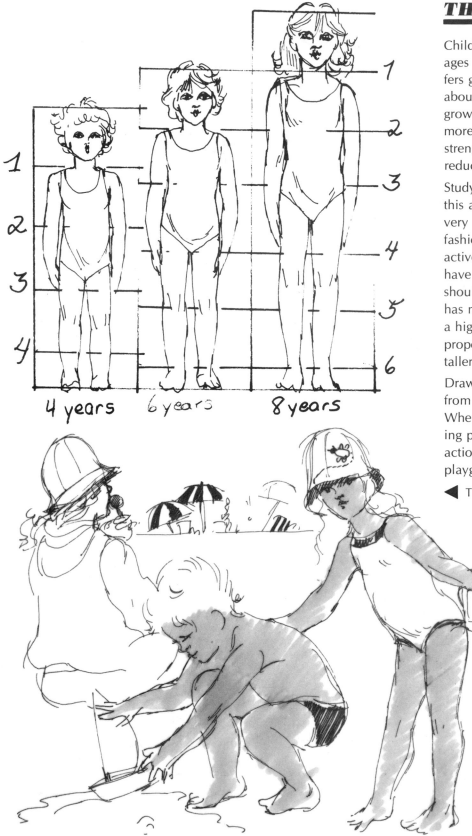

4 years   6 years   8 years

THE 4-YEAR-OLD

THE YOUNG CHILD

Children grow rapidly between the ages of 4 and 8 years. Proportion differs greatly because the torso remains about the same length, but the legs grow longer. The body begins to have more definition as the spine strengthens and the stomach is reduced.

Study the comparative proportions of this age group. Boys and girls have very similar figures at this age. The fashion ideal for a child is a slender, active body. Fashion children should have a sleek, well-fed look—but they should not be plump. The waistline has not developed. Dresses often have a high, empire waistline. The uneven proportion makes the girl's figure seem taller and slimmer.

Draw several proportion sketches from the diagrams for each age group. When you have mastered the changing proportions, begin to sketch quick action sketches from life. Go to a playground or park where children

◀ THE 4-YEAR-OLD

THE 8-YEAR-OLD
▼

THE 6-YEAR OLD
▼

are playing for live models. Try to capture the personality and movement characteristics of each age group. Combine the control and accuracy of the proportion exercises with the spontaneity and personality of the action sketches for convincing children's drawings.

Sketch children in a situation or activity. Use simple props like balls, toys, or sporting equipment. Humor is especially effective when drawing children. Children's books are often illustrated with charming figures and can give a fashion illustrator many ideas for sketching juvenile fashion figures. Many children's book illustrators are also fashion professionals.

The same rules of balancing the figure over the centre of gravity at the pit of the neck applies to posing children

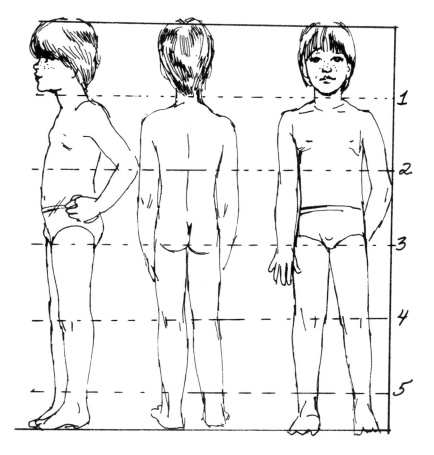

Children rarely pose gracefully. Artful awkwardness enhances the appeal of a pose at this age.

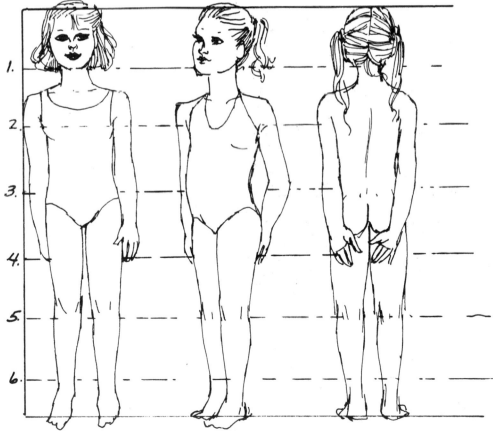

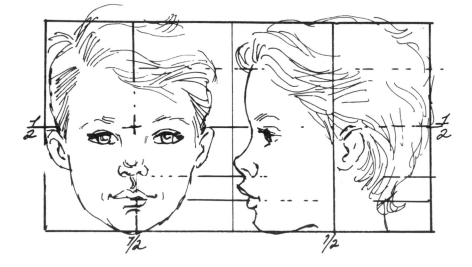

THE YOUNG CHILD'S FACE

The young child's head becomes narrower as the child grows. The features are still concentrated in the lower half of the face. The features have a softer, more natural look than an adult's. Notice the young child's eyes are smaller in proportion to the face than the toddler's and now have about one eye space between. The bridge of the nose is more defined, yet the tip still has a rounded innocent "pug nose" look. The lips and cheeks are full. The mouth is wider

than the toddler's, because the teeth are fully developed and the jaw has more definition. A child's expression is often shy or innocent.

Hairstyles should be simple and natural. Curls, braids, and bangs are typical for this age group. Ribbons or hair clips pull the hair off the face.

The proportion and drawing rules for the three-quarter profile follow the same rules as for the adult face. Study photographs and draw from life to develop your skills in drawing the child's face. Keep the lines fine and shadows light so the face looks young.

The loose, sketchy line of this drawing gives a natural, casual look to the illustration.

THE YOUNG TEENAGER

GIRLS

The young teenager has developed a specific masculine or feminine body. Girls have a definite waistline and small bust. Their shoulders have more width and the leg muscles are more shapely and defined than a child's. The figure is about six and one-half head lengths in proportion. The torso is still over half of the overall length of the body. Hairstyles are definitely feminine but emphasize casual, clean-cut, natural styling when you draw.

Poses can be more formal, with less emphasis on activity and spontaneous situations that were so appropriate for the younger children or boys of the same age.

Practice sketching the figure. Use a light pencil line and draw from the proportion diagrams. Sketch garments on your lightly drawn figures. Notice how garments ride over the tummy, often emphasizing empire or drop-torso styles. The uneven proportion makes the figure appear longer.

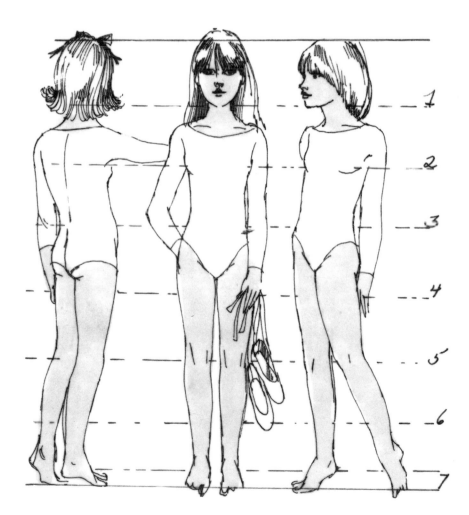

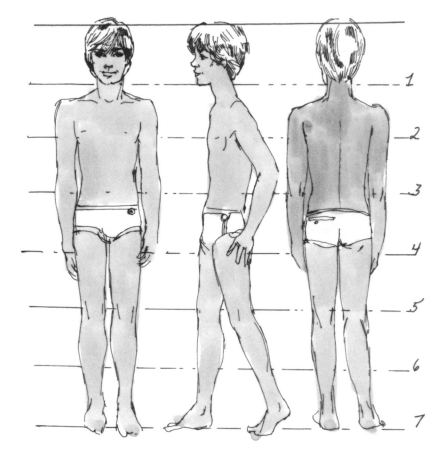

1
2
3
4
5
6
7

BOYS

Young teenage boys begin to develop a masculine silhouette. Their shoulders broaden and the torso becomes slender. Hands and feet grow and seem large in proportion to body size. Knee and elbow joints also seem too large. Muscles are more developed and give arms and legs a sharper, more defined shape. The crotch is lower for teenage boys than for girls of the same age. As the torso be-

▲

The movements of the body are controlled by the rules of axial-line balance. The axial line falls between the legs when the model's weight is equally placed on both legs. Children's poses should be casual and natural.

comes straighter and more slender, the waistline is lowered. Boys tend to wear pants low on their hips. Simple, natural hairstyles are most effective. Features are sharper. The nose is quite well developed and the mouth is firmer.

Emphasize action sketches and use a simple prop to carry through the theme of this active age group. Sketch from the basic poses to reinforce the proportion; then do several life studies to develop your sketching skills.

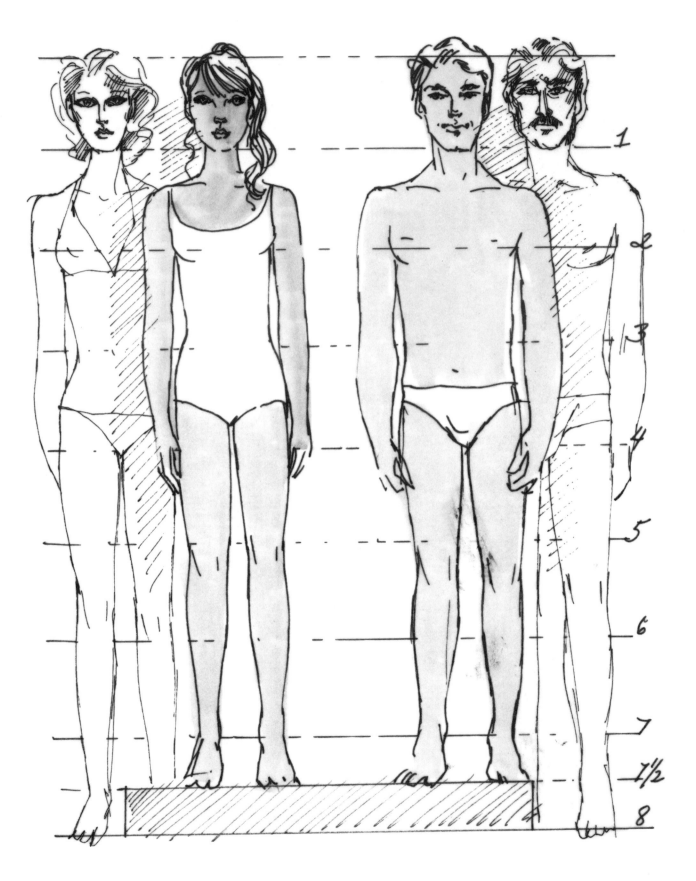

1

2

3

4

5

6

7

7½

8

THE OLDER TEENAGER

The older teenager has almost adult proportions. Seven and one-half head lengths works well for both boys and girls. Muscle and bone structure is not as developed as an adult's, so the body's curves are smoother and less defined. Girls do not have the extreme emphasis on bone structure that adult models have. The teenage girl has a small, high bust line and slim hips. Her crotch length is almost half the overall body length, but the legs will grow at least a half a head longer for adult proportions. The shoulders are narrower and the length of the neck is not as exaggerated as an adult's.

Teenage boys are beginning to develop their upper torso to adult proportions. The fashion ideal is slender and lithe. The torso proportion is longer for men than women. More growth occurs in the legs to reach adult proportions.

Facial structure is the same as an adult's, but the features and contours of the face are softer and rounder. A certain wide-eyed innocence and good humor should animate the teenage face, a reminder of childhood expressions.

Courtesy of Harper's Bazaar.

▼ ▲

STYLIZING, OR "CARTOONING," CHILDREN'S ILLUSTRATIONS

Illustrating childrens' fashions on cartoon figures is an effective design technique. The proportion and action of the figure should be realistic or slightly exaggerated. The features and clothing details can be stylized to give a whimsical, humorous look to the sketch.

Children's book illustrations offer a wealth of ideas for stylization and cartooning the juvenile fashion figure. Look for the illustrations of Hillary Knight (the Eloise series), Maurice Sendak, Gyo, Carl Larsson, and Steven Kellog, as well as those of many other notable artists, for ideas and inspiration for illustrating children.

Period children's illustration can also give the juvenile illustrator rich insight into how to style a drawing. Notice how contemporary many of the styles in these drawings from a 1913 *Harper's Bazar* are. The artists are Tony Nebb and Grayce Drayton.

▶
Using an animal's face on a child's body gives the illustration a whimsical quality.

CHAPTER
TWELVE

DRAWING
ACCESSORIES

Drawing accessories requires accurate rendering of details, a knowledge of simple perspective, and a creative approach to layout and presentation. Accessories are apparel items that are not classified as garments. These include jewelry, hosiery, shoes and handbags, belts, hats, and fabric accessories like scarves and shawls. Accessories must be drawn first by a designer, so they can be produced. Handbag buyers often sketch the items they buy so they can be identified when they arrive at the store. Accessories are an important fashion category that is often advertised, and the drawing is usually done by a specialized illustrator, particularly when the accessories are not shown on a figure. More general fashion illustrators often draw accessories on the figure.

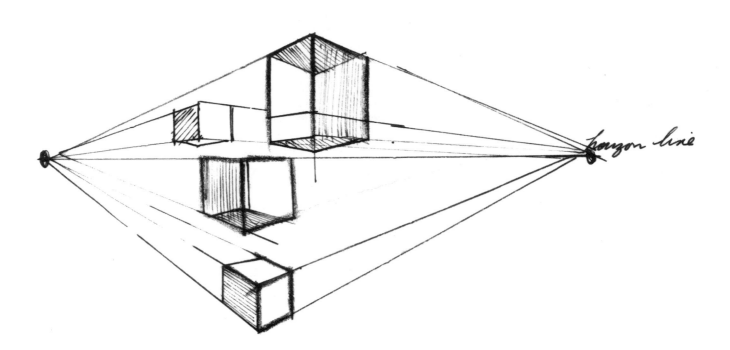

horizon line

SIMPLE PERSPECTIVE

The principles of perspective were developed during the Renaissance to depict depth, or the third dimension, in drawings and paintings. It is important for the accessory artist to know the rules of simple perspective.

Determine the eye-level line (also called the horizon line) by looking straight ahead at your paper. Place two parallel push pins at either end of the eye-level line. These represent the right- and left-hand vanishing points. All objects on this line will look flat. When objects are above or below this

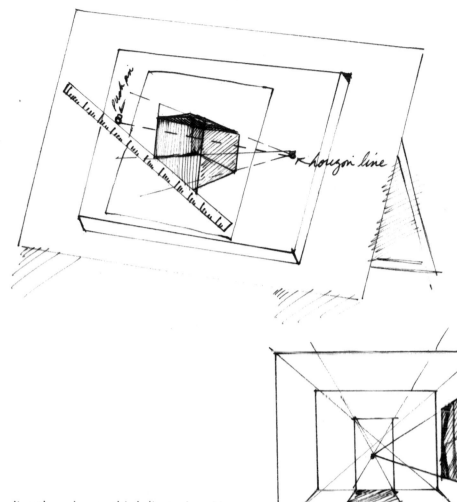

line they show a third dimension. Use your ruler as a guide emanating from the push pins at either end of the horizon line to develop the third dimension as the illustration shows.

One-point perspective has only one vanishing point and is used to draw from a flat plane which recedes into the drawing. This guide is good to use when drawing a single item.

Study the diagrams and practice drawing several glass cubes, accurately capturing their volume. Sketch everyday geometric objects until you can establish the perspective guidelines and accurately draw a three-dimensional object. Try drawing a single object with a variety of angles above and below eye level.

Draw frontal shapes of object and then determine a simple vanishing point

APPLYING PERSPECTIVE TO FASHION ACCESSORIES

Accuracy of detail and silhouette usually require a preliminary drawing to illustrate accessories. Follow these steps to learn how to develop an accurate drawing.

1. Arrange the object so you are viewing it from the most advantageous angle. Determine the eye-level line and establish your vanishing points. First draw the frontal plane (the area of the object that is closest to you). Use your ruler and the vanishing points to project the sides of the frontal plane into the third dimension.

2. When the silhouette of the object is drawn to your satisfaction, add the details.

3. Study the effects that can be achieved by lighting the accessory in various ways. Use a small, intense light to change the setting until the lighting pleases you.

4. Tone the various planes with lead pencils to explore the various surface planes of the object. Practice shading until you can create a smooth, even tone, of varying intensities. Notice how different tones add dimension to the object. Let the paper be the lightest value and shade down from there. The tonal differences will describe the shapes inside the object without a heavy outline around the various planes of the object.

5. Use the pencil-carbon transfer method to draw the accessory on illustration board. Use your tonal sketch as a guide when applying washes. Detail the finished drawing in ink, felt pen, or prisma pencil. Try to keep a fresh, sparkling quality to your finished drawing.

Gradually the experienced artist can eliminate step 4 and render the finished drawing from the object.

Refine shape and sketch in details

Transfer to Illustration Board

Lay in type, copy or background

Refine and Tone sketch

looking down slightly

- Arrange objects in a pleasing group
- Block in the basic shapes
- Establish eye level and horizon points

COMPLICATED PERSPECTIVE SETUPS

Multiple objects in a setting require careful planning before drawing. Arrange the objects until they relate to each other in a logical way. Review pages 203–209 for layout suggestions on arranging multiple objects. Try to establish a theme so the accessories tell a story suggested by a setting or figure in the drawing.

Experiment with the lighting so the objects are highlighted and accented appropriately. Many artists use a Polaroid camera to capture a setup so it is not lost before the drawing is complete. The photograph will also check the setup from various perspective angles. When you are satisfied with the arrangement and lighting of the objects, begin the preliminary drawing. Apply your knowledge of perspective to accurately draw the setup. Proceed as you did in the exercise on simple perspective.

▲
Experiment with the angle used to draw luggage and geometric accessories, in order to select the most pleasing and dramatic approach to an object.

Luggage and handbags
are usually drawn from an
angle—to give a view of
the inside or outer edge
of the item

▶

*The linear technique of rendering these
handbags and integrating them into the
foreground gives the illustration visual
unity.*

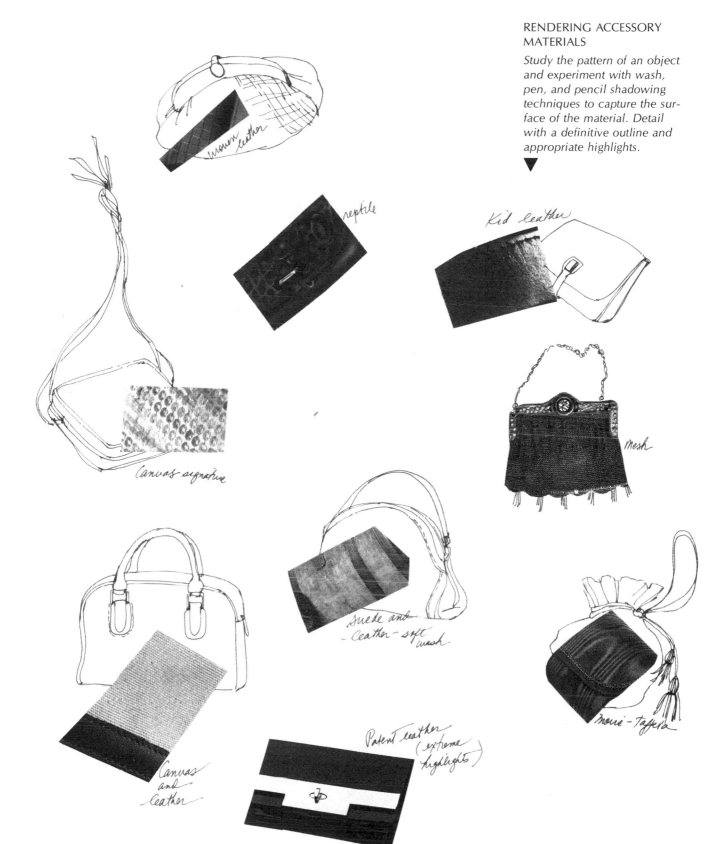

Study the pattern of an object and experiment with wash, pen, and pencil shadowing techniques to capture the surface of the material. Detail with a definitive outline and appropriate highlights.
▼

woven leather

reptile

Kid leather

Canvas signature

mesh

Canvas and leather

Suede and leather - soft wash.

Moire - taffeta

Patent leather (extreme highlights)

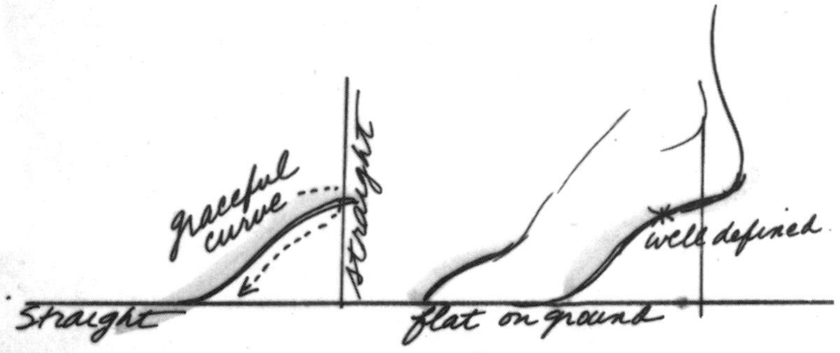

graceful curve — *straight*

Straight

well defined

flat on ground

1) Draw sole line —
heel guide line and
arch angle of shoe.
Observe profile
and height of shoe
accurately.

2) Draw shape of foot in
shoe — Arch front to
follow raised arch
line.

Low and
trim
lines

solid
heel

3) Block in details —
keep heel clean and
trim for a quality look.

4) Render to finish

SHOES

Illustrating shoes professionally is an exacting, specialized skill. Shoes must look new without looking stiff. Subtle exaggeration on the style lines and cuts are used to enhance the illustration. Shoes may be illustrated off or on feet. The heel height establishes the curve of the arch. The sole line should be a straight continuous line, beginning at the toe and gracefully curving into the arch and the back of the heel. The heel is aligned at an angle of 90 degrees with the floor line, though it may be styled to curve into the arch at differing angles.

Study the step-by-step diagram. Draw the foot several times until you have mastered a profile shoe. Select several of your shoes and practice drawing them in different positions. Draw them as if they were new. Review page 327 for help in illustrating shoe leathers correctly.

Boots have the same balance as shoes. The heel height determines the contour of the sole line. The top of the boot may have many style variations and details.

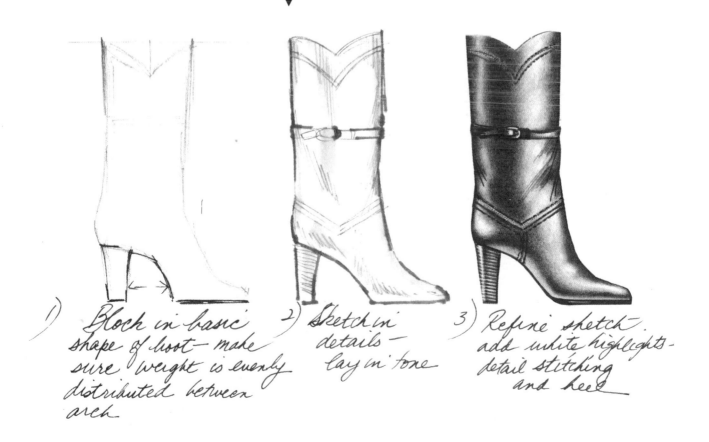

1) Block in basic shape of boot—make sure weight is evenly distributed between arch

2) Sketch in details— lay in tone

3) Refine sketch— add white highlights— detail stitching and heel

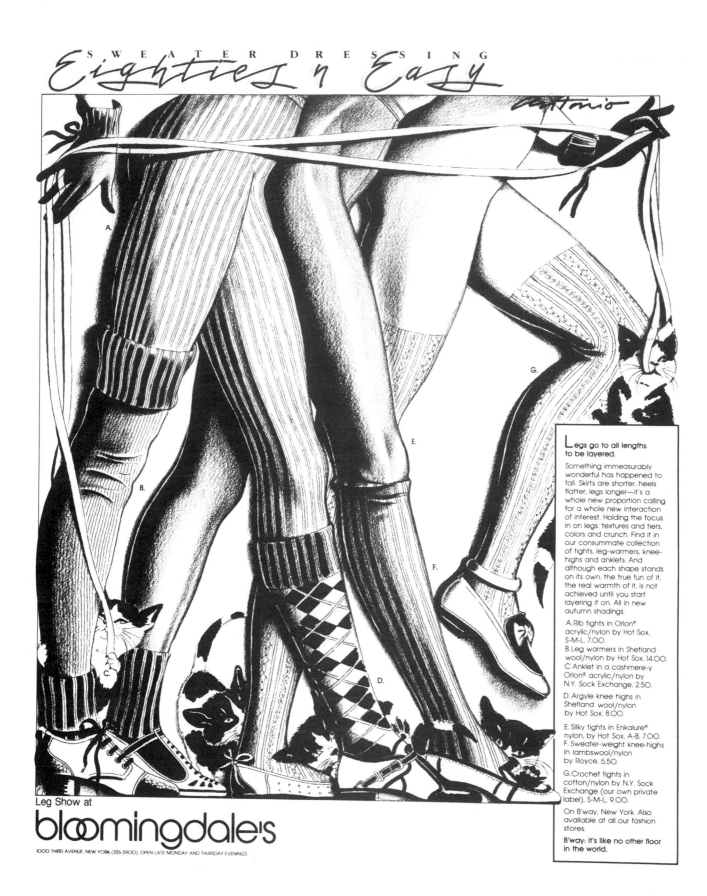

BELTS

Belts are made in a wide variety of different styles and materials. They range from neat functional sport belts to exaggerated cummerbunds and dramatic ties. They are most often illustrated on a figure, because they are so effective shown with a garment.

The rules of one-point perspective govern the circular ellipse silhouette of a belt shown alone. The buckle should be slightly wider than the belt. Tie belts are an inexpensive and popular accessory. Draw a bow or tie with softly curving ties and a full bow, so it looks new and fresh. When a belt is used on a loose garment, it creates a soft puff of fabric above and below, as it shapes the garment to the body.

◄ *This illustration by Antonio utilizes a complicated layout, enhanced by line and shadows, to create movement. (Courtesy of Bloomingdale's, illustration by Antonio, art direction by John C. Jay.*

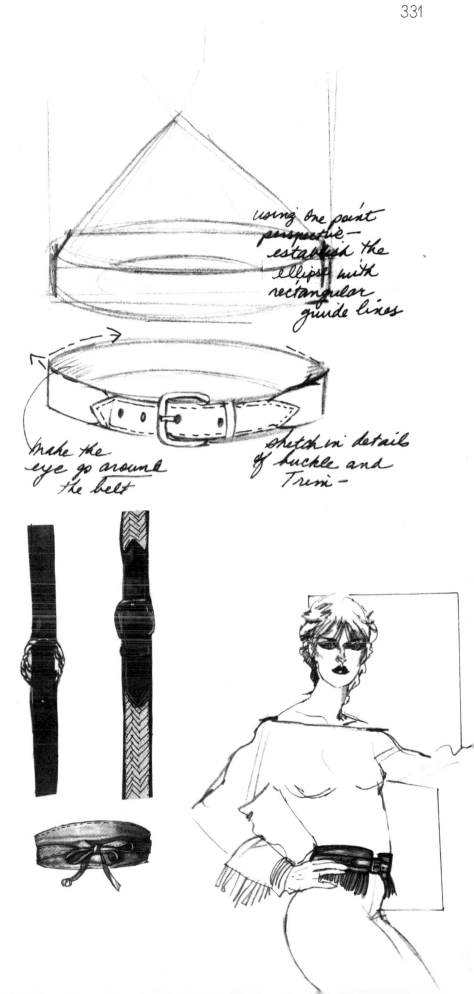

using one point perspective— establish the ellipse with rectangular guide lines

make the eye go around the belt

sketch in details of buckle and Trim—

JEWELRY

Rendering jewelry requires a precise drawing with accurate details. Study the smooth reflective surfaces of the metal before rendering the piece of jewelry. Notice how the shadows and midtones define the planes and details of the design. Control the light source so the highlights are focused in one area of the jewelry and contrast with mid-tones and dark tones. Use opaque gouache or china white paint to accent the highlights.

When drawing diamonds or other faceted precious stones, the sparkle is the most important element to capture. The cut of the stone dictates the shape. Notice how the setting is attached to the stone, and accurately render it. Start a clipping file of examples of jewelry illustration and photography to work from.

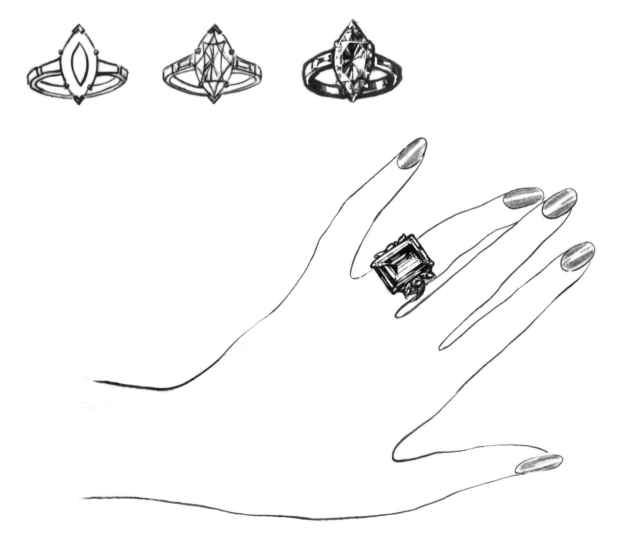

Detail glove style and seams

Long gloves give dramatic effect

Block in the hand

GLOVES

Gloves are made in leather or fabric and worn with a great variety of outfits. Once, every well-dressed woman completed her outfit with sparkling white gloves. Today, functional requirements of sports or cold weather—rather than fashion demands—dictate the use of gloves. Gloves follow the contour of the hand and fingers and are shaped with seams which add to the distinctive style of the glove. Elastic insets or crocheted pieces may be added to the fabric or leather to increase the flexibility of the glove.

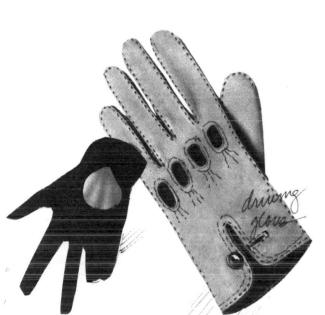

driving glove

ski gloves

FABRIC ACCESSORIES

Fabric accessories include scarves, shawls, separate collars, and ruffs. They may be illustrated alone, or on a body with other garments. Scarves are often illustrated as floats, because the graphics are dramatically visible. Before you begin your sketch, drape the scarf without too many folds, so the pattern is clearly visible. Focus your light source so the folds are accented. Draw the silhouette and undulations of the fabric. Keep the contours crisp and fresh. Block in the pattern details. Draw the pattern realistically, as it is interrupted by the folds of the fabric. Render the floating scarf in halftones and line.

Fabric accessories are effectively illustrated in combination with other garments and add fashion pizzazz to a basic garment. Focus on the accessory in an illustration by cutting down the frame of the picture as if you were cropping a photograph. This highlights the accessory. Make sure the accompanying garment is an appropriate backdrop and enhances the accessory.

1.) Block out general
silhouette and fold
patterns of the scarf

Black

Black

2.) Accurately
translate pattern
onto the
draped

scarf

silhouette
and
shade

1) Sketch in head with features — Draw an ellipse that represents the hat band and the general silhouette of the crown of the hat

2) Draw the entire brim — let it frame the face, and circle the head

3) Detail the flip of the brim and crown — erase guide lines

4) Detail, refine and render finished sketch

HATS

Hats are usually professionally drawn by a fashion illustrator, because an appropriate head must carry the hat. Hats are made in a wide variety of shapes and fabrications. They are functional, as well as decorative. Begin your drawing by establishing the band line of the hat as it encircles the head. Be sure to correctly judge the angle or tilt of the hat and how far down it is fitted on the head. Draw the shape and height of the crown. The brim line also encircles the head, but may have a different contour from the band. Hats may be shaped and trimmed with many different kinds of accessories. Render these in your final illustration. Hats are worn as occasional accessories. They should relate to the outfit they are shown with. Style the hair in a simple, complimentary way, so it does not detract from the shape and style of the hat. To become familiar with the way a hat enfolds the head, draw the diagrammatic exercises several times. Then begin to draw from life and photographs until you have mastered many hat styles.